Addiction as an Attachment Disorder

Addiction as an Attachment Disorder

Philip J. Flores, PhD.

JASON ARONSON
Lanham • Boulder • New York • Toronto • Oxford

To
Lisa Mahon,
my friend, mentor, teacher, confidant, and wife. Without her support, advice, and encouragement, this book would not have been possible.

Published in the United States of America
by Jason Aronson
An imprint of Rowman & Littlefield Publishers, Inc.

A wholly owned subsidiary of
The Rowman & Littlefield Publishing Group, Inc.
4501 Forbes Boulevard, Suite 200, Lanham, Maryland 20706
www.rowmanlittlefield.com

PO Box 317
Oxford
OX2 9RU, UK

This book was set in 11 pt. New Aster by Westchester book Composition.

British Library Cataloguing in Publication Information Available

Library of Congress Cataloging-in-Publication Data

Flores, Philip J.
Addiction as an attachment disorder / Philip J. Flores.
p. cm.
Includes bibliographical references and index.
ISBN 0-7657-0337-8
1. Alcoholism—Treatment. 2. Substance abuse.
3. Attachment behavior. 4. Psychotherapy. I. Title.
RC565 .F5678 2003
616.86—dc21 2002028042
Printed in the United States of America

∞™ The paper used in this publication meets the minimum requirements of American National Standard for Information Sciences—Permanence of Paper for Printed Library Materials, ANSI/NISO Z39.48-1992.

CONTENTS

CHAPTER 4: 68
Addiction: An Attempt at Self-Repair that Fails

CHAPTER 5: 101
Neurophysiology and Attachment

CHAPTER 7: 151
Rules for Effective Treatment: An Attachment Perspective

CHAPTER 8: 168
Early Treatment: Creating the Capacity for Attachment

CHAPTER 9: 203
Late-Stage Treatment Issues

CHAPTER 10: 221
Attachment and Group Therapy

CHAPTER 11: 240
Attachment and the Therapeutic Alliance

FOREWORD

Addiction is a disorder in self-regulation. Individuals who become dependent on addictive substances cannot regulate their emotions, self-care, self-esteem, and relationships. In this monumental and illuminating text Philip Flores covers all the reasons why this is so. But it is in the domain of interpersonal relations that he makes clear why individuals susceptible to substance use disorders (SUDs) are especially vulnerable. His emphasis on addiction as an attachment disorder is principally important because he provides extensive scholarly and clinical insights as to why certain vulnerable individuals so desperately need to substitute chemical solutions and connections for human ones.

Dr. Flores persuasively builds the case that we are creatures who are, by nature, more driven and governed by our need for human attachment and comfort than we are driven or governed by our need for instinctual pleasure and gratification as early psychodynamic theories of addiction suggested. Although Flores ultimately and repeatedly draws on attachment theory to guide his reader, he will frustrate those who seek a simplistic or reductionist formulation of addictive vulnerability. He is diligent and courageous enough to consider multiple and competing paradigms, and, more often, to think and write integratetively rather than resort to linear/either-or arguments about understanding and treating addictive disorders. Thus, he is unafraid to examine, compare, and critique controversial issues such as abstinence versus harm reduction, controversies about moderation management, and the cause-consequence controversies about SUDs and psychopathology. So even as he frustrates the doctrinaire, he stimulates us to expand our boundaries of understanding to more deeply, or in more depth, appreciate the complex underpinnings of addictive disorder.

Flores' perspective is multidimensional in the best biopsychosocial traditions but his perspective is primarily a psychodynamic one. He develops this perspective with refreshing and clear language. He avoids reductionistic thinking, and enlightens us as to how lifelong human interdependency is necessary and the norm, rather than developmental goals of separation and individuation embodied in outdated drive and conflict theory. Constantly appreciating the biological bases for the drive to attach, Flores, nevertheless, persistently and persuasively affirms why psychologically establishing and maintaining solid attachments assures human safety, comfort, and well being. As he indicates, "This is not just a good idea, it is the law." Attachment theory, according to Flores, parts way from classical psychoanalytic theory, which lays more emphasis on internal drives and unconscious fantasies. Rather, the imperative here, drawing on Bowlby's observation of the child-maternal bond, is what happens in the real world of interpersonal relationships throughout our lifespan, appreciating attachment as a "primary motivation." He even dares to broach a scientific theory of love in exploring the functions of attachment.

Dr. Flores' gifts as a clinician and scholar are made evident by his deft interspersing of rich clinical material with exhaustive citations and exploration of addiction and psychodynamic theorists. In the former case the ingredients of empathic listening and responding to patients' interpersonal needs are evident. In the latter instance, he stands intellectually tall because he rigorously cites and appreciates the theories and investigative findings of essentially all of the works of antecedent and contemporary scholars who have deliberated on the nature of addictive vulnerability.

This combination of clinical empathy and rigorous scholarship combine to breakthrough the all too frequent Cartesian divisions concerning debates about mind/brain relationships. Philip Flores makes it more easy and palatable to accept how biology, in this instance, of attachment, is inseparable from the human effects of psychological nurturance and interpersonal connectedness. He also makes clearer how interpersonal breaches and trauma early in life are embedded (i.e., "imprinted") in our brain and later reflected in adult life in errant and compulsive behaviors such as addictive ones.

Flores continuously and rightfully reminds us of the inseparability of the brain from the mind, the limbic system from the cortex, and the real world from the intrapsychic.

There are needed maps and menus here, but of a very sophisticated kind. Flores, in chapters on neurophysiology and society, guides us through the maze, starting with infancy and beyond, of interpersonal and societal challenges working their way into our minds and seating themselves in the limbic system and then working back the other way. He is constantly instructing how disruption and disorder at any of these byways profoundly affect mammals of all kinds; for us humans, they are the preeminent bases for narcissistic deficits in psychological structure and self-regulation, especially those resulting in addictive behavior. His writing is masterful in lucidly breaking through conventional wisdom to more fully appreciate how our emotional brain, as often as not, resonates with that of our human surrounds, often without words or cognition.

The important point that Flores makes is that emotional interpersonal bonds, seated in the brain as much the mind, are the most important stuff of our ties to the caring and comforting parts of self and others. In their absence we become behaviorally and addictively disordered. He champions a special brand of humanism, which begs that we appreciate, bridge and integrate an otherwise dualistic mind-body dichotomy. With exquisite precision he gets it down to the neuronal level and whether the earliest experiences of the newborn are adequately stimulating for his/her neurons to sprout ("bloom"), or if not age appropriately adequate, neuronal stunting (or "pruning") occurs. This is as good as it gets in appreciating how the real world shapes and influences the brain, especially the emotional brain.

Dr. Flores appropriately uses his review of attachment styles, and the societal and parental trends that influence them, as his springboard and guide to instruct us on essential aspects of effective treatment. Just as parental influences can dictate secure or insecure attachment patterns, the therapist can correct or perpetuate the troubled ways patients or clients relate to those around them. Flores skillfully and evocatively heightens the clinician's awareness of how individual and group treatment relationships become the lightening rod for illuminating and correcting what is disordered about how we connect (or don't connect) in interpersonal relationships.

Flores correctly points out that alcoholics' and addicts'

attachments to their substance is powerful, and requires equally powerful counterforces of caring others in the service of establishing abstinence as the primary order of business. Flores believes that a combination of AA and a positive connection to a clinician most often works best to achieve the needed abstinence as the first step. AA provides a context for creating a narrative and a fellowship with others that fosters modification of self-destructive behaviors and stimulates self-reflection. A feelingful connection to a clinician creates the all-important treatment alliance that initially holds the alcoholic-addicted individual to AA and other continuing influences; subsequently, it becomes the bedrock for therapeutic work and needed personality transformation in individual and group psychotherapy.

Whether cause or consequence, few clinicians working with alcohol-drug dependent individuals would argue that there is enormous suffering at the heart of addictive disorders. The worst fate, however, is not the suffering; the worst fate is suffering alone. Here again, in this book Dr Flores is masterful in linking how a focus on addicted individuals' disordered attachments is the crucial pathway to accessing patients suffering and countering their isolation and aloneness. Through integrating self-help and individual and group therapeutic approaches, Flores instructs how such treatment can alleviate the suffering and produce the necessary changes in character and personality organization that perpetuate their suffering.

Because addicted individuals are interpersonally disconnected, isolative, and counterdependent, they desperately need the engaging and connecting influences of AA and group and individual psychotherapy. Philip Flores persuasively makes the case for attachment oriented therapy (AOT) which he states is as much an attitude as it is a method of psychotherapy. He makes us appreciate how much psychotherapy has changed over the past century (and Flores contributes to that change in this volume), and thankfully so. The changes clearly suggest we need be less burdened by convoluted issues of technique or technical considerations, but simply and more essentially how the therapist behaves and "creates the proper emotional climate of the relationship." Could it be said more accurately and succinctly as to what makes for an effective treatment relationship?

In AOT empathic listening and emotional attunement to the patient's needs is the primary currency for therapeutic understanding, change, and maturation. The strength of Flores' paradigm of addiction as an attachment disorder is that it is a theory that effectively and wisely guides treatment, but at the same time when properly implemented or practiced, the treatment resonates with and further enhances the theory. Flores' work here is an extraordinary one because in parsimonious and clear language he makes a major contribution to the literature and practice of effective psychotherapy in general and effective psychotherapy for the addictions in particular. He fills in all the gaps between theory and practice covering wide and ranging issues of what practice and empirical findings have to teach about the critical ingredients of AA, group therapy and individual psychotherapy. This is a job well-done because it helps students and experienced clinicians alike to always be mindful of how they bring their humanity (in comforting and transformational ways) to the distress and suffering of others. His theory of addiction as an attachment disorder makes it particularly clear how especially important this is for those suffering with addictive disorders.

Edward J. Khantzian, M.D.
Clinical Professor of Psychiatry,
Harvard Medical School at
The Cambridge Hospital and
Tewksbury Hospital

1

Addiction as an Attachment Disorder

We don't have relationships; we take hostages.
Alcoholics Anonymous member

Feeling anxious about going to a party? Have a few drinks. Having difficulty talking to a member of the opposite sex? A little speed or cocaine will grease the larynx and make you funny and charming. Do you have to host an important dinner or gathering for your boss and a few important guests? A little Librium or Valium will do the trick. Or is the thought of going out and meeting some new friends just too overwhelming? Why not stay at home and get stoned. After all, the relationship with marijuana is more reliable and much easier to control than the uncertainty of human contact.

Recognize the pattern?

For better or worse, an increasing number of individuals within our present-day society have become increasingly reliant on psychoactive substances to help them manage the fears and difficulties stirred up with interpersonal relationships. Fortunately, most individuals are able to use the substances mentioned above in ways that do not cause them prolonged harm or dire consequences. However, certain individuals, because of intrapsychic deficiencies related to genetic and biological substrates, are more vulnerable to developing disabling dependencies and addictions to substances that many of us either learn how to use less destructively or stop using before the consequences of our use become too damaging.

However, the etiology of addiction is not a simple one-dimensional phenomenon. Evidence is mounting that prolonged substance use alters brain functioning, leaving many individuals unable to control their substance intake once they start. For some, this loss of control is rapid. For others, the erosion is more insidious and gradual. Substance use, which originally started as a way to help the individual manage the difficulties generated by interpersonal relationships, gradually impairs an already fragile capacity for attachment. Prolonged substance abuse, because of its toxicity, gradually compromises neurophysiology functioning and erodes existing psychic structure (Parsons and Farr 1981). Consequently, the interpersonal skills that abusers possessed early in their substance-abusing career depreciate even further. Managing relationships becomes increasingly difficult, leading to a heightened reliance on substances, which accelerate deterioration and addictive response patterns.

> Mike showed up at a therapist's office three months ago complaining of depression and suicidal ideation. Antidepressants and psychotherapy were recommended. Over the course of the next few weeks, it soon became apparent to Mike's therapist that Mike lived an isolated existence. He had little interpersonal contact, other than with his co-workers on the job, and over the last few months he had found himself withdrawing more and more from them. When asked when his depression was at its worst, Mike confided, "The weekends are killers. I get home on Friday and don't leave the apartment until it's time to go back to work Monday morning." Never one to make friends easily, Mike described how he had not been able to force himself "to risk rejection again," since being transferred on the job two years ago to a new city. Divorced five years prior to his move, he had never established any new commitments with anyone and found dating, "more and more difficult. I miss my children who still lived with my wife on the other side of the country and since she's remarried, the contact with them has diminished. They never call anymore."
>
> When the therapist asked what he did with his weekends, Mike explained that he would "rent a few movies and buy a couple twelve packs of beer." Exploration during the course of therapy revealed a picture of a man who was withdrawing more and more from personal relation-

> ships into a world that relied more on alcohol to buffer his feelings of loneliness and fears of rejection. Unknown to his intoxicated brain, his attempted solution to his loneliness was exacerbating his depression and creating a greater problem. His social skills, never fully developed to their complete potential, were deteriorating even more as the toxicity of his ethanol use increased, and eroded his confidence and capabilities. Suggestions to give up or reduce his drinking were initially met with panic and protest. "What? You expect me to sit home alone in that apartment without drinking. It's the only relief I get. I'd kill myself for sure if I didn't have something to take the edge off these feelings."

As Mike's case illustrates, not all addicts and alcoholics start off their substance-abusing careers with highly dysfunctional interpersonal skills. Many earned their dysfunctional styles through a prolonged period of escalating use that gradually compromised whatever skills they originally possessed. Whether impaired attachment capabilities are the consequence or cause of prolonged substance abuse is irrelevant as far as recovery is concerned because the approach to treatment remains the same. Attachment theory holds the position that it is impossible for individuals to completely regulate their affective states alone (Lewis et al. 2000). Consequently, until substance abusers relinquish their dysfunction attachment styles (e.g., insecure avoidant, insecure ambivalent, insecure disorganized) and develop the capacity for healthy interpersonal affect regulation (secure attachment and mutuality), they will forever remain vulnerable to substitute one obsessive addiction (e.g., alcohol, drugs, sex, gambling, work, etc.) for another.

ATTACHMENT THEORY AND SELF PSYCHOLOGY

Addiction treatment specialists familiar with attachment theory (Bowlby 1979a) and self psychology (Kohut 1978) recognize that an inverse relationship exists between addiction and healthy interpersonal attachment. It is rare, if not impossible, for a practicing alcoholic or addict to successfully negotiate the demands of healthy interpersonal relationships. This is a fact that experienced addiction specialists have discovered in their work with substance abusers, and Alcoholics Anonymous (AA) has always intuitively known. Since AA's establishment in the early 1940s, its members have been reminding each other, "We don't have relationships; we take hostages."

Recovering addicts and alcoholics have long recognized that their relationships typically are maladaptive, unsatisfying, manipulative, or "more trouble than they're worth." Inconsistencies, jealousy, distrust, disappointments, and countless other difficulties dominate their most intimate attachments. Developing new relationships and striking up conversations with strangers usually stretches their capacity for engagement far beyond their capabilities. In many cases, the use of chemicals early in their substance-abusing career initially served a compensatory function, providing temporary relief by helping lubricate an otherwise cumbersome inadequacy and ineptness in their interpersonal attachment styles.

Some controversy exists about whether alcoholics and addicts can ever be taught to moderate or manage their chemical use. This issue is discussed in Chapter Two. For now, it will suffice to say that attachment theory complements the abstinent-based treatment approaches that dominate the addiction treatment field (Miller 1995). And attachment theory is highly compatible with AA's stance on addiction: abstinence must be the first goal of recovery. Clinicians who work with this population on a sustained basis know how difficult it is to form a working therapeutic alliance with a practicing alcoholic or addict. Before chemically dependent individuals can become *attached* to treatment, they must first get *detached* from the object of their addiction. Because of the potent emotional rush that alcohol and drugs produce, they are powerfully reinforcing and inhibiting of the more subtle emotional persuasions in a person's life. Consequently, the vulnerable individual's attachment to chemicals serves both as an obstacle and as a substitute for interpersonal relationships.

CROSS-ADDICTION

The pattern of substituting one addiction for another has long been recognized in the addiction treatment field and is commonly referred to as cross-addiction. Early in the history of Alcoholics Anonymous, the twelve-step group became acutely aware that many of the newcomers to the program would successfully stop their drinking, only to become addicted to something else. Alcoholics who discontinue drinking may become dependent on pills or other drugs, and vice versa. Many addicts, if left unchecked, become cross-addicted to other addictive behaviors, such as eating disorders, gambling, sexual addiction, and nicotine addiction, once their primary addiction was interrupted. Addicts and alcoholics become increasingly anxious when the last door on their last addictive behavior is closed. Addiction specialists learned that shutting the last door is very important because as that last door closed, the addict instinctually moves through a previously unseen, and often-painful portal into the true transformational experience that AA calls recovery.

In AA, many alcoholics stop drinking, rid themselves of the abundant character defects that plagued their relationships, and turn their lives around. However, for every success there are many other individuals who are unable to remain sober and continue to act out their destructive patterns in a similar fashion with other obsessions and addictions. They suffer constant relapses, often substituting one compulsive problem (e.g., cocaine, marijuana, etc.) for another. Many become bulimic, overweight, or anorexic. Their eating becomes as compulsive and out of control as their drinking or drug use was. They become compulsive workers or gamblers, or use sex as they used chemicals to combat the emptiness, boredom, anxiety, and depression that constantly threatens to overwhelm them. They do not achieve the healthy sobriety or serenity that AA and recovery promise. They become what AA terms a *dry drunk*. They stop their alcohol use, but their compulsive tendencies do not diminish. Even the *Big Book of AA* (1939) recognizes that some are "too sick to get the program" and AA may not work for everyone: "There are such unfortunates. They are not at fault; they seem to have been born that way. They are naturally incapable of grasping and developing a manner of living which demands rigorous honesty. Their chances are less than average. There are those, too, who suffer grave emotional and mental disorders" (p. 58).

These "grave emotional and mental disorders" are often compulsive in nature because addiction and other compulsive disorders tend to coexist (Orford 1985). There is a high correlation among a variety of dysfunctional, destructive behaviors, including sexual compulsive/addiction, paraphilia, addictive relationships, kleptomania, compulsive spending, embezzlement, gambling, and self-injury. For instance, a number of studies have demonstrated a high correlation between nicotine dependence and alcohol dependence (Irons and Schneider 1996), between sexual compulsivity and cocaine use (Washton 1989), and among compulsive spending, eating disorders, and compulsive gambling (Carnes 1991). A survey of seventy-five recovering sex addicts found that 39 percent were also recovering from chemical dependency, 32 percent had an eating disorder, 13 percent characterized themselves as compulsive spenders, and 5 percent were compulsive gamblers (Schneider and Schneider 1991). Recently, evidence has surfaced suggesting a pattern of compulsive behavior and compulsive Internet use that is consistent with the growing body of research on behavioral addictions (Morahan-Martin and Schumacher 2000). Intake counselors frequently discover during an initial assessment that a person entering treatment for chemical dependency will also be suffering from numerous other compulsive disorders. A closely related phenomenon in early recovery is that patients report a tendency to switch addictions or intensify a concurrent addiction. Attachment theory (Flores 2001) and affect regulation theory (Khantzian 2001) provide a convincing theoretical explanation of why substance abusers are likely to substitute one compulsive behavior for another until the underlying defects in the self are repaired.

ADDICTION AS AN ATTACHMENT DISORDER

Addiction, therefore, can be viewed as an attachment disorder. Since it is biologically impossible to regulate our own affect for any extended period of time, individuals who have difficulty establishing emotionally regulating attachments are more inclined to substitute drugs and alcohol for their deficiency in intimacy. Because of a person's difficulty maintaining emotional closeness with others, certain vulnerable individuals are more likely to substitute a vast array of obsessive-compulsive behaviors (e.g., sex, food, drugs, alcohol, work, gambling, computer games, etc.) that serve as a distraction from the gnawing emptiness and internal discomfort that threatens to overtake them. Consequently, when one obsessive-compulsive type of behavior is given up, another is likely to be substituted unless the deficiency in self structure is corrected.

The recent work of attachment theory and self psychology have taught addiction specialists that dysfunctional attachment styles interfere with the ability to derive satisfaction from interpersonal relationships and contribute to internal working models that perpetuate this difficulty. Experiences related to early developmental failures leave certain individuals with vulnerabilities that enhance addictive-type behaviors and these behaviors are misguided attempts at self-repair. Deprivation of age-appropriate developmental needs leaves the substance abuser constantly searching for something "out there" that can be substituted for what is missing "in here."

Because attachment theory has given scientific authority to the importance of the study of the bond between children and their caregivers, it helped legitimize the investigation of the relationship between addiction and attachment. While classical developmental theory has always recognized the importance of early childhood experiences on adult psychopathology, it took attachment theory to place the significance of these early attachments in their proper perspective. Intimate long-lasting relationships are an integral part of human nature and the inability to establish long-lasting gratifying relationships is directly related to the quality of early attachment experiences. Difficulty overcoming ineffective attachment styles (Ainsworth 1989) can leave certain individuals vulnerable to addictive compulsions as compensatory behavior for their deficiency. Louie (1996) emphasizes the primacy of this biologically driven need: "Attachment is not just a good idea, it's the law."

DYNAMICS OF MULTIPLE ADDICTIONS

The novice therapist soon learns that many addicts, even successful, high-functioning ones, often manifest a pattern of multiple addictions and a type of symptom substitution that is compulsive in nature. These compulsive behaviors are driven by the addicts' inability to draw prolonged satisfaction from interpersonal relationships. Since attachment theory holds the position that affect regulation is impossible without external assistance and that we all are emotional regulators of each other, many addicts prone are to substitute one disorder for another until the deficit in self is repaired and dysfunctional attachment styles are altered. The dynamics surrounding this phenomenon are common enough that addiction specialists have categorized them:

Switching: Suspending one compulsive behavior but initiating a new one.

Masking: Onc addiction masks or excuses another.

Fusion: More than one addiction must be present for the other to work.

Ritualizing: One addiction is part of the ritual for another.

Numbing: Shame about one addiction is numbed by another addiction.

Disinhibition: One addiction lowers inhibitions for another addiction.

Alternation: An ingrained pattern of alternating from one addiction to another.

Intensification: Mutual addictions intensify each other.

A clinical example will help illustrate this problem. After a second female patient in less than two years filed allegations of sexual misconduct against a young male psychiatrist, he was ordered by administration to seek psychotherapy. Allan had been invited to join a private practice group three years previously because of the clinic's need to recruit a psychiatrist knowledgeable about the treatment of addiction. None of the other psychiatrists on staff had received adequate training about addiction in medical school. Allan's successful inpatient treatment for his own cocaine addiction five years ago and his successful recovery program, consistent abstinence, and committed involvement in twelve-step programs made him a desirable candidate at the time. He was a tireless worker, adored by his patients and dedicated to his work. His practice thrived because of his skillful management of substance abusers, and his caseload remained full with a long waiting list. Requests for consultations and supervision grew as rapidly as his reputation and expertise.

When Allan entered therapy, the treating psychologist was immediately struck by his appearance. He was a thin wiry man, meticulously dressed, and flawlessly groomed. Although Allan had difficulty sitting quietly—his leg bounced constantly and his fingers repeatedly stroked the large coffee cup that he carried everywhere—he laughed easily and his face beamed with ready excitement. With his boyish good looks and contagious smile, Allan could engage people quickly and easily. He was an easy person to interview. Completely open and nondefensive, he quickly revealed his history. He was diagnosed with attention deficit disorder (ADD) as a child and put on Ritalin when he was 5 years old, adding, "My mother was always the nervous type, and didn't know what to do with me until they got my medication right. I busted my ass all through high school, college, and medical school. I've always been hard working and busy, just like Dad. I never dated as a teenager." Allan cringed and rolled his eyes. "I was so shy and fat in college. But I guess I made up for all that in medical school when I lost a lot of weight and discovered girls." Allan laughed, arched his eyebrows, and did his best Groucho Marx impression. "I never drank or did any drugs as an undergraduate, but started taking speed in medical school to help cram for finals and stay awake during those killer hours I kept during my residency."

"The diet pills led to weight loss and I started exercising a lot, mostly running. Boy, now that's a terrific high. It took only a couple months and I really got hooked on

> exercise. I've completed a number of marathons and still manage to run a couple hours early in the morning every day. That's about when the girls started noticing me. I was always nervous around girls up until that time. I guess they frightened me. But once I discovered cocaine, everything changed. The two—drugs and women—just seemed to go together, and you know the rest." Allan laughed, smiled broadly, and took a giant slug of coffee.
>
> When asked about the two patients who filed complaints because of his conduct, Allan chuckled and shook his head. "You're right, I've got to be more careful. There's enough women out there. I don't need to start hitting on every 'pretty young thing' that shows up in my office, just because she flirts with me. I'll be more careful in the future."
>
> When asked if he was ever married, Allan smirked and shook his head. "You're kidding. Look at me. Do I look like someone who would have any trouble getting laid? Besides, I get bored easily. It must be the ADD."
>
> The therapist asked how many women he had had sex with in his life.
>
> Allan paused, and after a few seconds said, "I'm not sure . . . let's see, maybe two, no . . . maybe three . . . I guess it's closer to four hundred."

Allan's case is not an unusual one. His situation illustrates a number of the difficulties that commonly plague addicts and alcoholics. His early history of attention deficit disorder is the first sign of affect disregulation and suggests he may have been introduced too quickly into the world of the "pills to cure your ills" mentality. The absence of siblings and friends as a child left him extremely vulnerable to the constant heckling he received from schoolmates because of his weight, resulting in even more withdrawal and isolation. There is also evidence that neither of his parents (his mother was too anxious and his father too distant) could provide the emotional regulation and attunement that is required for the healthy development of a cohesive self. Their lack of availability and emotional responsiveness left a shy young boy with few options other than the choice to retreat into schoolwork and food as the only means of distraction and comfort available to him at the time. Even at this young age, troubling signs of the excessive need for the external regulation of affect were evident, suggesting deficits in internal sources of self-soothing.

His vulnerabilities and deficits in psychic structure made it inevitable that he would be susceptible to the seductive call of the siren song of amphetamine use in college. Amphetamines quickly became part of the ritual of his work addiction, and each addiction intensified and masked the other. Like every other coping strategy he employed in his life, his rapid weight loss, because of his excessive amphetamine use, fused with his addictive-like obsession for running. Drugs also helped mask his extreme shyness and led to switching and alteration between his sexual addiction and cocaine use. Each addiction served a disinhibiting effect on the other. Once outside circumstances forced him to relinquish his use of drugs (which had become fused with and part of the ritual of his sexual compulsivity), his sexual addiction and running intensified and became more compulsive and excessive.

Allan's situation demonstrates the dilemma facing every addict, alcoholic, and, ultimately, the therapist who is trying to provide treatment. Substance abusers continue to substitute one compulsive, potentially addictive behavior for another until they are forced to face the gnawing emptiness and intolerable anxieties that drive their substance use. This is why abstinence is such a crucial part of the alcoholic and addict's recovery. Until every addiction is relinquished, addicts or alcoholics will never be forced to develop the only source of healthy affect regulation that is available to them: healthy interpersonal attachment.

2

Substance Abuse as a Consequence of and Solution for Impaired Attachment Relationships

Physicians have for years been treating alcoholics as if they suffered from a Valium deficiency.
Joe Pursch, M.D.

Historically, the addiction treatment field has been divided into two divergent camps: the disease abstinence-based treatment model and the mental health model. This chasm has existed ever since the late 1930s, when Bill W. and Dr. Bob, two struggling alcoholics who had repeatedly sought assistance and failed to be helped by traditional methods of medical treatment, gathered together a number of other alcoholics to form the fellowship of Alcoholics Anonymous (AA). These men all shared a common disorder and frustration born out of their desperate need for help because of the medical community's inability to understand the true nature of their affliction. Their common struggle led to the birth of the self-help movement in this country. Seventy years have since passed and it appears that many in the mental health community have never forgiven AA for spurning the health care system that failed to help them.

Over the years, the mental health model's approach to addiction treatment was composed primarily of academicians, while the abstinence-based treatment approach remained the domain of clinical practitioners, most of whom worked in treatment programs that adhered almost exclusively to a pure abstinence-based model (Miller 1995). Researchers operating out of universities, and whose interest in working with addicts and alcoholics was merely passing or primarily academic, were producing a vast amount of research influenced by learning theory, suggesting that alcoholics could be taught to drink "normally." Since the results on controlled drinking and Moderation Management conducted by the academicians flew in the face of the day-to-day experience of the clinicians who worked directly with practicing addicts and alcoholics on a sustained basis, the chasm grew wider and more acrimonious.

Fortunately, there have been important exceptions to this split. An increasing number of dedicated professionals have demonstrated an increasing willingness to establish a more cooperative atmosphere between the two approaches (Brown 1985, Flores 1988, Khantzian et al. 1990, Minkoff 1995, Vaillant 1983). Recent advancements in the coexisting or co-occurring disorders field, especially in clinical treatment models applied with special populations, have produced more integrated approaches to assessment and treatment of people with addictive disorders (Jerrell and Ridgely 1999, McHugo et al. 1999). Most importantly, the pervasive adversarial attitude that separated the two disciplines has subsided, and the mental health and substance abuse treatment fields have begun to overcome historical barriers to cooperation (Meissen et al. 1999, National Association of State Mental Health Program Directors 1999, Ridgely et al. 1998). Consequently, initiatives and demonstration projects have provided a foundation for integration of these sometimes divergent approaches, resulting in the advancement of more effective treatment for the dually diagnosed (Group for the Advancement of Psychiatry 1993, National Association of State Mental Health Program Directors and National Association of State Alcohol and Drug Abuse Directors 1999).

ADDICTION—THE CART OR HORSE OF MENTAL ILLNESS?

Addiction has become recognized as one of the most significant health problems in this country. Previously, treatment for addiction was available only through AA or an occasional obscure hospital or treatment program in some distant part of the country that specialized in its treatment. Now it is rare to find any major metropolitan area that does not have at least one hospital or outpatient treatment program that specializes in addiction treatment. The increased need for more treatment facilities is a direct result of the increased use of alcohol and substances in our society (Ray 1983). The most crucial precipitating factor in addiction is the degree of availability and access to a particular drug. Thus, no matter how great the societal tolerance for addictive practice is, or how strong individual personality or genetic predispositions are, people cannot become addicted unless they have ready access to the drug.

Thirty years ago, addiction treatment was far less complicated than it is today. Treatment referred exclusively to alcoholism and the alcoholic, who in most cases was a Caucasian man in his late forties or early fifties. If necessary, he was first detoxed, then instructed to stop drinking and told to go to AA meetings. Now, it is rare to find an alcoholic, especially someone under thirty years of age, who isn't also using and abusing numerous other drugs. Cross-addiction, namely stopping the use of one drug and becoming addicted to another, is common practice for most substance abusers and alcoholics. The term *polydrug abuser* is a common diagnosis. It is now necessary to inquire about the substance abuser's drug of choice. Certainly, the onset of increased drug use in our culture has complicated the diagnostic and treatment picture.

Consequently, addiction treatment has become increasingly complex and fraught with controversy within the last twenty years. Multiple factors have contributed to this increased complexity, the least of which is the growing increase in the use of drugs, licit and illicit, in this country. The increased utilization of illicit drugs such as marijuana, heroin, and cocaine, along with the rapid proliferation of the use of designer drugs (LSD, Ecstasy, meth-crystal) by men, women, adolescents, and children regardless of race, creed, socioeconomic status, and ethnic background has complicated the treatment picture thoroughly. Add the pharmacological revolution taking place in our country, which has brought with it not only the many benefits that modern pharmacology provides, but also an ever-increasing potential for addiction and abuse of tranquilizers, amphetamines, and pain relievers, and the treatment alternatives become even more confusing. It is no wonder that addiction treatment specialists are caught in a labyrinth of contradictory attitudes and conflicting recommendations for treatment strategies and approaches. Compounding this difficulty even further is the growing number of afflictions or disorders that are now referred to as addictions to gambling, sex, work, and so on, even though they have nothing to do with the ingestion of chemicals.

In the 1970s, a growing number of health care professionals who had achieved their own sobriety by working the twelve steps of the AA program began to apply the disease-concept treatment approach to their own alcoholic patients, with startling success. The incorporation of the principles of AA into standard medical practices led to a significant change in the understanding of addiction and its treatment. The general acceptance of addiction as a disease and a primary disorder that must first be addressed has had a tremendous impact on the way that addiction is treated. From the disease perspective, addiction to chemicals, whether it be to alcohol or drugs, was no longer viewed as a symptom of a more serious core issue. Rather, it was seen as a primary condition that must first be arrested if any progress in treatment is to be achieved, and abstinence from all chemicals must be the first goal of recovery. Disease-concept–oriented therapists hold the position that substance abusers and alcoholics cannot benefit from psychotherapy as long as they continue to use chemicals. Not only has this stance legitimized the treatment of addiction and created a philosophy of treatment completely independent of the more classical and traditional approaches to psychological difficulties, it also has raised the question of whether addiction is purely a psychological phenomenon. The disease concept supported AA's lifelong contention that addiction is a disease and that total abstinence is a necessity if addiction is to be treated successfully (see Table 2–1, p. 34).

Prior to the acceptance of the AA treatment philosophy, intrapsychic conflicts and intrapersonal dynamics were usually viewed as the cause of addiction. However, the disease concept stood that view completely on its head. Depression, anxiety, and character pathology were viewed as symptoms—the result, not the cause, of addiction. Clinical and personal experience had taught addiction specialists that if they persuaded the alcoholic and substance abuser to abstain from the use of chemicals, their symptoms either completely subsided or at least greatly diminished in many cases.

George Vaillant's (1983) classic longitudinal study put a final nail into the coffin of the controlled-drinking versus disease-concept controversy of the late 1970s. Vaillant and Milofsky (1982) stated, "Thus, the eliotogical hypothesis that viewed alcoholism primarily as a symptom of psychological instability may be an illusion based on retrospective study" (p. 494). Consequently, Vaillant verified what everyone within the AA community and the addiction treatment field had known for years. Vaillant later wrote, "Prospective studies are gradually teaching psychiatrists the astonishing fact that most of psychopathology seen in the alcoholic is the result, not the cause of alcohol abuse. Put differently, alcoholism is the horse, not the cart of mental illness" (1983, p. 317).

ABSTINENCE: IS IT NECESSARY?

Not everyone has embraced the abstinence treatment approach. Many have rejected the disease concept as simplistic, and have questioned many of AA's basic assumptions. A number of addiction specialists contend that the reasons why someone initially gets hooked on drugs are primarily psychological and sociological, not pharmacological (Peele 1989, Ray 1983). Something in their personal makeup predisposes certain individuals to use substances addictively. Evidence suggests that few people become accidentally addicted to drugs. For instance, thousands of people have been chronically exposed to morphine in hospitals, and even demonstrate signs of physical dependence, yet show no evidence of continued use of narcotics after leaving the hospital. Complicating this clinical picture is the fact that many heavy drinkers are not alcoholic. Even though a substance has more potential to be abused if it produces a desirable effect (usually euphoria), usually the drugs that produce tolerance and physical dependence are more likely to be addictive.

A vast amount of contradictory evidence has been turned out in the past ten years by the more academically oriented researchers. Many of them challenge the basic assumptions and most cherished beliefs of the disease-concept–oriented treatment modalities. Looking at addiction from a learning theory perspective, many of these researchers (Kishline 1994, Marlatt et al. 1993, Sobell and Sobell 1973) have recommended controlled drinking and Moderation Management as alternatives to abstinence, presenting evidence showing that alcoholics can learn how to drink nonalcoholically.

While many theorists agree that the reason why people become dependent on drugs lies in the user, not the drugs (Ray 1983), there is another body of evidence that suggests that prolonged periods of substance use can produce physiological and neurobiological alterations in the brain, which in turn fuels the addictive process (Heyman 1995). Recent neurobiological research indicates that prolonged use of certain substances produces alterations in brain functioning, leaving certain vulnerable individuals unable to use substances nonaddictively (Leshner, 2001).

CRITERION QUESTION

The distinction between addiction and substance abuse is not always clearly defined. Is there a difference between a substance abuser and an addict or alcoholic? If there is, when does a heavy drinker become an alcoholic and when does a substance abuser become an addict? AA has struggled with this question for decades, and in their own colorful vernacular they posed the question: "At what time does a cucumber become a pickle?" At some time in the process of substance use, the substance abuser crosses an undefined line from which he or she cannot return. Just as a pickle can never become a cucumber again, the adaptation in brain circuitry and neurophysiology is altered in a way that the brain functioning of the substance abuser is changed forever. At some undefined point, substances and the ritual intertwined with their use have commandeered the motivational centers of the brain. Substance abusers are no longer in volitional control of their substance use, especially when they take that first drink or first pill. The alcoholic/addict is now under the control of powerfully induced and reinforced conditioned response patterns that are triggered by external cues and internal affect states.

Controlled drinking (Sobell and Sobell 1973), Moderation Management (Kishline 1994, Marlatt 1998), and natural recovery (Sobell, 1995) have all produced a vast amount of research challenging many of AA's most cherished and accepted positions on treatment. When examining research results and the conflicting claims of treatment outcome studies, enough cannot be said about the crucial necessity of distinguishing between those who are addicted and those who are substance abusers. To completely address the importance of the differential diagnosis, the important criterion question—How does one define an alcoholic?—must be raised. Most of the confusion that complicates research on this topic is tied to the controversy and disagreement on what constitutes an alcoholic. The *Diagnostic and Statistical Manual of Mental Disorders*, fourth edition (*DSM-IV*) provides little relief for this dilemma, preferring to address alcohol dependence rather than alcoholism despite the fact that many, if not most, alcoholics active in AA would not fit the criterion for alcohol dependence.

Like Democrats and Republicans, reasonable people who are aligned to either Moderation Management (MM) or Alcoholics Anonymous cannot always agree on who is an alcoholic and who is an abuser. Even the most conservative and strongest proponents of controlled drinking and MM Sobell and Sobell (1993) have finally reluctantly conceded (through some embarrassing and painful lessons) that true alcoholics should be excluded from MM.

Related to this issue, it would be helpful if one examined more thoroughly those prognostic indicators that seem to predict success or failure in the area of controlled drinking. Specifically, those individuals who are successful at Moderation Management tend to demonstrate less severe physical dependence, tend to be younger, and tend not to have a positive family history for alcoholism or drug addiction. Some would argue that these people were never really addicts in the first place, but only substance abusers. Even the staunchest and most devoted members of AA readily admit that not all heavy drinkers are alcoholics, and if they can learn to manage or control their drinking, more power to them.

Vaillant proposed years ago that, like hypertension, alcoholism runs on a continuum, and a person can have a little of it or a lot of it. His position closely parallels that of AA, as the organization contends that a distinction must be made between "high-bottom" and "low-bottom" alcoholics. High-bottom alcoholics, in AA's experience, do not suffer the severity of symptoms or negative consequences that low-bottom alcoholics do. Despite the vast difference between the two, both types respond to similar treatments and, as far as a diagnosis goes, no distinction should be made between the two when identifying someone as an alcoholic. Many high-bottom alcoholics (e.g., airline pilots, neurosurgeons, veterinarians, attorneys, priests, etc.) continue to function responsibly in demanding careers despite their alcoholism. Before they got into recovery and achieved abstinence, their drinking did not have to deteriorate to the point that they suffered the same degree of social consequences that is inflicted on low-bottom alcoholics.

Vaillant's research lends some support to why attempts to diagnose someone as an alcoholic based either on self-reports or on the amount of alcohol consumed are unreliable and highly subjective (i.e., many heavy drinkers are not alcoholic). Vaillant's classic study (1983) confirmed that the most reliable method for correctly assessing alcoholism is to cite the number and frequency of alcohol-related problems or social deviancy/consequences (e.g., DUI arrests, health problems related to alcohol consumption, public intoxication, legal difficulties related to alcohol consumption, etc.). Valliant demonstrated that there is a very high correlation between the severity of a person's alcoholism and social deviancy/consequences, and the assessment and identification of these related factors has a much higher reliability than the measurement "of ephemeral concepts of loss of control or alcoholism p. 37" and subjective reports on consumption levels.

Emerging neurological research (e.g., brain imagery) suggests that addiction is more than just a bad habit. No less than the director of the National Institute of Drug Addiction (NIDA) (Alan Leshner in 2001) and the director of the National Institute of Mental Health (NIMH) (Steve Heyman in 1995) contend that once a person crosses over a yet-undefined line, there is an alteration of neurophysiology that cannot be reversed. They contend that prolonged use of substances can alter neural synapses and the endogenous production of certain neurotransmitters that eventually result in permanent alterations of brain functioning. These alterations in turn affect the reward centers of the brain (hypothesized to be around the medial forebrain bundle, [MFB]) resulting in certain syndromes (e.g., reward deficiency syndrome), making addiction a brain disease.

Those who look to collaborative work to sustain their claims that controlled drinking works may wish to reconsider their reference to the work of Audrey Kishline (1994) to support the efficacy of MM. As the entire addiction treatment field learned recently, she crashed head-on into a car while driving the wrong way down the interstate and killed a 38-year-old man and his 12-year-old daughter. What made this tragic accident more noteworthy was that Kishline was the recognized founder of Moderation Management, and her blood alcohol level at the time of the accident was more than three times the legal limit. At her trial she was quoted in the popular press as saying, "MM has done more harm than good." She now describes the MM movement as "a lot of alcoholics covering up their problems."

What makes this tragedy even more troubling is the similarity between this incident and the Sobell and Sobell (1973) controversial study on controlled drinking that led to an embarrassing exposé on *60 Minutes* twenty years ago that revealed that most, if not all, of their "successfully treated" subjects had either died, relapsed, or joined AA. Charges (Pendrey et al. 1982) and countercharges (Marlatt 1983) on methodological flaws and the ethical implications of the findings were debated in professional journals for years. Special attention has been paid to the ethical dilemma that is posed when advocating controlled drinking for those at risk. Some say MM violates medicine's most hallow creed: First, do no harm. Although the merits and accusations about the Sobell study have never been definitively settled, both supporters and critics agree that their data have never been replicated, and probably represent at best, an anomaly (Nathan 1992).

George Vaillant best summarizes the position that needs to be carefully considered when looking at outcomes research for controlled drinking or MM. Longitudinal studies, not short-term cross-sectional studies, need to be done to evaluate claims of treatment success. Vaillant knows, as recovering alcoholics learn from their own personal experience, that alcoholics can control their drinking for weeks, months, and sometimes even years.

ADDICTION OR SUBSTANCE ABUSER: DIFFERENTIAL DIAGNOSIS

Assessing a person's level of involvement with substances is crucial when determining what kind of treatment is necessary. Is the person a recreational user or abuser? Is the person dependent, addicted, or suffering from a co-occurring condition? Many individuals go through periods of alcohol and drug experimentation in which they misuse, abuse, or excessively use substances. Not all of these persons become dependent, and not all dependency leads to addiction. Certain persons, because of intrapsychic or developmental deficiencies often closely related to their genetic and biological substrates, either are more vulnerable to developing a substance abuse disorder or are at greater risk of exacerbating present co-occurring conditions if they use substances excessively (Flores 2001, Khantzian 2001).

To help correctly assess the relationship between substance abuse and co-occurring conditions, it is necessary to examine the pattern of an individual's substance use history across a continuum. Flores (1997) suggests that substance abuse often follows a predictable and identifiable pattern that can be categorized into four general areas:

(1) Those individuals who experiment with drug and alcohol use and learn early how to control and modulate its use. These individuals, even though they may have had periods of heavy substance use, were never really addicted.
(2) Those individuals who learned later in their life that they could not modulate or control their use so they stopped either alone or with the help of a professional or a 12-step program. These individuals are referred to as "high-bottom" alcoholics in AA.

(3) Those individuals who learn much later in their life that they have to stop, but either cannot or, once they do stop, are unable to stay sober or clean and are plagued by constant relapses. They suffer repeated losses and often require outside consequences like cirrhosis of the liver or an intervention before they finally stop. Such individuals are referred to as "low-bottom" alcoholics in AA.

(4) There are others who never achieve any lasting sobriety or are unable to stay clean despite careful working of the 12 steps of the AA program. They either die from their condition or end up in the penal system or on the street. [p. 309]

There is a high probability that individuals in categories 3 and 4 are likely to suffer from co-occurring conditions. If these co-occurring conditions go unrecognized, and consequently untreated, these individuals' chances for successful treatment are going to be greatly diminished. In categories 3 and 4 there is a greater possibility that individuals may have a primary mental disorder (e.g., bipolar disorder, personality disorder, etc.) that in turn may interfere with their ability to maintain abstinence for any length of time. In many instances, stopping the use of substances may actually worsen their psychiatric symptoms. Severe character disorders (e.g., borderline, antisocial, etc.) are other examples of co-occurring conditions that can interfere with treatment and recovery.

The primary relationships between substance abuse and psychiatric symptoms were extensively reviewed in a document (TIP No. 9) published by the Center for Substance Abuse Treatment (1994). The Treatment Improvement Protocol (TIP No. 9) presented a list of possible relationships between substance use and psychiatric symptoms that must be considered during the screening and assessment process.

Substance abuse can cause psychiatric symptoms and mimic psychiatric syndromes.

Substance abuse can initiate or exacerbate a psychiatric disorder.

Substance abuse can mask psychiatric symptoms and syndromes.

Withdrawal from substance abuse can cause psychiatric symptoms and mimic psychiatric syndromes.

Psychiatric and substance abuse disorders can independently exist.

Psychiatric behaviors can mimic substance abuse problems.

The report concluded, "There is no single combination of dual disorders; in fact, there is great variability among them. . . . Patients with mental disorders have an increased risk for substance abuse disorders, and patients with substance abuse disorders have an increased risk for mental disorders" (p. 4).

THE RELATIONSHIP BETWEEN MENTAL HEALTH AND ADDICTION

Co-Occurring Disorders

Clients with co-occurring psychiatric disorders present unique challenges in therapy. Since many substance abusers require either detoxification or a structured treatment program to help prevent their downward spiral from becoming life threatening, they pose special difficulties in the early stages of their treatment. While substance abuse treatment facilities and personnel often rely on the mental health system for support, the two systems historically have had different approaches, administrative structures, professional requirements, and funding mechanisms. Consequently, clients have had to receive treatment in different settings, often with little coordination, based on therapies that were not always complementary. In addition, those who are dual diagnosed are a heterogeneous group for whom no single treatment mode is adequate.

It is essential that the therapist be prepared to assess and effectively identify an entire array of accompanying conditions when working with this population, since all axis I and axis II conditions are overly represented with alcohol and substance abusers (Miller and Brown 1997). Add to this the high probability for chemically dependent individuals to suffer from multiple addictions and their propensity to rapidly switch from one addiction for another, and the therapist often finds treatment with these patients to be complex and challenging (Flores 2001). The heterogeneity of problems accompanying addictive disorders is complicated by the heterogeneity of patients who will be seeking or requiring substance and alcohol treatment. Consequently, it is highly unlikely that a one-treatment-for-all, cookie-cutter approach will work for all patients suffering from addictive disorders.

Individual psychotherapy, especially with patients with coexisting disorders, is rarely applied as a stand-alone treatment modality during the early stage of recovery. As Kemker and colleagues (1993) suggest, "Professionals must accept that they cannot treat patients alone—the addiction is too deeply entrenched, the patient too alienated p. 299." Attachment theory holds the position that as long as the substance abuser continues to use substances, the establishment of a working therapy alliance will be difficult to establish or maintain. The prevailing reinforcing effects of chemical use are just too powerful and compelling, overriding anything the therapist may have to offer. However, since it is rare for practicing alcoholics or addicts to remain free from the consequences of their substance abusing behavior, it is inevitable that circumstances will eventually take a toll on their lives.

Attachment systems open up during a crisis. The inescapable problems produced by continual substance use create an opportunity that the therapist must quickly take advantage of, before the substance abuser's defenses seal over. Because of the severity of the crisis the substance abuser may be facing, a referral to a treatment facility may be required. Despite the crucial need for collaborative treatment and the additional support of other providers, it is crucial that the therapist not compromise the attachment relationship. Confronting the destructive nature of the substance abuser's chemical use without irreparably damaging the therapeutic relationship is a crucial skill that must be developed when working with this population.

John Wallace (1978), in a classic article, was the first to attempt to provide a systematic view of psychotherapy with the alcoholic by identifying critical issues and a number of strategic choices that must be made when treating the alcoholic client. Wallace pointed out that successful treatment of the alcoholic often required choosing a safe course between two equally hazardous alternatives. Walking the narrow ridge between too much support (i.e., continual analysis of the person's depression without introducing the question of the patient's alcoholism) or too much confrontation (i.e., forcing the alcoholic to either stop drinking or face termination of treatment) is a challenge that in some cases will test even the most skilled and experienced therapist. One has to go to only a few AA meetings to hear the all-too-familiar stories of alcoholics who nearly drank themselves to death while their therapist tried to uncover and explore the reasons why they drank. On the other hand, AA members will caution newcomers about the "AA Nazis" and "Big Book thumpers" who will insist on the "My way or the highway" approach, a stance that often drives many away from help rather than assisting them in their struggle.

Conjoint Treatment Requirements

The question of how treatment will be approached depends on a number of conflicting factors and variables. What type of treatment setting (e.g., inpatient, outpatient, day treatment, etc.), with what level of substance abuse and which kind of substance (e.g., late stage addiction, IV heroin use, crack cocaine, early stage alcohol abuse, etc.), with which level of motivation (e.g., court referral, voluntary admission, etc.), with which type of therapy (e.g., group, individual, AA, etc.), for which type of coexisting disorder (e.g., bipolar, anxiety disorder, personality disorder, etc.), in what stage of recovery (e.g., early, late, precontemplative, maintenance, etc.), and for what aim or purpose (e.g., abstinence, moderation, etc.) must be carefully considered. The answers to these questions have to be thoroughly evaluated to determine what role the therapist will take in approaching the patient.

When a substance abuser requires collaborative treatment, the treating therapist can often get lost in the shuffle. All too often the substance abuser's alliance with the therapist will not be honored, and the patient will quickly become absorbed into the treatment system. A comprehensive treatment program simultaneously provides group therapy, drug screening, medication if necessary, family therapy, education sessions, detoxification, neuropsychological screening, and introduction into twelve-step programs. The introduction of the patient into twelve-step programs can be especially troubling for therapists who are not familiar with the workings of the AA program. Kemker and colleagues (1993) wrote extensively about the difficulties facing the therapist who has to "face the task of integrating self-help and psychological models of treatment." The authors point out how one very crucial component of addiction treatment involves getting the patient to accept the diagnosis and to become acculturated to "the culture of recovery," p. 294.

But just as newly identified addicts and alcoholics must be introduced to an alternate treatment ideology, so must newly initiated professionals. Becoming familiar with twelve-step programs and the jargon of AA has a number of important implications for treatment. Matano and Yalom (1991) put forth recommendations that are very similar to those of Kemker and colleagues when they suggested that special considerations be given to integrating AA and twelve-step recovery principles into a psychotherapy format. Matano and Yalom warned that traditional approaches to addiction treatment are doomed to fail unless recovery and abstinence are accorded priority, and the patient accepts the identification as either an addict or alcoholic.

The acculturation into the culture of recovery carries some potential obstacles for the novice therapist. If therapists are going to work with this population on a sustained basis, Matano and Yalom encourage them to become familiar with the language and principles of twelve-step recovery programs, and caution them that until they do, they will be vulnerable to the misuse and distortion of AA concepts by patients who either apply them inappropriately or deliberately use AA jargon as a defense.

> Following his second DUI (driving under the influence) arrest in less than two years, Bob was ordered by the court to get an assessment as part of his plea bargain.

Thirty minutes into the session, Bob balked at the therapist's recommendation that he would benefit from psychotherapy. "No way." Bob waved his hand dismissingly at the therapist. "Listen, I've gone to a few AA meetings in my life and learned enough from AA that talking about how I might have been treated as a baby doesn't have anything to do with why I drink. I drink because I'm an alcoholic. As they say in the program, wallowing in self-pity doesn't help. Anyway, psychotherapy doesn't work for alcoholics, it only makes them drink more."

Bob leaned back in his seat, a satisfied smile on his face. "AA also has taught me to 'utilize, don't analyze.'"

The therapist didn't flinch. "It's great that you've gone to a few meetings. I was going to recommend that, also. As a matter of fact, the next time you go, I want you to seek out one of the old timers after the meeting is over and ask him about Bill W."

"Why? And who's Bill W.?" Bob asked. His face wrinkled up with irritation.

"Because he might tell you how the founder of AA and the chief architect of the Big Book was influenced by two of the most prominent psychologists of his time. Bill Wilson corresponded with Carl Jung and read extensively the book *Varieties of Religious Experience* by William James. Each of these men had a tremendous impact on Wilson's thinking about spirituality and greatly influenced the workings of the AA program. The old timer might also tell you how Bill W. twice entered psychotherapy with Henry Tiebout, M.D. Each time, he stayed in therapy for about fours years. Obviously, psychotherapy didn't interfere with his sobriety and recovery. If the founder of AA can benefit from professional help, I think you can too."

Matano and Yalom (1991) also recommend that the therapist be prepared to help alcoholics or addicts clarify and distinguish what they are responsible for and what they are not responsible for. For instance, since relapses are to be expected, alcoholics are not responsible for their disease or addiction, but they *are* responsible for their recovery. Alcoholics must learn that while they are not responsible for their frequent loss of control once they start drinking, they *are* responsible for taking that first drink.

> Mary showed up at the therapist's office after missing her last two appointments and promptly admitted that she had "slipped again." When asked what had happened for her to start drinking again after more than two months of abstinence, she shrugged her shoulders, looked down at her hands, shrugged, and mumbled, "I don't know, I just slipped."
>
> "No, Mary," her therapist replied softly, "you didn't slip, you relapsed."
>
> Mary looked up at him. "What's the difference?"
>
> "There's a big difference. A slip implies that something happened to you, unsuspectingly." Her therapist looked into her eyes and stated emphatically. "A relapse is different. You didn't drink because something happened to you. *You* did it. Let's call your relapse what it is—a premeditated drunk. You made a decision to drink, and if you keep denying responsibility for what you did, you'll never learn anything from this relapse and will likely repeat it all over again."

CHARACTER PATHOLOGY AND ADDICTION

The relationship between addiction and character pathology has important implications for treatment. In a classic longitudinal study addressing the relationship between character pathology and alcoholism, Vaillant (1983) discovered that alcoholism and personality disorders have a complex and different multifactoral etiology. He discovered that "as soon as one disorder is present, the second becomes highly likely," p. 159. Schuckit (1973) agreed and had previously summarized the etiological possibilities that exist between these two conditions:

> There are those who have character disorders and abuse substances because this is one common symptom of their personality disorder.

Chemically dependent individuals can manifest character pathology as a consequence of their chemical dependency.

There is a common shared factor that leads to both addiction and character pathology.

It is crucial to distinguish between these three possibilities because what will work in treatment for an alcoholic or substance abuser who manifests character pathology owing to the toxicity of the substance abused will require a far different approach than will a patient with a personality disorder who is abusing drugs. The stress and regressive pull that prolonged substance use has on the brain and the body often blurs the distinction between the two disorders. In many cases, an accurate diagnosis is impossible to make until the individual is substance free for a period of time. In my earlier text Flores (1988), I gave an example of the significant changes that can occur quickly when an alcoholic is correctly diagnosed:

> Alice was a 35-year-old Caucasian female who had been in outpatient treatment in a community mental health center for over five years. She had "worn out" six different therapists because of her violent outbursts and demanding provocative behavior. She had been diagnosed as a Borderline Personality Disorder five years earlier, and none of the outpatient staff wanted to carry her on their caseload, so they referred her to an outpatient group at the clinic in the hope that this would rid them of a very troublesome patient. As Alice attended her weekly sessions, it became clear that her explosive tirades in group and difficulties outside of group usually followed severe or prolonged drinking episodes. Six months into treatment, the group leaders, who had a thorough background in addictions, began to point out these patterns in her behavior. Initially, she rejected their observations, but eventually conceded the possibility that they might be right and responded more favorably after other group members began to share similar observations. Unable to deny the

> consensual observations of the entire group, Alice succumbed to the opinion that she stop drinking and seek treatment for her alcoholism. After completing a thirty-day outpatient treatment program, she returned to the group and continued to attend meetings at Alcoholics Anonymous.

The change in her behavior was dramatic. She was able to tolerate other members' disagreement and proved receptive to feedback from others for the first time. Where previously she reacted to disagreements by vehemently attacking others, she now was able to see alternative viewpoints. Her behavior change was so apparent that staff members who had treated her previously began to make appreciative comments about the changes in her demeanor and behavior as a consequence of her group treatment. Little did they realize that it was her abstinence from alcohol and her involvement in AA that permitted her to respond favorably to therapeutic intervention. In actuality, it was the proper diagnosis of her alcoholism that led to her primary condition being treated appropriately. Instead of committing the frequent error of futilely trying to combat the affective storms produced by her addiction, the group leader required that she stop drinking and use the group to reinforce this requirement. The troublesome borderline features of her personality quickly subsided.

AXIS I DISORDERS

The interactions between substance/alcohol abuse and other psychological disorders are complex. For instance, there is mounting clinical evidence that patients who present with mental health problems have a significantly greater prevalence of substance abuse histories than the general population (Miller and Brown 1997). However, the reverse is also true. Research has clearly demonstrated that alcohol and drug use may, in many cases, provoke depression or anxiety disorders. In other cases, chronic emotional difficulties like social phobia or anxiety disorders may lead some individuals to self-medicate with alcohol and other substances (Kushner and colleagues 1994). Individuals diagnosed with alcohol or substance abuse disorders have a much greater lifetime risk for other diagnosable psychiatric disorders (Regier et al. 1990), and patients who seek treatment consistently manifest significantly higher rates of mental health disorders (Brown et al. 1994). However, it has been found that many of these diagnosed emotional and mental health conditions diminish or completely abate when substance and alcohol use is stopped or reduced (Miller and Brown 1997).

Trauma and Addiction

Within the last few years, a vast amount of evidence has been accumulated that suggests that the incidence of untreated sexual trauma is alarmingly high for addicts and alcoholics (Bollerud 1995). Women with substance abuse disorders are especially likely to suffer from psychological trauma stemming from emotional, physical, or sexual abuse. One preliminary study by Bollerud (1995) placed the figure as high as 75 percent. Other research has shown that women become addictive for reasons that are quite different from men's, and treatment has to be tailored specifically to their needs (Covington 1997). Despite the fact that women's issues with addiction derive from different experiences, Bollerud recognizes that it is difficult to accurately diagnose both addictive and trauma-related disorders because there is so much overlap in their symptoms. Nevertheless, she recommends that the addictive disorder be given priority and be dealt with aggressively, and she supports a twelve-step abstinence-based approach. She cites evidence that trauma patients—even those suffering from dissociative disorders—who use AA have better recovery rates.

THE RELATIONAL MODELS: AN INTEGRATION

It is important to have a comprehensive meta-theory of addiction that not only integrates diverse mental health models with the disease concept, but also furnishes guidelines for clinical practice that are compatible with existing treatment strategies. Any proposed theory—no matter how comprehensive and intellectually satisfying it is—will not maintain credibility if its basic premises fly in the face of applied practical experience and the fundamental realities of successful clinical applications. Since most addiction specialists who deliver treatment adhere to an abstinence-based treatment approach that is closely aligned with twelve-step treatment philosophy, any theory is doomed to be ignored if it contradicts the direct clinical experience of those who work with this population.

Attachment theory accomplishes this aim. With its rich heritage and solid grounding in psychodynamic theory, it provides a respected theoretical perspective that helps legitimize the recommendations of the abstinence-based treatment approach. Most importantly, attachment theory's basic premises do not conflict with any of the principles of the AA program. Lewis and colleagues (2000) support this position:

> An addict's bulwark against relapse involves more communion that cognition, as Alcoholics Anonymous and its multiple variants demonstrate. Gathering like people together to share their stories imbues a wordless strength, what Robert Frost called in another context "a clarification of life—not necessarily a great clarification, such as sects and cults are founded on, but a momentary stay against confusion." The limbic regulation in a group can restore balance to its members, allowing them to feel centered and whole. [p. 214]

An attempt to synthesize and integrate the seemingly divergent perspectives of AA and attachment theory can lead to a more thorough understanding and appreciation of the therapeutic stance that must be taken when treating addiction. Such an investigation can also supply a firmer theoretical foundation for those dissatisfied with AA because of its perceived lack of rigorous scientific underpinnings. The integration of these diverse approaches can also furnish a more expansive view of AA, alleviating some of the misgivings that critics have of the program. It is hoped that this will not only provide needed clarification and elaboration, but also help establish a more harmonious relationship among these conflicting perspectives.

Accepting attachment theory as a credible alternative explanation for the etiology and treatment of addiction also permits the recognition of additional contributions from other related perspectives. Psychodynamic theory went through an exciting evolution in the last half of the twentieth century. In contrast to a "one-person" psychology (i.e., a neutral therapist tries to understand the unconscious determinants of the patient's aberrant behavior), the relational models are a "two-person" psychology. From this perspective the patient's psychology is inextricably connected to context, which is to the psychology of the therapist or person with whom the patient is interacting. While the understanding that is developed in the psychotherapeutic context is related to the patient's personal history, it remains the case that the behavior demonstrated is always a function of the current situation and psychological states of every participant in the relationship. Relationships, therapeutic and social, are shaped by the projections, assumptions, hopes, wishes, and fears of all participants. The development of the relational models has shifted the focus away from intrapsychic struggles to an exploration of the interpersonal or relational difficulties that contribute to a person's present situation. Most importantly, the relational perspective has ushered in more innovative ways for understanding addiction and the difficulties that the typical addict and alcoholic brings to treatment.

Self psychology (Kohut 1977) was the first theory to offer a comprehensive theoretical description that bridged the gap between the abstinence-based treatment specialists and the psychodynamic-oriented psychotherapists. Kohut's formulations were influenced by and an extension of the earlier work of the relational models that were developed by Bowlby (1973) and others (e.g., Guntrip 1974, Fairbairn 1952, Winnicott 1965) at the Tavistock Clinic in London. The object relations school helped shift psychoanalytic thinking from classical drive or instinct theory to a relational approach with its greater emphasis on adaptation, developmental arrest, and deficits in self structure. This shift has profound implications for treatment that will be explored in the following chapters of this book.

Bowlby (1988) and Kohut (1977) are the first credible theories that provided a practical alternative rationale for the addiction cycle that is not only compatible with the disease concept, but also expands it by providing a more complete and intellectually satisfying theoretical explanation of why AA works as it does. Both attachment theory and self psychology not only help broaden the theoretical implications for treatment, but also are in complete harmony with AA and complement the way twelve-step programs treat chemical dependency. Kohut and Bowlby's perspectives also provide inherently an valid alternative explanation for why twelve-step programs work as they do and how the curative forces in these programs have a direct relation to the strategies that need to be emphasized when treating patients suffering from substance abuse disorders.

TABLE 2–1.

TWELVE STEPS OF THE ALCOHOLICS ANONYMOUS (AA) PROGRAM
1. We admitted we were powerless over alcohol—that our lives had become unmanageable.
2. Came to believe that a Power greater than ourselves could restore us to sanity.
3. Made a decision to turn our will and our lives over to the care of God as we understood him.
4. Made a searching fearless moral inventory of ourselves.
5. Admitted to God, to ourselves, and to another human being the exact nature of our wrongs.
6. Were entirely ready to have God remove all these defects in character.
7. Humbly asked Him to remove our shortcomings.
8. Made a list of all persons we had harmed, and became willing to make amends to them all.
9. Made direct amends to such people wherever possible, except when to do so would injure them or others.
10. Continued to take personal inventory and when we were wrong promptly admitted it.
11. Sought through prayer and meditation to improve our conscious contact with God as we understood Him, praying only for knowledge of His will for us and the power to carry that out.
12. Having had a spiritual awakening as the result of these steps, we tried to carry this message to alcoholics, and to practice these principles in all our affairs.

From Alcoholics Anonymous (1939).

3

Attachment Theory: Implications for Treatment

Attachment is not just a good idea: it's the law.
Lewis, Amini, and Lannon (2000)

Addiction from an attachment theory perspective holds one basic and simple premise about treatment: until substance abusers develop the capacity to establish mutually satisfying relationships, they remain vulnerable to relapse and addiction. To succeed in treatment, the addicted individual must learn how to establish healthy relationships. While this overly simplistic portrayal of attachment theory gets to the heart of the matter, it does not do justice to the intricate complexity of accomplishing such a modest maneuver. To keep the significance of attachment theory's primary premise in perspective, it is important to remember that attachment theory holds the position that substance abuse is both a solution and a consequence of a person's impaired ability in developing healthy attachments. Consequently, if addicts or alcoholics are to achieve abstinence and sobriety, they must first detach from their primary destructive relationship to substances and then develop the capacity for healthy interpersonal attachments.

Those familiar with Alcoholics Anonymous (AA) will immediately recognize the striking similarity to the program's position that abstinence be given the utmost priority (it is the first step of the twelve-step program) in treatment. Seventy years of experience has taught AA members that attachment to treatment is impossible as long as the alcoholic remains attached to alcohol. Newcomers to the program are strongly encouraged by AA members to "keep it simple" and "just don't drink and go to meetings." AA intuitively recognizes that without substituting some alternative behavior for drinking, maintaining abstinence is extremely difficult. From an attachment perspective, the AA community furnishes the support and emotional regulation that newly recovering alcoholics need while they make the difficult transition from detachment to alcohol to attachment to recovery.

> Tom, a 42-year-old account executive, arrived for his first appointment complaining of depression and job-related stress. The first part of the session was focused on "the tremendous amount of pressure I'm under at work."
>
> When queried about the other areas of his life, Tom shrugged and shook his head. "What other areas of my life? I haven't got time for anything else but this mess I've got to clear up at the firm." He gave the therapist a piercing look. "If I don't do it, who will?"
>
> "It sounds like you've always had to go it alone," the therapist replied.
>
> "Damn right," Tom sighed, and leaned back in his chair. "There's two or three people gunning for my job. They'd love to see me screw this thing up. I certainly can't count on them."
>
> "What about the home front?" the therapist asked. "Any help there?"
>
> "You mean my ex-wife?" Tom sat up in his chair and sneered. "Shit, she's a big reason I'm in this mess. She's never been any help."
>
> The next fifteen minutes were spent exploring the extent of Tom's isolation. His two daughters had just left for college and he had been living alone in an apartment since his divorce two years ago. His past was dominated by the same theme. Tom's parents died in an automobile accident when he was 6. He and his two younger sisters were sent to live with an uncle "who adored the two girls, but hated my guts." Gradually, the topic of Tom's drinking was addressed. He readily admitted to concerns about his drinking, confessing that he had suffered a couple blackouts and a second DUI violation a year earlier.

"Have you ever considered that you might be an alcoholic?" the therapist asked.

Tom gave him a wry smile. "To be honest with you, I have been concerned about by drinking, lately. I may have a drinking problem, but I don't think I'm an alcoholic."

"Well, you know that's an important distinction to make."

"What distinction?" Tom arched an eyebrow.

"Whether you're an alcoholic or someone with a drinking problem." The therapist leaned forward in his chair.

"What's the difference?" Tom asked.

"Well for one thing, it determines how we approach the problem. If you're an alcoholic, by definition you cannot drink normally and the only treatment that works is total abstinence." The therapist gave him a reassuring smile. "Now, on the other hand, if you're a problem drinker, you may have some other options."

Tom sat silently for a few seconds, pursed his lips, and looked up at the therapist. "What do you think I am—a problem drinker or an alcoholic?"

"Based on what I've heard, I think you're probably an alcoholic." The therapist held up his hand and began counting on his fingers. "One, you've been having blackouts; two, you have two DUIs; three, your ex-wife complained about your drinking and there is some evidence it contributed to the marriage failing; four, you have expressed your own concerns about your behavior when you drink; and finally, there is some evidence that your father may have been an alcoholic. There is evidence that alcoholism is genetically transmitted and runs in families. You have a lot of red flags that I would encourage you not to ignore."

Tom sat pensively and stared at the floor for a couple minutes before asking. "What do you think I should do?"

"I'd recommend we schedule an appointment for next week and in the meanwhile, you go to a few AA meetings."

"AA?" Tom looked aghast. "Isn't that . . . ?"

The therapist waved his hand to cut Tom off. "Listen, I know what you're thinking. What am I doing going to a room with a bunch of down and out drunks?" The therapist reached into his drawer and pulled out an AA meeting list. After circling three addresses and times of particular meetings, he gave the list to Tom. "Here, try these three. See which one you like the best. Choose your meetings like you would choose your therapist. There are good AA meetings and there are bad AA meetings. The most important factor for determining a good meeting is whether you feel comfortable there and whether you can relate to the people. I think you'll find these three meetings to be compatible with your issues."

When Tom returned for his next session, there was a marked change in his affect and demeanor. He told the therapist that he had been to five meetings since the last appointment and felt better than he had in years. Tom's enthusiasm was evident. He had fallen in love with the program. At the second meeting, he had run into an old friend whom he hadn't seen since college when they were drinking buddies. They were both surprised to see the other there. At the next meeting, he ran into a senior partner at his firm. After a couple of uncomfortable moments, they warmed up to each other and readily agreed to protect their anonymity from others on the job. However, Tom said that he noticed an important difference in his relationship with the senior partner at work.

"I feel less isolated there, now. I feel I have an ally."

ATTACHMENT AND BIOLOGY: HISTORICAL INFLUENCE

Unlike most relational theorists (e.g., Guntrip and Fairbairn), who depended on data obtained from the treatment of their adult patients, Bowlby relied on data drawn from observations of the behavior of young children in real-life situations. Because his observations did not fit completely with the leading psychodynamic perspectives (e.g., Klein 1948) of the day, he searched for an alternative perspective to capture the full scope of what he saw as a primary drive for attachment. Bowlby turned to the science of ethnology (e.g., Lorenz 1953) to help place the importance of emotional regulation and attachment in its proper perspective. Bowlby's position contrasted with the Kleinian emphasis on the etiological prominence of fantasy and intrapsychic conflicts between impulses as the basis of psychopathology. From Klein's perspective, pathology is rooted in the conflicts that result from internally generated fantasies. Relationships with others are seen as epiphenomena of purely autogenerated internal processes rather than as an integral part of interpersonal interactions. Bowlby, in contrast, was much more interested in the actual events of real interactions that took place in the child's external world.

Drawing on the work of Lorenz (1953), Bowlby saw similarities between Lorenz's concept of imprinting and attachment. Goslings in the wild follow their mother goose, but not because they recognize her as a parent who will lead them to food or away from danger; rather, baby geese follow any object (even Lorenz) if they saw it moving early in their lives. Lorenz correctly concluded that evolution had equipped goslings with a hardwired neural rule to become fixated or imprinted to the first moving object, which was usually the mother. "Imprinting is a manifestation of rudimentary neural systems dabbling in relatedness and its rigidity owes much to the primitive nature of these circuits. Human relationships show similarly lawful properties. Even though primate attachments are more flexible than a gosling's, they bend less than people expect" (Lewis et al. 2000, p. 68).

Bowlby hypothesized that a similar process occurred with attachment. Until the early 1950s, a popular belief had been that children primarily bond to their mothers because they fed them. Bowlby dispelled the erroneous assumption, called "cupboard love," by drawing on the work of Harlow (1958) and Spitz (1945) to substantiate his theory. René Spitz reported on the fate of orphaned children reared in foundling homes and institutions, as well as infants separated from mothers in prison. While the physical needs of the children were adequately met in these sterile environments, the children failed to thrive because they were not held or furnished with the proper amount of emotional responsiveness. Death rates at the so-called sterile nurseries were routinely 75 percent. Spitz discovered that the lack of human interaction—handling, cooing, stroking, baby talk, and play—is fatal to infants.

Harlow's (1958) famous work in the 1950s provided further support for Bowlby's emphasis on the importance of attachment. As undergraduate psychology students will remember, young monkeys, when given the choice of two surrogate mothers, prefer the terrycloth figure to the wire mesh cylinder outfitted with a feeding milk bottle. During times of stress or threat, baby monkeys would always run to the cloth figures as a means of obtaining soothing and nurturance. If the cloth figures were removed, the baby monkeys would rock alone in the corner.

IMPLICATIONS FOR TREATMENT

Attachment theory has a number of important implications for addiction treatment. To utilize the theory's contributions, it is important to summarize its positions:

1. Attachment is a fundamental motivation in its own right and cannot be reduced to a secondary drive.
2. Actual real-world happenings matter more than unconscious fantasies or internal drives.
3. The degree to which people can regulate their own emotions is determined by the length and strength of their earliest attachment experience.
4. Separation and individuation, free from attachment needs, are not legitimate goals for normal development or therapy.
5. The need for attachment and selfobject responsiveness is a lifelong process, not just phase specific.

6. Attachment of child to parent is different from attachment of parent to child. When parents (or therapists) use children (or patients) to meet their own unmet attachment needs, psychology results.
7. Caregiving and affiliative relationships (mutuality) are separate developmental stages that are reached when the self is fully developed.
8. Attachment theory holds the position that just as a biochemical intervention (medication) will alter behavior, so too will environmental interventions (removal of stress-inducing stimuli, providing secure attachment, etc.) produce alterations in an individual's neurology and biochemistry.

We now discuss each of these positions in detail.

1. *Attachment is a fundamental motivation in its own right and cannot be reduced to a secondary drive.* Attachment theory, like self psychology, can be considered an offspring of object relations theory. While these three theories share important similarities, they hold different allegiances to classical drive theory. The most decisive factor that differentiates attachment theory from the other two theories is the degree to which it differs from classical drive theory on the importance of attachment. Attachment theory holds firmly to the position that the pains, joys, and meaning of attachment cannot be reduced to a secondary drive. Attachment is recognized as a primary motivational force with its own dynamics, and these dynamics have far-reaching and complex consequences (Bowlby 1973).

Bowlby recognized that natural selection favors mechanisms that promoted parent–offspring proximity in an environment of evolutionary adaptation. Attachment is not just psychologically driven, but is propelled by powerful biological needs for interpersonal closeness. A primary biological function is to secure assistance and survival in the case of adversity. This is true for all social mammals and applies to parent–offspring relationships in other species, not just human beings.

2. *Actual real-world happenings matter more than unconscious fantasies or internal drives*. One fundamental disagreement

between attachment theory and classic psychodynamic theory concerns Bowlby's dissatisfaction with drive theory's tendency to place more importance on fantasy and internal psychic experiences than it does on the impact of real-life events. Bowlby did not agree that internal experiences should take precedence over external reality. Like Foulkes (1975), he criticized the notion of therapy that reduces all complex phenomena to pure intrapsychic processes. Therefore, attachment theory was formulated to better explain observed facts in ways more coherent with overt behavior. Bowlby set out to develop a theory that better explained observed facts in ways that were more coherent with overt behavior. Bowlby emphasized that psychopathology originates in the real experience of interpersonal life and that classical drive theory took too many liberties with its theoretical musings.

Bowlby also challenged the fundamental tenets of psychoanalytic orthodoxy. He did not believe the dynamic and economic points of view were tenable because they were based on an energetic discharge model that relied on out-of-date nineteenth-century physics and biology. Like Fairbairn (1952), Bowlby viewed classical Freudian theory as rooted in an anachronistic model taken from nineteenth-century physics. Bowlby suggested an innovative and necessary shift to modern developments in biology, evolutionary theory, ethology, cybernectics, and information systems to support his position.

The way the word *object* was used in the psychoanalytic literature troubled Bowlby. He preferred the term *attachment figure*, because he felt it better captured the bi-personal nature of attachment relationships. He believed *object* had been applied to connote a wide range of concepts, leading to inaccuracies and divergent interpretations. As Marrone (1998) pointed out, "The word 'object' has different meanings; it can be a 'thing' or the 'target' of a drive or intent," p. 109. *Attachment figure* reflected more accurately Fairbairn's (1952) idea that the primary motivational force in all social mammals is relationship seeking. Attachment figures serve a function similar to Kohut's selfobjects because attachment, like selfobject transferences, can in itself be reparative.

3. *The degree to which people can regulate their own emotions is determined by the length and strength of their earliest*

attachment experience. Because attachment theory has given scientific authority to the importance of the study of the bond between children and their caregivers, it helped legitimize the investigation of the relationship between addiction and attachment. While classical developmental theory has always recognized the importance or early childhood experiences on adult psychopathology, it took attachment theory to place the significance of these early attachments in their proper perspective. Intimate, long-lasting relationships are an integral part of human nature, and the inability to establish long-lasting, gratifying relationships are directly related to the quality of early attachment experiences. Difficulty overcoming ineffective attachment styles (Ainsworth 1989) can leave certain individuals vulnerable to addictive compulsions as compensatory behavior for their deficiency.

4. *Separation and individuation, free from attachment needs, are not legitimate goals for normal development or therapy.* Attachment theory applied to addiction and treatment has important implications in our society, in which people strive for independence, autonomy, and self-sufficiency, but all too often at the cost of alienation from self and others. Nowhere is this difficulty played out with more consistency than with alcoholics and addicts. They are notoriously counterdependent individuals, living their lives in the extreme ends of the attachment–individuation continuum. Autonomy is purchased at the price of alienation and the absence of mutuality in their relationships. Attachment theory not only represents a movement away from one-person psychology, but also contains a fundamental interpersonal conception of human beings as always being situated in relations with others. Effective therapy, like attachment theory, is based on the implied notion that the essence of being human is social, not individual.

Object relations theory has taught Bowlby that introjected self and object representations carry within them intense affect, and that these internalized introjects contribute to a person's propensity to project their internal experience onto the external world (Ogden 1982). Through the power of projective identification, individuals are likely to coerce, induce, and provoke others in their external world to be unwitting contributors to their internal struggles and expectations. This becomes a "life script," a self-fulfilled prophecy that drives people's interpersonal interactions in such a way that their external world begins to conform to or fit their internal expectations and experiences. Paradoxically, a perverse sense of comfort results from the familiarity of the experience, which serves to satisfy the need or drive for consistency, thus reducing anxiety temporarily.

Addressing this issue, Bowlby formulated an alternative model of internalization because he believed the way psychoanalysis defined the process implied something of a mechanical nature, which consisted of making internal what had been external. Bowlby's internal working model (IWM) is a representative model of internalization highly compatible with Piaget's theory (1954) of representation and shares some similarities to object relations' description of internalized self and object representations. However, IWM is more theoretically compatible with intersubjectivity theory (Stolorow et al. 1987) because it places more emphasis on *how* the interpersonal field is created by both individuals within a relationship.

> Confidence that an attachment figure is, apart from being accessible, likely to be responsive can be seen to turn on at least two variables: (a) whether or not the attachment figure is judged to be the sort of person who in general responds to calls for support and protection; [and] (b) whether or not the self is judged to be the sort of person towards whom anyone, and the attachment figure in particular, is likely to respond in a helpful way. Logically these variables are independent. In practice they are apt to be confounded. As a result, the model of the attachment figure and the model of the self are likely to develop so as to be complementary and mutually confirming. [Bowlby 1973, p. 238]

The emotional availability of a caregiver is the crucial factor in determining the makeup of an IWM. As Kohut suggested, how the parent "is with" the child is more important than what the parent does. Stern (1995) holds a very similar view because he believes it is the nature of the relationship—"the experience-of-being with"—that is internalized and not just the object or self representation. Marrone (1998) writes that Bowlby defined internalization as "something that has been neither entirely outside nor entirely inside . . . What is represented in the person's mind is the relationship and not the parent as a separate entity" (p. 44). Much like Winnicott's classical description that "there is no such thing as just a baby," IWM holds the position that the primary unit of existence is not the self and object representation, but the relationship and the rules that govern that relationship. On the basis of repeated experiences, the infant learns what to expect from the parent. The rules governing these expectations are internalized along with mental representations and guides a person's thoughts, feelings, and behavior in subsequent close relationships. The implied rules of "how I have to be in order to stay in relation with you" defines the structure of the IWM and becomes the determining force that fuels the repetitive nature of people's relationships.

> Dan, a 38-year-old self-proclaimed cocaine and sex addict, had been clean and in therapy with a female therapist for nearly three years. Transference issues were difficult to work through, but Dan had gradually made consistent progress in his capacity to change the rules that dominated his relationships with women. Abstinence and a good-enough holding environment eventually allowed him to come to an understanding of what had driven his addictions. Ten minutes into this session with his therapist, Dan proceeded to unravel, with unusual clarity, the climate in his home that had come to dominate his internal world.
>
> "I don't think I've told you all there is to know about my family. I've only given you the surface stuff. You don't know the real reasons why I never see my father and avoid my sisters, and my mother when she was alive."
>
> The therapist nodded in agreement as Dan continued. "I never told you why we had to leave Indiana when I was 9 and move in with my grandmother in Ohio."
>
> His therapist sat quietly, intently watching him as he proceeded to tell her that he knew she represented all the women in his life who had ever wielded power over him. Dan explained how this awareness provided him little

relief from his complaisance with them. Perhaps, he told her, it was because there had been so many angry women early in his life who held this advantage and because their power came in so many forms and disguises that he was unable to alter his conditioned visceral response to them. Dan confessed that his stomach churned the same way it did with her as it did with Mrs. Swartz, his second-grade teacher, who seemed to take great pleasure in making an example of his appearance to the other children in class whenever his mother would shove him off to school with dirty clothes and unwashed hair. His grandmother, like his mother, never tired of reminding him that he was as worthless and useless as his father.

He paused and looked into her face for some clue. She gave it to him by softly saying, "Go on."

"Well, I had no way of fighting those accusations because she was right. My father was a real asshole—distant, self-centered, and totally immoral."

"Immoral?" the therapist asked.

"Yeah, my father tried to screw every women he ever met. He embarrassed us all with his behavior. Although he was a physician, and a brilliant man in many ways, he had no backbone and even less integrity and moral character. It didn't help that I looked like him. That was my curse. It seemed to give all the women in my family even more reason to use me as a punching bag for all their frustrations with him. The comparisons never stopped even after Dad managed to abandon me and the rest of the family when he ran off and married one of his wealthiest patients. This was just as well because the medical board was already in the process of suspending his medical license because he was always trying to screw his patients—literally and financially. Some of them, and especially their husbands, didn't appreciate that very much. I don't think he ever realized that most people didn't find him as charming and desirable as he thought he was. Oh, before I forget, there was also this little problem of his tendency to overprescribe drugs for himself and others."

Dan was now in a deep reflective mood, his eyes

slowly moving side to side as if he was watching the reels of a private motion picture untangle in his mind. He kept talking. “It took me a few years to figure out that my mother was no innocent bystander, but an eager recipient of many of these prescriptions. She was no better than him. They truly deserved each other. During the divorce, which was messy and public, there were lots of unproven allegations and wild rumors about wife swapping, drug orgies, pornography, and sex clubs. It all created quite a sensation in our little rural community and the local newspaper had a field day with all the disgusting dirty details. Soon after the trial, Mom had to move all of us to Columbus, Ohio, to live with her mother in order to escape the ridicule and embarrassment. Dad, despite his medical practice, had squandered all his money on drugs, sex, and rock ’n’ roll, so Mom was penniless. She deteriorated pretty fast after that. Got into her medication—as she called it—to help settle her nerves and stayed addicted until she died two years ago. Looking back now without my own addiction clouding my memory, it helps explain why she staggered around the house half-clothed most of the time. My mother was never very bright, but she had been attractive when she was younger. I’m sure that’s why Dad married her. She lost all of that as she grew older and got pretty disgusting those last few years. It was during her drug stupors that she was most likely to wander around the house naked or crawl into my bed at night bawling and saying that I was now her little man. All of this could quickly turn into anger and physical attacks depending on how drugged up she was that night.”

Dan paused, then looked at the therapist again to see if he should continue. She gave a sign he took as yes.

“The house, which had always been filled with a strong sexual tension—you could cut it with a knife—got even more intense when my two older sisters reached puberty. Following Mom’s example, Jeanie and Paula soon became adept at using sex as a weapon. They knew the power it wielded over men and they were not going to let any man do to them what Dad had done to Mom. They also derived a lot of pleasure from teasing me about my body and sex. I was never safe in the bathroom or my bedroom from their invasive comments about my genitals and body. They really worked me over pretty good sometimes."

Feeling he had said too much, Dan stopped and sat back. His therapist sensed he was finished for a while, so she said, "I've heard some of this before, but not all of it all together like this. It was much worse than I thought."

"I think you're right. Hearing myself say it all together like this reminds me how bad it really was. It was much worse than I let myself admit most of the time."

5. *The need for attachment and selfobject responsiveness is a lifelong process, not just phase specific.* Attachment theorists recognize that both one-to-one and group or network attachments are necessary because originally they serve a biological function to ensure survival. During early development, attachment helped secure assistance for the infant during times of threat or danger. However, as the individual grows older, affiliative relationships with peers and groups became more important because they involve greater reciprocity and a semantic order (Lichtenberg et al. 1992). Affiliative relationships are not based purely on physical proximity, but are mediated by a complex set of meanings and representatives. If long-term recovery is to be achieved, the capacity to establish affiliative relationships is crucial. One reason AA works as well as it does is that it provides alcoholics the opportunity to substitute affiliative relationships for their addiction.

There is a very subtle interplay among attachment, attunement, and emotional stability. Attachment theorists have long recognized an important paradox about attachment: secure attachment liberates (Holmes 1996). This is as true for the securely attached child as it is for the securely attached individual in treatment, whether treatment is provided by AA or an individual therapist. Just as securely attached children will move greater distances away from their caregiver, taking more risks exploring their surrounding environment, securely attached patients will take more risks, exploring their inner world during therapy.

Marrone (1998), quoting Stern, supports this position:

> Stern (1985) asserted that the essential state of human existence is togetherness rather than aloneness, with a most basic sense of connectedness, affiliation, attachment and security as givens (p. 240). He further recognized that, for infants, the "quality of relatedness"—that is, attachment—extends beyond the initial mother–infant bond and develops throughout childhood, applying to peers as well as mother. Stern also clarified how attachment and security are affectively intertwined. [p. 158]

6. *Attachment of child to parent is different from attachment of parent to child. When parents (or therapists) use children (or patients) to meet their own unmet attachment needs, psychology results.* Karen Walant (1995) criticizes our society's overemphasis on separation and individuation, claiming that our preoccupation with autonomy at all costs has contributed to the erroneous belief that we can regulate our own emotions. Parental instinct has been sacrificed for cultural norms that have made dependency a pathology and needing shameful. Looking at substance abuse from the perspective of attachment theory, she views addiction as a secondary substitute that individuals have adapted as a means to cope with the traumatic effects of early, unmet developmental needs. To counter the effects of what Walant calls "normative abuse," she recommends a shift in our approach with these patients to one that is more relational and intimate. This allows addicts and alcoholics to become part of something greater and more satisfying than their isolated existence. She emphasizes the need for an "immersion experience"—moments of complete understanding between patient and therapist—as the means for dislodging the alienated, disconnected self.

Attachment theory contends that infants and their parents are biologically hard-wired to forge close emotional bonds with each other. These attachments serve important emotional regulatory functions. Animal studies have demonstrated that secure attachment can produce alterations in biochemistry and neurophysiology (Lewis et al. 2000). All social mammals regulate one another's physiology and modify the internal structure of one another's nervous system through the synchronous exchange of emotions. This interactive regulatory relationship is the basis for attachment.

Emotions have a commutative function (starting first with the mother and the infant). The central nervous system of all social mammals is an open feedback loop. All social mammals interact and alter one another's neurophysiology. The nature of the impact is the basis of attachment. The memory of it is recorded in the change that takes place.

7. *Caregiving and affiliative relationships (mutuality) are separate developmental stages that are reached when the self is fully developed.* Because addiction is both a consequence of and a solution to the absence of satisfying relationships, the emphasis on the ability to make attachments with others becomes crucial if treatment is to be successful. Maturity in development implies the ability to perceive self and other as separate with needs and wishes of their own with whom one can develop empathic, reciprocal relationships, based not on demands but on mutuality. As relational theory (Jordan 1986) reminds us, mutuality or affiliative relationships become a critical part of an individual's development and growth. Mutuality is especially difficult for most substance abusers who have grown up encouraged to value competition, performance, achievement, individualism, and autonomy over attachment. The exploration of intimacy and mutuality leads to an awareness of the responsibilities of relationships and how they can be a source of both pleasure and frustration. Substance abusers must learn that mature relationships cannot be determined unilaterally by one person, but must be achieved through an interactive process of mutual agreement and consent. Crucial themes like dominance or submission and dependency or autonomy will have to be painfully worked through and negotiated in relationships.

Mutuality requires the recognition of the other as different, separate, and equal. Dealing with the conflicts and narcissistic injuries these differences produce is a developmental skill that most substance abusers have failed to master. Compliance or rebellion and acquiescence or domination are usually the only options available in these patients' limited repertoire of responses. If long-term sobriety and abstinence is to be maintained, they must learn how to resolve conflicts in their relationships rather than abandoning them or allowing them to degenerate into sadomasochistic patterns. Resolving disagreements leads to psychological structure building, and optimal frustration is the vehicle that permits the self to gradually internalize the functions previously provided by the selfobject. Psychic structure is laid when the ruptured bond between the self and the person providing selfobject functions is restored (Harwood, 1998).

> Michael, a 35-year-old recovering cocaine addict and self-proclaimed sex addict, had been actively participating in a weekly outpatient therapy group for over two years. Upon entering the group shortly after his discharge from an inpatient treatment program, he complained repeatedly of the lack of excitement and pleasure in his life. Despite his constant lamenting, he managed to stay clean and off of drugs even though his sexual acting out increased during the first year and a half in the group. His outside relationships were marked by multiple sexual encounters and short-term trysts. As his commitment to the group continued, he gradually developed more meaningful relationships outside of group. Eventually he became involved in a monogamous relationship with a women that had entered its six month, and he announced to the group he had started taking guitar lessons, proudly proclaiming that for the first time in his life he was enjoying something other than "sex, drugs, and rock 'n' roll." He also took on the group role of cheerleader, often announcing after each group, "Wasn't this a great group tonight?"
>
> His honeymoon with the group ended when two members left the group and were replaced by two new women. The composition of the group had been remarkably stable up to this point, and one of the new members was an aggressive and at times highly invasive woman. One night while Michael was speaking to the group about his difficulties with his long-term relationship, this new member, Alice, began to interrogate him, firing off a series of intrusive questions mixed with judgmental commentary about his behavior. After a few minutes of this, the group leader asked Michael how it felt being interrogated. He replied, "Oh, I'm fine with it. I don't mind at all." He smiled at Alice and the group leader without any outward sign suggesting otherwise and the group continued.

> Michael did not attend the next two group sessions, calling each time with a credible excuse. After sitting quietly and withdrawn through much of the session upon his return to the group, the group leader asked if the change in the group composition had contributed to his silence and absence. Michael denied it, but was not convincing enough to prevent the rest of the group from pressing him on the issue. The group noticed a difference in his demeanor. Michael finally conceded he did feel "a little funny," but could not explain his feelings. After much effort by the group, Michael eventually described his experience as a child in a home dominated by a mother and two older sisters who were very intrusive and sexually shaming of him. When asked if he had felt any of that with Alice, Michael said he couldn't be sure. Further exploration led to a "vague recognition" that Alice did remind him of his older sister and that it "probably" did bother him that she had interrogated him three weeks ago. When asked by another group member why he had not said so when asked by the group leader, Michael volunteered, "I couldn't be sure what I was feeling." Over the course of the next few months, Michael was encouraged by the group to use his vague sensations as possible signals, especially when he wanted to hide or stay away from the group. This eventually led to an increased capacity for empathy and affect recognition.

The long-term goal of therapy is helping the alcoholic or addict develop the capacity for mutuality and attachment, which helps break the substance abuser's cycle of alienation and isolation. However, as important as attachment is, the maintenance of a sense of separateness is equally so. The polarity between attachment and autonomy has to be carefully managed. Secure attachment can only be established once insecure and ambivalent attachment styles are relinquished (Ainsworth 1989). If late-stage treatment requirements are successfully achieved, substance abusers will begin to understand and experience healthy mutuality. They also will learn the important task of resolving conflicts without resorting to alcohol or drugs, ensuring a better chance of maintaining satisfactory relationships. Pines (1998) discusses why this is important:

> Healthy human beings grow within a culture of embeddedness where others provide reciprocity, gratification, and the impetus for continued growth. Within the culture of embeddedness processes of attachment and relatedness develop. From attachment and relatedness develop both autonomy and connectedness, the psychological double helix of human life. From this fundamental biologically rooted sense of reciprocity leading to a sense of fairness develops the drive to get it right and to get satisfaction from doing so. Getting things right means also putting things right when they have gone wrong; that is, the drive for reparation and the origins of the sense of "getting things wrong" from which comes the sense of human guilt without which human relationships become impossibly destructive. [p. 27]

Viewing addiction and substance abuse as an attachment disorder with a problematic expression of the need for selfobject responsiveness helps explain why AA works as it does for this population. Substance abuse is the result of disturbances in attachment and reactions to injury of the self. As self psychology reminds us, the experience of the bond between the self and selfobjects is crucial for psychological growth and health. No one ever escapes their need for satisfying relationships, and the degree to which we are unable to form healthy interpersonal intimacy determines the degree to which we are vulnerable to substitute substances for human closeness.

8. *Attachment theory holds the position that just as a biochemical intervention (medication) will alter behavior, so too will environmental interventions (removal of stress-inducing stimuli, providing secure attachment, etc.) produce alterations in an individual's neurology and biochemistry.* The mind–body dualism that has dominated science since the time of Descartes is being challenged by attachment theory. When patients are emotionally engaged in therapy, their brain is being altered. Evidence is mounting that shows effective psychotherapy alters neurophysiology. There is also a growing body of scientific research suggesting that all mental processes have corollary changes in

physiology, even though our technology is not advanced enough to accurately measure all the subtle changes that occur. Consequently, attachment is not just an abstract concept; it is a complex physiological process. Animal studies show this to be the case. Secure attachment creates stable neurophysiological homeostasis, and the lack of it produces disruptions in neurophysiological systems. An increasing body of research is suggesting that attachment theory is not so much a psychological theory as it is a biological theory.

The theory holds the position that our emotions and our neurophysiology are an open feedback loop, which requires input and external regulation from attachment figures or selfobjects. We cannot independently regulate our own affect. The degree to which we can regulate ourselves is determined by the length and strength of our earliest attachment experience. The more secure and stable the earlier attachment, the more success we have at self-regulation. With the absence of secure attachment, we remain more vulnerable to disruption and affect destabilization.

> The false dichotomy that exists between the mind and the body is most pronounced when working with trauma survivors. Emma, a recovering alcoholic, began to identify vague memories of childhood sexual abuse after achieving nine months of sobriety in AA. The intrusive recall of repressed trauma promptly compelled her to seek therapy. She feared she might start drinking again, and realized her alcoholism had served a compensatory function by keeping away the painful affect associated with her sexual abuse. Six months into therapy with Dr. Davis, the therapy was producing effective but painful results. A transcript from her session illustrates her struggles.
>
> Dr. Davis waited for Emma's sobbing to stop; however, her tears showed no signs of slowing down. Instead, they gathered momentum, surging up from somewhere deep inside of her.
>
> Despite efforts to compose herself, Emma could not stop her body from heaving convulsively as she gasped for breath in between sobs.
>
> The drama was painful for her therapist to witness.

Emma looked like her body was trying to expel some vile poison that contaminated it to the core of its molecular structure.

The more she tried to stop crying, the more something within her refused to cooperate. Her body's natural striving for cleansing itself clashed with Emma's stubborn determination to wrest power from an imagined adversary. Even in the midst of the safety of her hospital room, Emma fought to gain composure, to be appropriate.

Dr. Davis knew Emma's struggle to control herself was futile because there was really no self to control. He wanted to shout at her: "Let go! Can't you see you're fighting yourself? You're imposing a dichotomy where none exists." He wanted to explain to her that her solution to the problem was creating a greater difficulty than the problem. "Your 'self' is an intellectual construct that creates the illusion that there is a you separate from your body." Her therapist knew that mind and body do not act upon each other, because they are not other; they are one.

Similar dramas had been played out countless times during the fifteen years he had practiced psychotherapy. He knew Emma's efforts only made matters worse, but to tell her this in the middle of her sobbing would have been not only insensitive but also useless. An intellectual explanation would require her to think, which was a big part of Emma's problem. She lived most of her life in her head. He preferred to support the truth of the body and the authenticity of her emotions. Emma did not need an explanation; she needed an experience. Knowing this, he said gently, "Breathe."

Emma followed his suggestion and inhaled deeply. The convulsive resistances of her body subsided, once they did not have to fight against the imposed restrictions of her mind. She wept more freely, allowing her tears to flow and be spent, naturally.

When her outpouring paused, he prompted her once more, "Keep breathing."

She was holding her breath again. His reminder permitted her to relinquish control once more. Emma exhaled slowly, allowing additional pollutants and toxins to be released. Her efforts provided an increased opportunity for her feelings to wash through her. She cried quietly, more gently.

Dr. Davis waited patiently until the tears ended completely of their own accord.

After she finished crying, Emma looked up at her therapist and smiled awkwardly. She reached for the box of tissues on the table to her left. Holding the box on her lap, she pulled out a couple of tissues and dried her eyes before blowing her nose.

Her therapist looked away. While watching Emma cry did not strike him as intrusive, staring at her while she blew her nose felt more invasive. The release of one's mucus was more private, more personal.

Finally, Emma spoke. "God, don't you ever get sick of me crying?"

He ignored her question. "First of all, I don't consider your feelings pitiful, just painful."

Relief washed over her face. Emma held eye contact and smiled, before slumping back in her chair and running her hands through her hair. "When will I ever be able to talk about these things without my guts being ripped inside out?"

"All things in their own time." He leaned forward in his chair. "When your body's finished grieving, it'll let you know. Until then, permit your emotions to run their course. The worst thing you can do is cut yourself off from your feelings once more. If you do, you'll start drinking again."

Emma grimaced. "That's not the answer I wanted, Doctor."

He nodded. "I know. That's part of the problem."

She tilted her head to the side and feigned innocence. "And what do you mean by that remark?"

He hesitated and smiled at her knowingly. "If you weren't so damn arrogant, all this would be easier on you. Your pride makes it hard for you to let yourself be vulnerable with me."

"Don't take it personally Dr. Davis. I don't let myself

be vulnerable with anyone." Emma forced a laugh. "I've done more shameful blubbering with you in the last six months than with anyone else in my entire life."

Dr. Davis returned her smile. "It would help if you would learn to make a distinction between your shame and your pain."

Emma examined his eyes. "You're right. I'm always judging myself."

"Yes, just like your mother did when she asked you what you did to cause your uncle to touch you. Old habits are hard to break."

"It's just that I can get so disappointed in myself."

"Are you feeling that now, here with me?" Dr. Davis asked.

"Yes, I am. You come here every day and help me figure out what I'm feeling. You'd think I'd learn by now how to do this myself."

"Your difficulty identifying your feelings appears to be another indictment about your worth."

"Of course." A faint smile crossed her face. "As you keep reminding me, I keep my shameful feelings from overwhelming me by trying to be perfect."

He nodded.

"Feeling is just something I don't do very well," Emma said with a thin layer of disgust in her voice. "I don't have much practice at it."

"There's another thing you don't have much practice at," Dr. Davis replied.

"What's that?" Emma asked.

"You don't have much practice letting yourself depend on people. It's quite an accomplishment for you to show your vulnerabilities and allow me to help."

Emma eyes filled with tears again. These tears were different though; they were tears of appreciation. Of course, he was right. He had identified the real issue. She had great difficulty with her perceived neediness.

An overwhelming appreciation for Dr. Davis washed over her as he spoke. Sometimes, like today, she felt understood and completely in harmony with him. A vague, almost forgotten childhood memory returned to her. It was associated with a familiar feeling of being picked up, held, and wrapped in a soft, warm blanket.

She looked at him fondly. Emma wanted to say more. She wanted to tell him how hard all this was, letting herself depend on and be cared for by someone. Despite her compulsion to explain it all to him, she didn't because she knew he was fully aware of her struggle. Her awareness produced an unexpected luxury: a feeling of being known by someone in a way that didn't require words.

From the position of attachment theory, Lewis and colleagues (2000) encourage us to remember that "dividing the mind into 'biological' and 'psychological' is as fallacious as classifying light as a particle or a wave," (p. 167). They write on the jacket of their book how the need for attachment is driven by powerful biological forces that requires another person's emotional resonance if stability is to be maintained:

> A primordial area of the brain, far older than reason or thinking, creates the capacity that all humans share . . . The workings of this ancient, pivotal urge reveals that our nervous systems are not self-contained. Instead, our brains link with those of people close to us, in a silent rhythm that makes up the very life force of the body. These wordless and powerful ties determine our moods, stabilize and maintain our health and well-being, and change the structures of our brains. In consequence, who we are and who we become depend, in a great part, on whom we *love*.

Lewis and colleagues must be congratulated for taking the risk of introducing the subject of love for scientific scrutiny. Most mental health professionals are notorious for avoiding the subject, especially as it applies to therapists and their patients. Volumes are written about aggression, hate, envy, fear, and a myriad of other emotions that dominate the therapeutic encounter. But love remains a taboo subject. The fear of appearing soft-minded does not prevent Lewis and colleagues from venturing into an area that many avoid because the word *love* is fraught with messy misconceptions and undefined pronouncements.

ATTACHMENT: A GENERALIZED THEORY OF LOVE

One way out of this dilemma is to look at attachment as a scientific way of operationalizing love. Attachment theory provides a language and method for making sense of the nebulous process we call love. Attachment theory can also be thought of as an attempt to legitimize a topic that, like the weather, everybody talks about but does very little about. Because of its emphasis on emotional bonds and the functions that attachment serves, it would be helpful to think of love simply as simultaneous mutual regulation.

As attachment theory and self psychology continue to remind us, we are object-seeking animals. We are driven innately from birth for close human contact. To the degree that we are deprived of this and do not possess the ability to accomplish this task, we are emotionally deficient and vulnerable to addiction. The familiar and popular bumper sticker that idealistically advocates "Hugs, Not Drugs" as a solution for our country's drug problem may be a lot closer to the truth than we sometimes realize. The implication of this wistful statement is simple and straightforward. Close interpersonal contact can provide an effective alternative to drugs as a means of altering and stabilizing one's neurophysiology.

Critics of this position perceive these statements as more examples of the naive and misguided belief that therapists can "love their patients into health." Despite the unenviable task of trying to defend an approach that can be overly sentimental, idealistic, and indulgent, there may be some wisdom to be garnered from this posture if the rush to judgment and ridicule is tempered by an investigation into the ways that attachment theorists defined attachment. In the process of scientifically studying the effects of early loss on children, Bowlby discovered that interruptions in parental bonds have far-reaching consequences on a person's development and their later adult relationships. Because Bowlby never allowed conjecture or an investment in a preferred supposition to take precedent over actual observed behavior, attachment theory has identified a sequence of overt interactions that typically occurs between social mammals. The force that drives these interactions is commonly referred to as love.

If there are any doubts about how this topic has any relation to addiction, here is how Caroline Knapp (1996) described her own alcoholism in her book, *Drinking: A Love Story*:

> A love story. Yes: this is a love story.
>
> It's about passion, sensual pleasure, deep pulls, lust, fears, yearning hungers. It's about needs so strong they're crippling. It's about saying good-bye to something you can't live without.
>
> I loved the way drink made me feel, and I loved its special power of deflection, its ability to shift my focus away from my own awareness of self and onto something else, something less painful than my own feelings. I loved the sounds of drink: the slide of a cork as it eased out of a wine bottle, the distinct glug-glug of booze pouring into a glass, the clatter of ice cubes in a tumbler. I loved the rituals, the camaraderie of drinking with others, the warming, melting feelings of ease and courage it gave me. [p. 5]

Attachment is not just feeding. Attachment is also different from bonding. It is a complex developing process that is similar to what is called love. Attachment theory is also a theory about relationships. It provides a way of thinking about relationships, especially as they are shaped by threat and the need for security. In a compelling book that draws on an abundance of recent scientific discoveries and seventy years of collective clinical experience, Lewis and colleagues (2000) unravel the mystery and nature of love by examining it from an attachment perspective.

> Because loving is reciprocal physiological influence, it entails a deeper and more literal connection than most realize. Limbic regulation affords lovers the ability to modulate each other's emotions, neurophysiology, hormonal status, immune function,

> sleep rhythms, and stability. If one leaves on a trip, the other may suffer insomnia, a delayed menstrual cycle, a cold that would have been fought off in the fortified state of togetherness. [pp. 207–208]

COMPULSIVE CARETAKING

Lewis and colleagues (2000) define *love* as *simultaneous* mutual regulation. To prevent love from being confused with what Bowlby and attachment theory identifies as *compulsive caretaking* and the twelve-step community calls codependency, it is necessary to distinguish between healthy mutuality and the chronic sacrifice of self in order to maintain an attachment. Love, from an attachment theory perspective, implies a capacity for giving and receiving in relationships. The healthy need for confirmation and attention should not be mistaken for the excessive dependence on approval or affection from others that many codependent individuals persistently demonstrate in their relationships. All developmentally mature individuals have a healthy need to be loved and appreciated. Codependent individuals' longing for affection or approval is frequently disproportionately related to the real emotional significance that others play in their lives. Codependent individuals often have an indiscriminant hunger for appreciation or affection, regardless of whether they care for the person or whether the relationship with that person has any real meaning for them. In fact, the more they know someone, the less likely they will be able to feel any genuine affection or love for them. They are more concerned with the approval from others who do not know them well. It is as if they are driven to substitute quantity ("I must be loved by everyone") for quality. Consequently, they are often unaware of their boundless craving for approval from others who they don't know or even like.

Most importantly, there is a marked contradiction between their wish for love and their capacity for feeling, receiving, or giving it. Easily hurt by slights or minor disagreements, they can brood and take secret solace in the perceived injustices they judge others have inflicted upon them. They hide their excessive demands, resentments, and anger behind a sacrificing facade of unjust suffering because of another's behavior. While they may be overly considerate and eager to be helpful to anyone, their actions are more compulsive than generated out of any spontaneous radiating warmth. Despite actions and behavior that might suggest otherwise, they can appear worried or concerned, but they cannot genuinely give of themselves. Buber (1961) eloquently describes how the subtleties of compulsive caretaking lack any authentic warmth:

> In man's existence with man, it is not solitude, but the essential relation, which is primal. Nor is it any different if we set aside the problem of origin, and undertake the pure analysis of existence. In mere solitude man remains essentially with himself, even if he is moved with extreme pity; in action and help he inclines towards the other, but the barriers of his own being are not thereby breached; he makes his assistance, not his self, accessible to the other; nor does he expect any real mutuality, in fact he probably shuns it; "he is concerned with the other," but he is not anxious for the other to be concerned with him. In an essential relation, on the other hand, the barriers of individual being are in fact breached and a new phenomenon appears which can appear only in this way: one life open to another—not steadily, but so to speak attaining its extreme reality only from point to point, yet also able to acquire a form in the continuity of life; the other becomes present not merely in the imagination or feeling, but in the depths of one's substance, so that one experiences the mystery of the other being in the mystery of one's own. The two participate in one another's lives in very fact, not psychically, but ontically. This is certainly something which comes to a man in the course of his life only by a kind of grace, and many will say that they do not know it; but even he to whom it has not come has it in his existence as a constitutive principle, because the conscious or unconscious lack of it plays an essential part in determining the nature and character of his existence. And certainly, in the course of their life many will be given the opportunity of it which they do not fulfill in their existence; they acquire relations which they do not make real, that is, which they do not use to open themselves to another; they

> squander the most precious, irreplaceable and irrecoverable material; they pass their life by. But then this very void penetrates the existence and permeates its deepest layer. The "everyday," in its inconspicuous, scarcely perceptible part, which is nevertheless accessible to an analysis of existence, is interwoven with what is "not the everyday." [p. 170]

A clinical example illustrates how compulsive caretaking and the inability to establish mutuality in a relationship becomes easily intertwined with addiction.

> Donna called to schedule an appointment with a therapist who had treated her five years ago for her alcoholism. During her initial return visit, she explained that she has continued to remain alcohol and drug free since terminating therapy, had more than eight years of sobriety, and still attended AA meetings on a regular basis. After assuring her therapist that her alcoholism was no longer the issue, she than proceeded to describe the reasons for rescheduling an appointment.
>
> "I don't know if you remember, but the reason I first came to see you was because I was stuck in this dead-end marriage with this alcoholic and you pointed out to me that my own alcoholism was so tied into our drinking together that I would never be able to get out of that marriage unless I first got sober."
>
> "Yes," the therapist nodded, "I remember that well."
>
> "Well . . ." Donna squirmed nervously in her chair, "I don't know how long it's been since I've seen you . . ."
>
> "Five years," the therapist interjected.
>
> Donna looked up and forced a weak smile. "As I was saying, in the five years since I last saw you, I've been married two more times, divorced my second husband, and I'm here today because I'm thinking of leaving my third marriage." Donna hesitated and examined the therapist's face for some sign of judgment or disapproval. When she saw none, she continued. "But before I do this another time, I need to find out what's wrong with me."
>
> "You think there's something wrong with you?" the therapist asked.

"I do." Donna folded her hands in her lap and worked to compose herself. "If there's one thing I've learned in AA, it's that if I don't look at how I'm contributing to the problem, there's no way I can come up with a solution. I keep asking myself, what's the one consistent variable here in all these three failed marriages?" Donna looked up at the therapist and frowned. "It's gotta be me."

"It's good to hear your willingness to look at the way you're contributing to the problem. But," the therapist patted her medical chart, which sat on the corner of his desk, "if I recall correctly, you have a tendency to take on all the blame and often feel that everything's your fault when it isn't. So, let's talk about how you're contributing to the problem, because the way you think you are may be far different from the way you actually are."

Donna smiled. "I'd forgotten how much I always felt known and understood by you." The smile quickly faded and her forehead wrinkled. "But this time I know it's me. I just can't seem to be satisfied with anything. I'm doing the same thing in this marriage that I did in the first one and that I did in the second one."

"Well, if you're right and you did the same thing in these last two marriages that you did in the first, that means you have picked someone who is emotionally unavailable for you and that you're trying like hell once again to get them to give you something that you don't feel you deserve or are worthy of."

A confused look washed over Donna's face. "And what is that?"

"Love." The therapist sat silently for a second, waiting for his comments to sink in. "Donna, remember we spent the last year of therapy talking about how uncomfortable you were when anyone gave you anything emotionally."

"Oh?" Donna blushed. "Yeah, now I remember."

The therapist leaned forward. "You know, I always wondered if that was the reason you left therapy when you did."

"What?" Donna looked at the therapist with a blank look on her face. "I don't understand what you mean."

"I wondered if you left therapy when you did because you were uncomfortable with the support and caring you felt you got from me."

Donna pulled at her lower lip as she pondered her therapist's observations. "Mmmm . . . maybe you're right."

"I thought you might not be ready to leave treatment, but didn't want to pressure you to stay because that would have been exactly what your husband was doing and what your father had done when you tried to leave home."

"Now that I think about it, there is a similarity between all three of these guys." Donna continued to pull at her lower lip. "They all needed me."

"Well, that's the pattern. You need someone to take care of and they all needed someone to take care of them," the therapist said. "It was a match made in heaven."

"Actually, it was a match made in hell. I eventually get angry and resentful," Donna frowned. "They don't understand why in the hell I'm changing the rules on them and pull away even further."

"Let me guess," the therapist offered, "they picked you. You didn't pick them."

Donna's hands balled into a fist. "Oh, shit. Am I that damn predictable? You're right. You told me once that I'm always the interviewee; I'm never the interviewer. I'm so preoccupied with, 'Am I good enough for them' that I never ask if this person is good for me."

"Your feeling that you are unworthy of love drives you to find men who match your insides and leads you to try your damnedest to earn the right to get them to give you what you are uncomfortable with receiving."

The session ended with Donna making a renewed commitment to deal with her feelings of low self-worth and compulsive caretaking. She promised her therapist that she would deal with the uncomfortable feeling that came up in therapy with him and gave him permission to challenge her if the intensity of their relationship prompted her to consider leaving therapy before this issue was resolved. Donna needs to be in relationships, as we all do, to maintain our emotional equilibrium; it's just that her internalized and unmodified implicit rules of relatedness prevent her from being able to experience any of the benefits of healthy mutuality and secure attachment.

Bowlby (1980) has aptly described the characteristics and features that drive the compulsive caring for others, which dominates the life of someone like Donna.

> Often they select someone who has had a sad or difficult life, as a rule including a bereavement. The care they bestow may amount almost to an obsession; and it is given whether it is welcomed, which it may be, or not. It is given, also, whether the cared-for person has suffered real loss of some kind or is only believed to have done so. At its best this caring for another person may be of value to the cared-for, at least for a time. At its worst, it may result in an intensely possessive relationship which, whilst allegedly for the benefit of the cared-for, results in his becoming a prisoner. In addition, the compulsive caregiver may become jealous of the easy time the cared-for is thought to be having.
>
> Because a compulsive caregiver seems to be attributing to the cared-for all the sadness and neediness that he is unable or unwilling to recognize in himself, the cared-for person can be regarded as standing vicariously for the one giving the care. [1980, pps 156–157]

The clinical example of Donna's plight helps illustrate one of the most important ultimate goals of therapy. Until a person, addicted or not, can develop the capacity to receive or give love, he or she will always be vulnerable to affect dysregulation. Fromm gives a clear expression to this goal in the following passage:

> Whatever complaints the neurotic patient may have, whatever symptoms he may present are rooted in his inability to love, if we mean by love a capacity for the experience of concern, responsibility, respect, and understanding of another person and the intense desire for that person's growth. *Analytic therapy is essentially an attempt to help the patient gain or regain his capacity for love.* If this aim is not fulfilled nothing but surface changes can be accomplished. [1950, p. 87; italics in original]

Examining the far-reaching consequences of love and secure attachment has numerous implications, not only for child development, but also for adult psychopathology and addiction. Because evidence is mounting that shows secure attachment or love alters the way our brain develops and functions, the false distinction between physiology and psychology that medical science has perpetuated is now being challenged. This has important implications for treatment since one of the most consistent variables that continuously rear itself in research study after research study is the significance of the therapeutic alliance on successful treatment outcome. Attachment, alliance, bonding, friendship, mutual physiological regulation, and love are nothing but semantic attempts to define and explain all the intricate subtleties and nuances involved in intimate relationships. The theme of the relationship between neurophysiology and attachment will be explored at greater length in Chapter Six.

4

Addiction: An Attempt at Self-Repair that Fails

To be ourselves, we must complete ourselves.
Will Durant (1926)

As comprehensive and compelling as Bowlby's work is, his theory fails to thoroughly address all the subtle nuances that make up successful addiction treatment. Because Bowlby's observations evolved from the study of children, his formulations do not always translate easily into direct clinical application. Bowlby's observational data and ethological framework need to be expanded with concepts drawn from other sources if their full potential for addiction treatment is to be realized. The work of the relational models, especially the contributions of self psychology, helps compensate for attachment theory's limitations by placing Bowlby's model within a more practical paradigm that has increased relevance for addiction treatment.

Although there is no evidence that Kohut and Bowlby were openly influenced by each other's writings, they shared a unified allegiance to psychodynamic theory in general and object relations theory in particular. It appears that their individual theories were parallel developments, achieved separately without the other's direct influence. Because Kohut's clinical work was primarily with adult patients (Bowlby collected his data exclusively from children) who demonstrated disturbances in their capacity to maintain narcissistic homeostasis, he added an important perspective that was lacking in attachment theory, especially as it applies to addiction treatment. A brief review of Kohut's contributions illustrates the significance and strength of the relationships between the two theories.

SELF PSYCHOLOGY

Heinz Kohut's (1972) work with patients whose central disturbance involved feelings of emptiness and depression is in many important ways an extension of Bowlby's observations concerning the difficulties that occur when a child's developmental need for secure attachment is disrupted. Kohut extended psychoanalytic thinking beyond its standard concept of drive theory so that narcissistic vulnerabilities could be better understood as a consequence of the patient's inadequately formed or damaged sense of self. Like Bowlby, Kohut emphasized the critical importance of parental responsiveness in the development of internal mental structures for self-control and the eventual emergence of individuality and the capacity for mutuality. Kohut stressed that a child's nuclear self is formed during infancy and embodies the fundamental self-esteem, ideals, and ambitions of the child. The nuclear self is bipolar, organized around two anchor points of ideals and ambitions. In his final book (1984), Kohut added a third constituent of the self, which involves the maturation of the alter ego or twinship needs.

Attachment with a primary caregiver allows the various agencies, drives, and conflicts of the mental apparatus to become unified into an integrated sense of self. Kohut (1977) defined the self as "a unit, cohesive in space and enduring in time which is the center of initiation and a recipient of impressions" (p. 99). However, the formation of the nuclear self does not take place in relation to overt praise and rebuke. Rather, it is the empathic, nonverbal, intuitive responsiveness of the mother to her child's needs that validates healthy striving for autonomy and identity. The atmosphere the parent creates either integrates or fragments the nuclear self. It is not so much what the parents do as much as who they are that determines developmental outcome.

> Sarah had entered treatment because of her husband's threat "to divorce me and never let me see the children

again if I don't do something about my drinking." It quickly became apparent during the first few sessions that the only attachment figures in Sarah's life were her children. The threat of losing them was a far more powerful motivating force than the pull of the compulsion to drink. She readily agreed to meet once a week for psychotherapy and attend AA meetings. Although Sarah was an elegantly attractive, intelligent, and educated woman, she never worked outside of the home and described her relationship with her husband as "empty and cold." Her drinking had always been solitary; she consumed wine or vodka only after her husband had gone to bed at night or the children were safely at school during the day. Despite her friendly smile, quick wit, and pleasant demeanor, she had no close friends. When asked why, she replied, "I don't think most people find me very interesting."

Therapy limped along for months. Sarah's attendance was sporadic. Many sessions were dominated by long periods of painful and uncomfortable silence. Encouragement to attend AA meetings was met by weak protests that "the people there didn't seem friendly or inviting."

All of this dramatically changed one day during the middle of a session, after her therapist had cautioned her again that her isolation was not good for her recovery or her depression. She uncharacteristically flared at him angrily. "What's wrong with you? Can't you see what I am?" She threw her arms open wide. "Look at me. Do I look like someone that you or anyone else would find interesting?"

"As matter of fact, I do," her therapist replied.

She stared at him, dumbfounded. Uncertainty washed over her face. "Well, it's all an act; nothing but smoke and mirrors. I can only maintain this on a superficial level. Eventually, like everyone else, you'll tire of me and see me for what I am."

Following this confession she burst into tears, buried her head in her hands, and sobbed.

Her therapist waited for her crying to stop before he

leaned forward and gently assured her. "Sarah, I see this is painful to face, but it's important you let yourself speak to it and feel what this brings up for you. I understand that you feel what you say is true about yourself, but that's not been my experience of you. Where does this feeling come from?"

Sarah leaned back into her chair and wiped the tears from her eyes. A loud sigh escaped from her chest. "You know, I haven't thought of this for years." She sat up and looked into the therapists' eyes. "I don't think I ever told this to anyone, but when I was a young girl . . . about 5 or 6, I use to hide behind this big chair we had in the living room, so no one would find me or see me. I'd close my eyes and try to make myself disappear. I did this for years."

Sarah proceeded to describe in painful detail an emotionally barren home that was in stark contrast to her parents' high-profile social standing in a small rural community in southern Mississippi. Her father owned the only movie theater in town and her parents were prominent members of the small community, loved and respected by all who knew them. Sarah was the polite, precocious only child they would parade out for the towns folk to admire like a porcelain china doll. At home, the climate was much different. Her father found her to be an embarrassment because she was an unplanned child who was born when he was in his early fifties and her mother was in her early forties. Her parents provided her with all the finest clothes, education, and trappings that money could buy, but both felt awkward and uncomfortable in her presence. Her father especially found her early childhood exuberance intrusive and annoying because it interfered with his tranquil and somewhat stately lifestyle. Sarah frequently overheard him complaining to her mother, "Can't you keep *your* child quiet, she's an embarrassment to me." Most evenings were spent at their large country home, which sat in the middle of ten acres of isolated farmland, with her parents sitting together on the front porch, engaged in quiet intimate conversations over cocktails, while Sarah played quietly and alone in her room.

Following this important revelation, therapy progressed more rapidly over the next few months as Sarah came to alter her internal working model, which included a strong component along the lines of "there is something lacking in me that is capable of provoking love from anyone." Her relationships with her therapist deepened, and her friendships, both inside and outside of AA, became richer and more satisfying. As people became an increasing source of emotional regulation, her need to drink became less of a driving compulsion.

EMPATHY

From the perspective of self psychology, a child needs empathic attunement from parental figures in order to develop a cohesive self. A cohesive or "bipolar self is a developmental achievement of transforming the archaic grandiose self in self-assertive ambitions and the idealized self into mature values and ideals" (Stone 1992, p. 335). Minor or sporadic emphatic failures are not deleterious. In fact, periodic lapses facilitate the crucial process of transmuting internalization. Optimal frustration within the context of a holding environment provided by a "good-enough mother" actually facilitates the building of psychic structure and the internalization of functions previously provided by external objects. Since Kohut attributed the lack of empathy and attunement as a primary contributor to psychopathology, he reasoned that the use of empathy as a therapeutic tool was crucial in the restoration of the self. Empathy or "vicarious introspection" becomes the primary mode of data gathering for self psychologists. The therapist's task is to identify the selfobject functions that the patient requires, which are activated and demonstrated in the transferential relationship. Since it was the parents' original failure to adequately serve this function that initiated the child's misdirected search for regulation through dysfunctional channels (e.g., alcohol, drugs, sex, etc.), one key element in the repair of the developmental arrestment can be provided if the therapist makes him- or herself available as a selfobject.

NARCISSISM

One of Kohut's primary contributions to psychoanalytic theory is a change in the way narcissism is conceptualized. Kohut legitimated narcissism as a normal developmental process necessary for a healthy, age-appropriate need for object relatedness and attachment. Classical drive theory regarded narcissism more as selfishness or stubborn self-centeredness, reflective of an individual's unwillingness to delay gratification. The insistence that "I must have everything my way" is very similar to AA's position when it warns its members of the dangers of the alcoholic's inflated ego. From Kohut's perspective, narcissistic needs are not regarded as selfish, but reflective of a disturbance in the relationships between the self and its most significant others or selfobjects. Narcissism can be viewed as a roundabout way of attempting to provide for oneself what was not provided by others.

SELFOBJECT

Another person "is a selfobject when it is experienced intrapsychically as producing functions that evoke, maintain, or positively affect the sense of self" (Wolf 1985, p. 271). A selfobject is neither a self nor an object; rather, a selfobject is a subjective aspect of a function performed by a relationship. Selfobject transferences, like substance use, are really attempts at self-repair. The vulnerable individual is attempting to complete a process initiated in childhood but uncompleted. Kohut believed that we never give up the hope for completing ourselves. In a similar fashion, Paul Ornstein (personal communication, 1982), speaking to the importance of maintaining the therapeutic frame and the therapeutic alliance added, "The self is always searching for the right environment to complete itself."

Kohut made the important distinction between healthy and pathological narcissism. Phase-appropriate, empathic responsiveness to the child's selfobject needs is essential for the cohesion and development of the self and leads to healthy self-esteem. Without the idealizing or mirroring selfobjects, a child is likely to grow up with narcissistic vulnerabilities leading to disturbance and difficulty with affect regulation, increasing the potential for addictive behavior. Consequently, the vulnerable individual is left without the internal structure necessary to manage the emotional injuries and disappointments (affect dis-regulation) that are sure to follow later in life. As Bacal (1985) writes, "The defects in the self produced by faulty responses of self objects lead this individual to establish what Kohut called transference like states, where he looks for self objects in his later life to provide him with the responses which he missed in order to repair the self" (p. 488). From this perspective, Bacal is suggesting that transferential relationships are essentially attempts at self-repair. Bacal's position is similar to the self-medication hypothesis of Khantzian (1982). Both Khantzian and Kohut postulated that the use of substances and archaic selfobject relationships share a similar function: each is a compensatory driven behavior reflecting desperate and futile attempts to shore up the defective self.

SELFOBJECT RELATIONSHIPS AND TRANSFERENCES

Evidence gathered by Kohut and others (e.g., Stolorow et al. 1987, Wolf 1988) over the years in their work with patients suffering from narcissistic vulnerabilities has led to the identification of seven common selfobject tranferences:

1. *Mirroring:* A response that confirms the child's innate sense of vigor, importance, and uniqueness. It is the "gleam in the mother's eye" as she is empathically attuned with the child's feelings and interests. From this experience, the child develops healthy narcissism and grandiosity. This results in healthy self-esteem with an

appropriate sense of assertiveness and drive for mastery and achievement.

2. *Idealizing:* If the child is presented with a strong, soothing selfobject who allows and provides idealization, the capacity for healthy ideals, values, and principles is internalized.

3. *Alterego or twinship*: A firm sense of self, resulting from the optimal interactions between the child and selfobjects makes up this third constituent in relation to the first pole (mirroring), from which emanates the basic strivings for power and success, and the second pole (idealizing), which harbors the basic ideal goals and values. The core of the personality is determined by the tension arc in the intermediate area of basic talents and skills, which is established between ambitions and ideals. The selfobject requirement consists of the need to belong to something greater than oneself, a human among humans, and is the antithesis of alienation and isolation. It reflects the desire to be part of a community.

4. *Adversarial:* The need to compete and exert one's full potential without fear of destroying the other person. For a child, it's the need to be able to play aggressively without fear of destructive retaliation. For an adult, it is the confidence that the other person will tolerate your anger and work through disagreements without the relationship being destroyed. The experience helps the person develop resiliency.

5. *Efficacy:* The experience of having importance and significance in relation to another person. It is the feeling that one's presence, responses, and actions can have a positive impact on another person, that one can be of help and of importance to someone.

6. *Self-delineating:* A relationship with an object that promotes individuation and the separation of the self without the threat of loss of attachment. Often, it is a relationship that allows the other person to be who he or she is, without undo pressure to behave in a certain way in order to maintain the attachment relationship.

7. *Witnessing:* The need for a selfobject to be a witness and provide emotional understanding for the injustices or wrongs that were inflicted on the individual. This relationship is especially important for trauma survivors.

AA AND SELFOBJECT FUNCTIONS

Self psychology's concepts of mirroring, idealization, and another person serve the function of a transformational or corrective twinship and provide alternative ways to explain how AA is helpful to its members. *Mirroring* takes place when members feel they are seen for who they truly are and when they have a positive influence on others. Those suffering from deficits in this area (mirror-hungry personalities) will often have their previously unmet needs for healthy grandiosity, exhibitionism, and respect gratified by the attention that their continual sobriety brings. *Idealization*, whether of a sponsor, the group, or of one's higher power, is in evidence when members tell of feeling bolstered by identification with some greater source of strength and wisdom. Members with longer periods of abstinence and sobriety serve as important role models that spur others on to emulate. *Twinship* is operating when members speak of the healing effect of belonging to the group and finding peers with similar experiences. Many of the other selfobject functions are provided through continual twelve-step work (helping others) and sponsorship.

> After his parents died, Cecil was raised by a series of aunts and uncles who lived in a rural area of the Midwest. At age 17, he promptly joined the Navy and spent the next four years traveling the world until he was honorably discharged at the age of 22. He began drinking in the Navy and continued throughout his adult life without any suggestion of problems for the next twenty years. Two failed marriages left him cautious about committing to any woman again, even though he had a long string of short-term relationships over the last ten years. He worked for the airlines and his job required that he move every few years.

Cecil showed up at a therapist's office one day complaining of "depression and lack of meaning in my life." He quickly announced that he had gone to a few AA meetings since being transferred to the city and concluded he was an alcoholic. In fact, an AA member had given him the therapist's name and had urged him to set up an appointment. Antidepressants were promptly prescribed and Cecil agreed to enter an outpatient therapy group.

During the course of the next few months Cecil religiously attended both AA and the group. With continual sobriety, he was able to identify a pattern to his drinking. "I never felt comfortable with my father or with men unless I was drinking with them." He proceeded to paint a picture of a man who surrounded himself with drinking buddies and for whom the local tavern became the one place where he felt he could count on connecting with others.

Eventually, AA began to serve a very similar function to that of the local tavern. He found a "home group" and a bunch of men that he admired and looked up to. Cecil developed a relationship with a sponsor and began to faithfully work the steps of the AA program, frequently reading the "Big Book" and "the daily meditations." He admitted, "You know, I never did get into this God thing that my aunts and uncles tried to force down my throat, but this higher power and spirituality make sense to me."

A few months later, he excitingly announced to the group that a "bunch of doctors and lawyers at the meeting invited me out to have coffee with them. They were asking me what they should do about working the steps. One of the lawyers even asked if I'd be his sponsor."

THE REPARATIVE APPROACH

In an attempt to explain the importance of self psychology as a treatment approach, Howard Bacal (1992) wrote, "One simply cannot apply unmodified classical drive theory in the clinical situation and expect that the patient will feel understood" (p. 56). Bacal challenged the "considerable discrepancy between what effective classical theorists preach and what they practice" (p. 56). His criticism has relevance because it is an attempt to bring classical psychodynamic theory in line with the practicalities of treating the addicted patient. Self psychology helps accomplish this task because it offers a unique perspective, not only for addiction, but also for all psychopathology. Self psychology departs from Freud's classical drive theory with its emphasis on intrapsychic conflicts and moves the focus of attention to relationships and the age-appropriate developmental needs that were unmet, which leads to arrested emotional development. Until this is repaired through the restoration of psychic structure, individuals will remain susceptible to seeking external sources of gratification because their internal self structure is unable to provide this needed capacity.

Ormont (2001), writing from a modern analytic perspective, convincingly argued that since the developmental failures (parenting figures did not provide needed maturational input, creating a gap that leaves the child with developmental personality deficits) occurred before the maturation of language, preoedipal patients cannot respond to words or interpretations. Characterological change does not take place through interpretation, but through experience, "microinternalizations" of the therapist's functions as a selfobject. No further psychic growth, Ormont contends, is possible without these experiences.

Therapy from this perspective needs to be geared to preoedipal patients' developmental arrest, which leaves them with the inability to use feelings as signals and the incapacity to regulate their emotions. Developmentally arrested patients require a corrective emotional relationship to repair the deficit in their psychic structure. Therapy, from this perspective, takes on a goal very similar to that of the transformational experience that AA requires of its members if sobriety and recovery are to be achieved. Ormont (2001) writes about the importance of such a treatment approach:

> Like the child, the patient has a maturational need to internalize the admiration of a nourishing figure who derives pleasure from the pursuit of mastering challenges and overcoming obstacles. The child-patient has a need to merge with the ideal-

> ized parent surrogate, to share in the security, standards, and calm of the analyst. The movement is from narcissistic need to a capacity to take care of oneself. [p. 345]

THE RESTORATION OF HEALTHY SELF-ESTEEM

Healthy self-esteem is the end product of sufficient age-appropriate responsiveness and parental emotional attunement. Healthy parental role models provide the other necessary component of idealization that leads to healthy narcissism, which is basic to emotional health and consists of a subjective sense of well-being and confidence in one's self-worth. People who feel a balanced valuation of their importance and potential and can relate in mature ways to others will usually have a sense of meaning and know how they fit in the world.

In contrast to this, even though the majority of cocaine addicts and alcoholics appear to be very successful and are high achievers in their professional lives, those who work with these patients on a consistent basis are struck by how fragile their basic sense of self-worth has been. Despite their exaggerated striving for financial and intellectual success, their need for approval and acceptance leaves them consistently vulnerable to injury, rejection, shame, and humiliation. Kohut and Wolfe (1978) state:

> Individuals whose nascent selves have been insufficiently responded to will use any available stimuli to create a pseudo excitement in order to ward off the painful feeling of deadness that overtake them. Adults have at their disposal an even wider armamentarium of self-stimulation—in particular, in the sexual sphere, addictive promiscuous activities and various perversions, and in the non-sexual sphere, such activities as gambling, drug and alcohol induced excitement, and a lifestyle characterized by hyper-sociability. If the analyst is able to penetrate beneath the defensive facade presented by these activities, he will invariably find depression. [p. 418]

HEALTHY AND UNHEALTHY NARCISSISM

Self psychology has consistently viewed healthy narcissism or mature narcissism as reflective not of the decrease of emotional investment in one's self but of a person's inability to establish mutually satisfying relationships with others in which giving and receiving are balanced. As Ornstein (1981) writes, "When . . . the self attains the capacity for becoming a relatively independent center of initiative . . . it is then also capable of recognizing the relatively independent center of initiative in the other" (p. 358). In the case of healthy narcissism, the person can hold a healthy respect for his or her uniqueness while at the same time being able to be in reciprocal resonance with the unique qualities and independence of another. Such a person can give as well as take and does not need to be one-up or one-down in a relationship.

In contrast, pathological narcissism requires either the presence of an idealized other (e.g., "My worth is enhanced by your power") or a mirroring selfobject (e.g., "My worth is confirmed by your admiration of my power") in order for the afflicted individual to maintain narcissistic homeostasis. Selfobjects in both categories occupy precarious positions, prone to devaluation or contempt if they should fail to provide their required functions. True reciprocal mutuality in a relationship is usually too taxing, overwhelming the narcissist's capacity for acceptance of imperfections in self and other. Consequently, the give and take that is part of healthy mature relationships cannot be maintained.

The narcissistic individual is like the magician in the circus sideshow who is constantly employing sleight of hand as a distraction to get others to pay attention only to what he wants them to see so that they do not notice what is being hidden. Grandiosity as a defense should not be confused with grandiosity as a healthy component of psychic structure. As Bacal (1992) suggests:

> Grandiosity, in my view, is not always an appropriate designation for the self state that it refers to. I believe that what Kohut meant by this term would better be separated into two ideas.

> The one would reflect the sense of personal conviction of one's unique importance. This would be a self-percept that presumably arises out of optimal experiences of mirroring by self-objects. It is affectively toned in a healthy way. The other, which would be closer to the traditional notion of grandiosity, would reflect a self-percept that is inflated beyond what the individual would normally experience. This may properly be regarded as a pathological self state; and it is associated with a disavowed sense of low self-esteem. [p. 72]

Narcissism from this perspective ceases to be a source of healthy self-respect and self-esteem and becomes a defense—a false self or grandiose self that guards against painful feelings of shame and low self-worth. As Morrison (1989) convincingly demonstrated, shame or humiliation is always the underbelly or driving force behind a narcissistic defense. AA has long recognized that the alcoholic's grandiosity or self-centeredness and lack of humility are the most important obstacles that have to be modified if sobriety is to be maintained. Using technically incorrect terms drawn from psychodynamic concepts, AA nevertheless captures the essence of the problem that must be addressed in recovery. Long before Kohut's theoretical formulations of grandiosity and narcissism, early pioneers in the treatment of alcoholism were writing of the necessity of "the surrender of the inflated ego" in an alcoholic's recovery (Tiebout 1954). Bateson (1971) wrote that the biggest obstacle to alcoholics' recovery was their reluctance to relinquish their "false pride." While the terminology may be different, the basic premise is similar. Early theorists recognized that narcissistic features such as grandiosity were a primary corollary in the addiction process.

False pride, inflated ego, and grandiosity are consequently viewed as defenses against feelings of inferiority and inadequacy. As Tiebout (1954) suggested, there has to be a reason why one has a need to inflate oneself. If an alcoholic or addict felt or believed these defenses were enough, there would be no need for inflation of self or false pride. From this perspective, if a person possessed a firm sense of self-esteem, confidence, pride, or healthy narcissism, there would be no need for grandiosity.

When individuals suffer from an absence of healthy self-esteem, they are left with an intolerable affect state often referred to as shame.

Morrison (1989) writes, "The self's experience of shame is so painful that the narcissistic constrictions of perfection, grandiosity, superiority, and self-sufficiency are generated to eliminate and deny shame itself. . . . Shame, then, can be viewed as an inevitable feeling about the self for its narcissistic imperfection for failure, for being flawed" (p. 66).

The cycle of remorse, shame, and self-loathing that substance abusers experience the morning after a humiliating night of chemical abuse spurs them to make the false promises and vows to never let something like this happen again. Attempts at control inevitably fail, exacerbating the self-loathing and contributing to the rigidity of the defenses. Because of repeated failures, shame and remorse become intensified. Substance abusers are forced to combat the painful affect with their only available resource, namely, alcohol or drugs.

Khantzian (1994) believes that AA is corrective for the alcoholic because the program is able to penetrate the narcissistic defenses of false pride. The primary reason alcoholics suffer, according to Khantzian, is because they cannot control their drinking and they cannot control themselves. Unable to admit their vulnerabilities, they remain isolated, alone and cut off from others and themselves. What they need to do (admit their vulnerabilities to another), they cannot do because of the shame and their characterological grandiose defensive posture. AA works because once initiation into the program occurs, contact with others is sustained, and through continued interaction with others alcoholics are able to alter the dysfunctional interpersonal style that up to now has dominated their life. Khantzian explains that only through this maintenance of contact with others can the disorders of the self be repaired. He identifies the four aspects of the disordered alcoholic as (1) regulation of emotions, (2) self-esteem or a lack of healthy narcissism, (3) mutually satisfying relationships, and (4) self-care. He agrees with Kurtz (1982) and other interpreters of AA that it is shame that makes the engagement and attachment difficult, if not sometimes impossible, for many practicing alcoholics.

A NEW DEFINITION OF *ADDICTION*

The treatment of narcissism has many similarities to and applications for the treatment of addiction—especially if addiction is viewed as an epiphenomenon of narcissistic defenses against shame, fear, and other painful affect. Narcissism, like addiction, is a retreat into a grandiose-self or false-self personality organization as a way of avoiding the need for attachment. Addiction from this perspective is the result of unmet developmental needs, which leaves certain individuals with an injured, enfeebled, uncohesive, or fragmented self. Vulnerable individuals are unable to regulate affect and in many cases are even unable to identify what it is they feel. Unable to draw on their own internal resources because there aren't any, they remain in constant need (object hunger) of self-regulating resources provided externally "out there." Since painful, rejecting, and shaming relationships are the cause of their deficits in self, they cannot turn to others to get what they need or have never received. Deprivation of needs and object hunger leaves them with unrealistic and intolerable affects that are not only disturbing to others, but also shameful to themselves. With few other options open to them, substance abusers turn to alcohol, drugs, and other external sources of regulation (e.g., food, sex, work, gambling, etc.).

Consequently, addicted and alcoholic patients are always vulnerable to compulsive, obsessive, and addictive behavior, constantly substituting one addiction for another until the vulnerabilities in the self structure are repaired and restored. Repair and restoration of the self can be accomplished only within a healing and healthy relationship. The patient needs a consistent, nurturing, mirroring, and holding environment that can contain and manage negative, destructive impulses while giving the patient the opportunity to identify, internalize, and incorporate a healthy set of introjects and internal object representations.

However, once the psychic structure is repaired and restored, it can be maintained only if, like any living organism, it is provided with an environment where it is continually nurtured, fed, and allowed to flourish and grow. That can be accomplished only if substance abusers learn how to establish and maintain healthy intimate interpersonal relationships outside the therapeutic milieu. Since relationships can also become compulsive and addictive, substance abusers need to experience themselves in relation to others to fully understand how they contribute to their difficulties within the interpersonal sphere. Until that is accomplished, the absence of continued satisfying relationships in the substance abusers' lives always leaves them with an internal feeling of emptiness and a susceptibility to search for external sources of gratification.

SELF PSYCHOLOGY AS A DEFICIT THEORY

Some may have difficulty with the generalization and the lumping of all addictions under one category. While there are many addictions and they each have their own special characteristics, all the addictions have their genesis in common endopsychic sources. An important aspect of any theory is its ability to identify and unite complex and seemingly unrelated phenomena into one simple singular truth. Self psychology and attachment theory do this. Kohut (1977) postulated that all addictions share a singularly underlying similarity: they are all misguided attempts at affect regulation and self-repair generated by inadequate psychic structure. Until psychic structure is built, the addict and alcoholic will have difficulty establishing intimate attachments and be inclined to substitute a vast array of obsessive-compulsive behaviors that serve as distractions from the gnawing emptiness that threatens to overtake them. Consequently, when one obsessive-compulsive–type behavior is given up, another is likely to be substituted unless the deficiency in self structure is corrected. Kohut stated:

> The explanatory power of the new psychology of the self is nowhere as evident as with regard to these four types of psychological disturbance: (1) the narcissistic personality disorders, (2) the perversions, (3) the delinquencies, and (4) the addictions. Why can these seemingly disparate conditions be examined so fruitfully with the aid of the same conceptual framework? Why can all these widely differing and even contrasting symptom pictures be comprehended when seen from the viewpoint of the psychology of the self? How, in other words, are these four con-

> ditions related to each other? What do they have in common, despite the fact that they exhibit widely differing, and even contrasting, symptomatologies? The answer to these questions is simple: in all of these disorders the afflicted individual suffers from a central weakness, from a weakness in the core of his personality. He suffers from the consequences of a defect in the self. The symptoms of these disorders, whether comparatively hazy or hidden, or whether more distinct and conspicuous, arise secondarily as an outgrowth of a defect in the self. The manifestations of these disorders become intelligible if we call to mind that they are all attempts—unsuccessful attempts, it must be stressed—to remedy the central defect in the personality. [1977, p. vii]

Vulnerability of the self is the consequence of developmental failures and early environmental deprivation. The absence of secure attachment leads to ineffective attachment styles, which perpetuate through adulthood. Substance abuse, as a reparative attempt, exacerbates dysfunctional attachment styles because physical dependence and chemical use toxicity exacerbate the deterioration of existing physiological and psychological structures. Prolonged stress on existing structure leads to exaggerated difficulty in the regulation of affect, which leads to inadequate modulation of appropriate behavior, poor self-care, and rigidly ingrained patterns of object relatedness, which lead to increased character pathology. Kohut (1977) clarified the relationship between addiction and psychic deficits:

> The calming or stimulating effect which the addict obtains from the drug is . . . impermanent. Whatever the chemical nature of the substance that is employed. . . . No psychic structure is built, the defect in self remains. It is as if a person with a wide open gastric fistula were trying to still his hunger through eating. He may obtain pleasurable taste sensations by his frantic ingestion of food but, since the food does not enter that part of the digestive system where it is absorbed into the organism, he continues to starve. [p. viii]

SELF-MEDICATION HYPOTHESIS AND AFFECT REGULATION

Building on the early theoretical observations and formulations of Kohut (1977), Khantzian (2001) provides an alternative explanation for the addiction process that not only is compatible with the disease concept, but also expands it while providing useful and practical theoretical formulations that can enhance an addict's and alcoholic's treatment and recovery. The self-medication hypothesis has important implications for psychotherapy. It not only provides an explanation of why substance abusers have a propensity to switch addictions, it also complements the way AA and other twelve-step programs treat chemical dependency.

In his earlier work with narcotic addicts, Khantzian (1982) first recognized that opiates were the drug of choice for certain individuals because of the drug's specific pharmacological effects. Khantzian discovered that heroin addicts prize their drug for its antiaggressive effects. It helped them soothe and calm their intense feeling of rage. He eventually discovered this to be similar for other drugs that reduce anxiety, depression, or other painful affect states. Chemically dependent individuals are in a sense acting as their own uncertified physicians to fix or repair what they are missing. Consequently, Khantzian hypothesized that it isn't pleasure so much that addicts are seeking; rather, they are attempting to regulate their emotional selves and escape, even momentarily, from the constant feelings of deprivation, shame, and inadequacy that dominate their lives.

In his later work, Khantzian found that all substance abusers were predisposed to abuse or become dependent on a particular drug because they suffered a particular impairment in affect regulation. He hypothesized that addicts were drawn to a certain drug because it matched their idiosyncratic deficits in regulating specific feelings. Although most addicts have experimented with many different drugs, they learn that a particular drug has a special appeal for them because of the drug's ability to regulate troublesome affect states. For instance, narcotic addicts are drawn to opiates because of their ability to relieve states of dysphoria associated with aggression, anger, and rage. Chronic depression, bipolar illness, hyperactive syndromes, and attention deficit disorder (ADD) are symptoms highly represented in cocaine addicts. Addicts who felt bored, empty, dead inside, or that life was meaningless were frequently drawn to stimulants. Later experience showed Khantzian that counterdependent, restricted, and inhibited individuals were likely to be drawn to alcohol and sedatives. Highly anxious and fearful people suffering from chronic anxiety are prone to use the benzodiazepines and likely to become dependent on minor tranquilizers like Valium and Xanax, while the more isolated and schizoid individuals were attracted to marijuana and the hallucinogens. As Khantzian (1982) wrote, "This self-selection is related to the distinctive psychoactive actions of various drugs. . . . In the course of experimenting with different drugs, an individual discovers that the action of one drug over another is preferred" (p. 587).

The self-medication hypothesis has proved to have important implications for treatment even though many of its earliest assumptions have not been substantiated by later research. The recognition of the self-medicating function of abused substances helped shift the focus from a pleasure-seeking to a pain-relieving approach to understanding why alcoholics and addicts abuse substances. This shift enabled clinicians to engage in a more positive, compassionate psychotherapeutic relationship.

AFFECT REGULATION THEORY

Affect regulation theory carries with it the implication that everyone, not just addicts and alcoholics, needs selfobjects to help provide affect regulation. Certain individuals, because of genetic and environmental variables, are more vulnerable to disruption because they suffer more severe deficits in this capacity. Vulnerable individuals are more dependent on outside sources or do not have the necessary interpersonal skills to obtain regulation the way our species is genetically hardwired to get it—through other people.

Because of Kohut's and Khantzian's persuasive reasoning, affect regulation theory helped shift psychoanalytic thinking about addiction from the more classic drive or instinct theory to the relational models (Fairbairn 1952, Guntrip 1974) with its greater emphasis on adaptation, developmental arrest, and deficits in self structure. Building on the early theoretical observations of Kohut (1977), Khantzian provided an alternative explanation for the addiction process that is not only compatible with the disease concept, but also expands it while providing useful and practical theoretical formulations that can enhance the substance abuser's recovery and treatment. Attachment theory, with its emphasis on the psychobiological aspects of the attachment experience, helped legitimize many of the aspects of affect regulation theory. Both attachment theory and affect regulation theory challenged a formerly unspoken bias that dominates our culture and the mental health model: dependency is bad.

DEPENDENCY AND PATHOLOGY

Bowlby cautioned therapists about their tendency to confuse healthy attachment needs with dependency. Too often, clinicians use the term *attachment* to explain adult pathology (West and Sheldon-Keller 1994). A person's need for reassurance, comfort, and understanding, especially during times of distress, must not be construed as pathological or regression to immature behavior, especially when someone is threatened by loss. Many therapists are too quick to impose these views or agree with patients' self-assessment when patients admit with embarrassment that they are "too needy." These value judgments are built into the idea of dependency. They are often reflected in a therapist's appraisal, which are reinforced by a culture that equates independency with maturity and mental health. In the rush to combat the demon of dependency, patients are often retraumatized, feeling much as they did when their critical parents shamed them for seeking comfort or assurance.

To be dependent on someone is not the same as being attached. Attachment is an emotional bond that forms over time with caregiving, familiarity, and continuity. Someone can be attached and not dependent. Consequently, it is also possible to be dependent and not attached, which is what codependency is all about. As attachment theory implies, *dependency* not only is a confusing and pejorative term, but also reflects a strong bias in our culture toward an obsession with autonomy and independence at all costs, which is not in line with the biological realities of our species.

> David had sought therapy because of complaints of depression related to a deteriorating marriage and recent job loss. An active member of AA for nearly four years, David feared his crisis at home and his difficulties finding a new job might jeopardize his recovery. A similar pattern with both his marriage and job were quickly identified. He was a bright, good-looking, energetic man who had little difficulty finding either new relationships or new employment. However, he had extreme difficulties maintaining either beyond six months. David would quickly become disappointed and critical of his boss, often perceiving him as inadequate or undependable. Similar reactions would get played out with the women in his life. Observations to this effect by his therapist were quickly rejected. Attempts to show how these patterns were related to a father who abandoned him as a child and left him in the care of a physically disabled and incompetent mother whom he could not trust to provide for his basic needs were initially dismissed as "pure coincidence." Just as progress was being made toward him developing some clarity about this pattern, he abruptly terminated therapy.
>
> Six months later, David called back, "to meet just a couple times for a little tune-up." During the meeting, the therapist encouraged him to join a therapy group. The therapist hoped that the transference intensity related to David's fear of dependency on one person might be diluted by shifting and spreading it out to the other members of the group. David reluctantly agreed, and over the course of the next few months, he quit two more jobs because of "incompetent management." The group gradually began to confront him about his pattern. David eventually conceded that "there might be some truth to the group's observations about how I respond to my bosses."
>
> Things proceeded smoothly in the group for a couple

months. David eventually started a new relationship with a woman and shortly thereafter announced to the group that he was leaving treatment. Members' comments that he was repeating his six-month cycle were met with denial and explanations that "this is different."

A year and a half passed before David called again to schedule an appointment. He wanted to join another group. He explained proudly that he held the same job now for nearly two years and had just gotten a promotion. His new position provided him with more opportunity "to run my own show. I don't have anyone that I have to keep running things by for approval." However, his relationships with women had not improved. When encouraged that he directly deal with his dependency fears if he entered another group, David balked. "I don't want to be tied down to any commitments."

The therapist did not hear from David again. However, a year later, a close colleague confided in him that he had a former patient of his who was posing a repeated difficulty in a therapy group. Without revealing the patient's name, it was clear that David was in the process of engaging in the same counterdependent behavior he had demonstrated repeatedly with his previous therapist. The mixture of fear and repulsion that dominated David's unmet dependency needs prevented him from tolerating and benefiting from what he needed most—a healthy reliance on other people.

Critics of AA (e.g., Jones 1970, Tournier 1979) often express concern that the addict and alcoholic may become too dependent on the program, and they judge the alcoholic's reliance on AA with concern and suspiciousness. Even if one accepted the premise of this argument, isn't it preferable to have a dependence on an organization that promotes health, sobriety, and helping others rather than a drug that promotes sickness, death, and immeasurable suffering to oneself, one's family, and society? For some reason, many professionals fail to understand how their devotion to their church, tennis club, or professional organization is any less dependent than an AA member's devotion to AA. Weinberg (1975) expresses a similar sentiment:

> Even if one accepted the premise (which to be consistent would also seem to rule out devotion to an organized religion or to psychiatric cults such as psychoanalysis), the author is hard pressed to consider this argument as reasonable. Since one cannot deny that alcohol dependency is extremely harmful to the individual, his family, and society, whereas AA dependency means sobriety, stability, and helping others as a result of living the program, what is the alleged harm in substituting the latter for the former? [p. 34]

AA members are in fact told, "You did not get sober just so you could go to AA meetings for the rest of your life." Dependency is actually discouraged in the program. What often gets passed off as dependency by AA's critics is actually the alcoholic's investment of himself in relationships within the AA fellowship. Often, this is the first time that the AA member has engaged in any type of meaningful human contact while not drinking or being intoxicated. Weinberg (1975) stresses the importance of this involvement:

> The close ties to an accepting group of peers which are generated over time may serve as a powerful incentive to resist the first drink and avoid facing loss of esteem in the group. Finally, AA groups frequently sponsor social events—picnics, dances, etc.—which help foster group involvement and also provide the alcoholic with an atmosphere which combines fun with sobriety, a combination often unknown to him for many years if at all in his adult life. It is of great importance to learn or relearn such an association, because there is little incentive in staying sober if one cannot have any fun in life without drinking. [p. 42]

It is unfortunate that so many professionals view it as a negative turn of events. A common suggestion is to get the addict or alcoholic to face the world as it really is. In contrast to the accusations that suggest that AA fosters pathological dependency by substituting one dependency for another is the consideration that the emergence of such dependent behavior actually signals an important change in a positive direction. It is fortunate that alcoholics become hooked on the people in the AA program. Such an occurrence is often the first evidence of alcoholics' ability to engage in one-to-one relationships, which allows them to accept their need for help and to find new people with whom they can identify. This process takes time. If this process is not interrupted, the addicted individual will eventually develop a healthy capacity for mutuality and secure attachment.

Closely related to this principle of healthy dependence on others is the maturation of narcissistic needs for selfobjects and affect regulation. Kohut differentiated between archaic needs for selfobjects (which is a reparative process that involves the building of psychic structure) and mature needs for selfobject responsiveness (which involves the mutual regulatory process that goes on between two healthy individuals who provide the type of regulation that keeps each other functioning at an optimal level). Early in recovery, alcoholics and addicts typically need archaic selfobjects. Their reliance on the excessive use of grandiose defenses is intertwined within the fabric of values expressed by the drug and alcohol subculture. Recovery and abstinence interfere with the narcissistic fixations of their chemical-using lifestyle. Treatment works best when it provides a course for recovery that facilitates the maturation of healthy narcissism. Sometimes this may require that the individual develop an idealized attachment to the program.

An idealized attachment to a program allows an individual's narcissistic needs to be met in a healthy fashion. It can be a reparative experience if the substance abuser internalizes the admired values expressed in the philosophy of the program. Since AA's values are often enthusiastically held by its members, they represent a direct confrontation with the tenets held by the drug and alcohol subcultures. By idealizing the values of the AA program, alcoholics and addicts not only become less enamored with drinking and drug use, but also develop a healthy dependence on those they idealize. Since these new objects of admiration are more dependable and far more empathic than their previous drinking or drug-using friends and earlier parental figures, alcoholics and addicts are more willing to risk relying on another human being. It is within this climate that a sense of hope can be generated, a beginning faith that personal change is possible, that with the help of new objects for identification a more adaptive patterning of relationships can emerge.

SELFOBJECT TRANSFERENCES: IMPLICATIONS FOR TREATMENT

As a result of insufficient selfobject responsiveness, the substance abuser lacks self-worth and suffers from chronic feelings of poor self-esteem and shame. It is within the matrix of environmental responsiveness and emotional attunement that a specific process of psychological structure formation develops. Structure building cannot occur without a previous stage in which the child's mirroring, twinship, and idealizing needs have been responded to efficiently. Structure is laid as the consequence of minor, nontraumatic failures in the responses of empathic selfobjects. Specifically, structure is built when the ruptured bonds between the self and the person providing selfobject functions is restored (Harwood 1998). Resolving disagreements in an ideal atmosphere of optimal frustration permits the self to gradually internalize the functions previously provided by the selfobject. Optimal frustration reflects the ideal environmental situation within which these minor, nontraumatic failures occur.

Empathic failures, within the context of optimal frustration, lead to a gradual replacement of the selfobject functions by the individual's developing capacity to soothe and calm oneself. Kohut called this process transmuting internalization. If affect regulation and self-soothing are internalized, the person will be less dependent on external sources for gratification. The more the holding environment provides opportunities for empathic failures to be worked through and repaired, the greater the frequency that ruptured bonds with the caregiver will be reestablished, and subsequently the stronger the structure formation will be (Beebe, 1993).

> Dorothy was sober for more than two years and active in AA when her female therapist referred her to a mixed group of men and women to give her an opportunity to work on her issues with men. The only daughter in a family of four sons and a father who was a major in the Air Force, Dorothy was the constant recipient of ridicule and mockery. Since the therapy group was co-led by a man and a woman, Dorothy was able to align herself with the

> women in the group and use them as a buffer as she dealt with her male siblings in the group. However, her biggest challenge came from her dealings with the male leader in the group. Any failures, imagined or real, on his part to defend or understand her were met with emotional storms of protest and outrage. With the group, and especially the women, serving as a bulwark against overwhelming fears of retaliation, Dorothy received the encouragement and support she required in order to work through all injuries as they occurred. With the male therapist's consistent patience, each repair allowed psychic structure to be established, providing her with a greater capacity not only to stand up for herself, but also to tolerate shortcomings in men without viciously attacking them.

Psychic structure, from a self psychology perspective, is not an entity or an agent, but a capacity, indicating a class of psychological functions pertaining to the maintenance, restoration, and consolidation of self-experience. Psychic or self structure represents the capacity or ability to integrate and organize fragmenting affect into meaningful experience. Structure formation—the acquisition of patterns and meaning—is developed out of the internalization of functions previously provided by external objects and reflects the ability to take over these functions without relying excessively on selfobjects. The deficits in psychic or self structure that require external augmentation are usually the result of developmental failures related to unmet age-appropriate attachment needs. Conversely, the successful formation and establishment of self structure is a developmental outcome reflecting the capacity for affect regulation.

In treatment, optimal frustration should not be confused with deliberate attempts on the therapist's part to frustrate the patient. Frustration naturally occurs in any genuine ongoing relationship. Optimal refers to the climate established in the holding environment that most favorably allows for the reestablishment of ruptured bonds in an atmosphere of optimal responsiveness. If a proper treatment environment is created, structure formation will be the natural by-product of the spontaneous interactions that occur within the therapy relationship.

PARALLELS BETWEEN PSYCHIC STRUCTURE AND INTERNAL WORKING MODELS

There exists a complementary relationship between Kohut's definition of psychic structure and Bowlby's internal working model. Following Kohut's work on selfobject transferences, substance abusers are viewed as having been deprived of the opportunity to adequately internalize the admiring, encouraging, valued, and idealized qualities of good-enough parental figures. Absence of this experience inhibits further developmental growth, interfering with the gradual internalization of the selfobject function. Until these capacities become internalized, vulnerable individuals—through the force of the repetition compulsion—will continue to re-create their past in the present. Attachments to external bad objects (e.g., a cold and critical mother, drugs, alcohol, etc.) in the external world are extremely difficult to relinquish until internalized object and self representations are worked through or modified. Ogden (1983) states:

> Resistance is understood in terms of the difficulty the patient has in giving up the pathological attachments involved in his unconscious internal object relations. . . . This tie is based on one's need to change the bad object into the kind of person one wishes the object were. . . . The second category of the bond to a bad internal object . . . takes the form of a crusade to expose the unfairness of, coldness of, or other forms of wrong doing on the part of the internal object. [p. 236]

The attachment to the tantalizing, internalized, split-off, good object and self representations is the collected bond that fuels the addictive process. The needy but undeserving good self representation is a bottomless pit that can never be satisfied, and the tantalizing good object can never fulfill its promise of perfect love, acceptance, and complete nurturance without any limits or disappointments. The overindulgent, overgratifying, and inconsistent mother can be as damaging to the child's development as the cold, critical, and rejecting mother. In the former case, frustration tolerance is never internalized and impulse control is never mastered. Ogden states, "One type of tie to a bad internal object is the attachment of the craving self to the tantalizing object. The nature of the tie to the object is that of the addict for the addicting agent and is extremely difficult to relinquish" (p. 236).

Disturbances in attachment during the formative years of development increase the potential for psychopathology and establish an internal working model that impacts future attachment styles. In a similar fashion, attachment-oriented therapy can be defined as a way of eliciting, exploring, integrating, and modifying internal working models. It is helpful to think of all interpersonal interactions as operating on two levels. There are the observable interchanges occurring between individuals in the external world, and the internal exchanges of self and object representations occurring within each person's internal working model. Each level of interaction influences the other. Just as a person's external behavior is modified by interactions with others, adaptations in internal self and object representations are also occurring. This approach to treatment operates on the principle that internal structural change is necessary if external behavioral change is to be long-lasting and something other than compliance.

LIFELONG NEED FOR SELFOBJECTS AND AFFECT REGULATION

Bowlby (1979) saw the need for healthy relationships that provided mutual affect regulation as an integral part of human behavior "from the cradle to the grave." Kohut agreed, and said that we never outgrow our need for selfobjects, and that therapy is only complete when the person can form healthy attachments outside of the therapeutic milieu. Another very important aspect of attachment theory and self psychology is their compatibility with AA. Each perspective defines addiction as failed attempts to regulate affect and repair deficits in psychic structure. Developmental failures leave the vulnerable individual with an inadequate capacity to form intimate attachments, leading alcoholics and addicts to substitute things and substances for people. Both theories view the disease concept as a metaphor and provide alternative explanations for why AA works and why abstinence is required.

However, as attachment theory reminds us, regardless of our age or emotional development, we will always require some degree of emotional regulation from others. The denial of the need for others is what leads individuals to seek gratification (e.g., drugs, alcohol, food, sex, work, gambling, etc.) outside the realm of interpersonal relationships.

AA AND NARCISSISM

Viewing addiction as a disorder of the self and narcissistic phenomena as the problematic expression of the need for selfobject responsiveness helps provide an alternative explanation for why AA and other twelve-step programs work as they do for the chemically dependent individual. Self psychologists hold many basic tenets that they believe are essential if narcissistic disturbances are to be repaired. Kohut viewed the narcissistic disorder as the expression of a reaction to injury of the self, and regarded the experience of the bond between the self and the selfobject to be crucial for psychological health and growth. Kohut is implying that there is an inverse relationship between individuals' early experience of positive selfobject responsiveness and their propensity to turn to alcohol, drugs, and other sources of gratification as substitutes for these missing or damaging relationships. Conversely, if they are to successfully give up these misguided attempts at self-repair, they must learn how to substitute healthy interpersonal relationships in which needs for selfobject responsiveness (mirroring, merger, and idealization) are satisfied in a gradual, gratifying way.

AA and other twelve-step programs accomplish this in a number of ways. First and foremost, AA provides a predictable and consistent holding environment that allows addicts and alcoholics to have their selfobject needs met in a way that is not exploitive, destructive, or shameful. Because of unmet development needs, addicts or alcoholics have such strong and overpowering needs (object hunger) for human responsiveness that they feel insatiable and shamed by their neediness. Through their identification with other alcoholics and addicts, they come to accept in themselves what they could not previously because they believed their badness was unique.

> This principle was brought home clearly one day at a conference led by John Bradshaw, the noted author, lecturer, ordained Protestant minister, and self-proclaimed recovering alcoholic. Bradshaw was speaking on one of his favorite topics—toxic shame—when he told the audience about his personal experience when he first entered AA. "My alcoholism had gotten so bad that I was forced by the shear humiliation of my situation to attend an AA meeting. Halfway through the meeting I was so overwhelmed by the shame that my drinking had caused in my life that I was compelled to stand up and tell everyone all the horrible things I had done in the last few years of my drinking. I must have carried on for over fifteen minutes with an outpouring of every despicable, disgraceful act that I could remember that I had committed while under the influence of alcohol. When I stopped talking and forced myself to look around at the faces in the room, I expected to see people pulling away in disgust."
>
> Imagine Bradshaw's surprise when the other alcoholics in the room did not reject him like his congregation did or abandon him as his church had done when they discovered all those horrible truths about him. "Instead," Bradshaw announced, "of running away from me in repulsion, everyone ran toward me, gave me their phone numbers, and told me to call them anytime I needed to."

Addicts or alcoholics can only tolerate acceptance at this level of emotional vulnerability because they feel understood on a very basic, empathic level. Empathy and emotional attunement are not only the cornerstone of treatment for self psychology, they are also the foundation from which chemically dependent individuals can begin to feel the kind of responsiveness and gratification they had been missing and were previously unable to tolerate in their lives.

As Kurtz (1979) has eloquently argued in his book, *Not God,* alcoholics must come to terms with their narcissistic defenses and quit playing God:

> "Not-God" means first "You are not God," the message of the AA program. . . . The fundamental and first message of Alcoholics

> Anonymous to its members is that they are not infinite, not absolute, *not* God. Every alcoholic's problem had *first* been, according to this insight, claiming God-like powers, especially that of *control*. But the alcoholic at least, the message insists, is *not* in control, even of himself: and the first step towards recovery from alcoholism must be the admission and *acceptance* of this fact that is so blatantly obvious to others but so tenaciously denied by the obsessive-compulsive drinker. [p. 42]

Figure 4–1 sums up Kurtz's position. Parallel to attachment theory and self psychology, Kurtz says it's the alcoholic's denial of his need for people that leads to his eventual denial that he's an alcoholic. Consequently, recovery is dictated by reversing this process. First, the alcoholic must admit that he is an alcoholic and then he must ultimately admit he needs people.

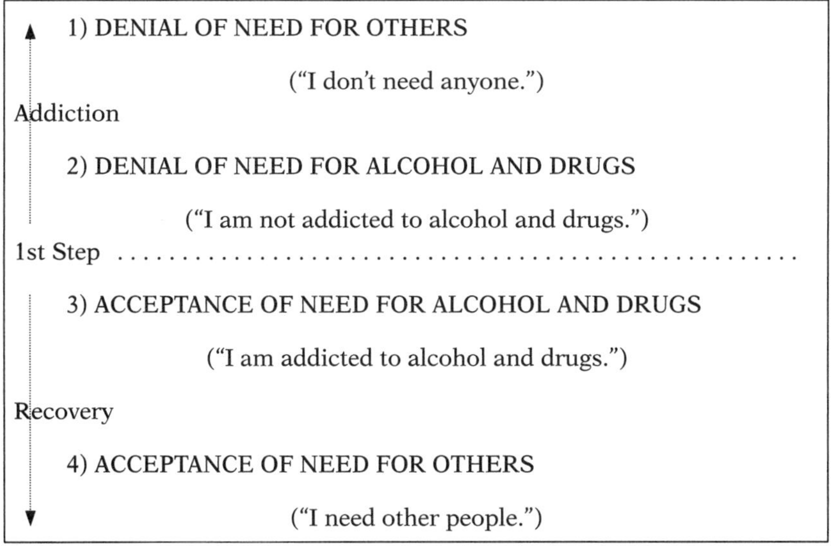

Figure 4–1

In an existential sense, the confrontation between what substance abusers tried to be and what they really are (not-God) results in their ceasing to live their life in bad faith (i.e., alcoholic) and become more authentic ("Hello, I'm Joe, a recovering alcoholic"), with all the limitations that authentic life imposes on them. As archaic ways of getting one's needs met are gradually relinquished for more mature ways of establishing close human contact (removal of character defect by working the program), the alcoholic or addict is able to internalize more self-care and monitoring of affective states (transmuting internalization). The central issue in this process is the acceptance of one's self as one is, which requires dealing with shame about the self that was previously hidden.

AA, as a holding environment, also becomes a transitional object; a healthy dependency that provides enough separation to prevent depending too much on any single person until individuation and internalization are established. Gradually, alcoholics or addicts are able to give up the grandiose defenses (narcissism) and false-self persona for a discovery of self (true self). As David Treadway (1990) points out, the self-help movement is, regardless of its successes or failures, driven by people's attempts to regain the "lost spirit of community."

5

Neurophysiology and Attachment

> Medicine lost sight of this truth: attachment is physiology.
> *Lewis, Amini, and Lannon (2000)*

> But dividing the mind into "biological" and "psychological" is as fallacious as classifying light as a particle or a wave.
> *Lewis, Amini, and Lannon (2000)*

The development and introduction of Bowlby's formulations concerning the significance of attachment were not only creatively innovative for his time, but also controversial. When he first presented his theory, not everyone readily agreed or accepted his initial conclusions about the extensive significance of attachment bonds. It took a series of ground-breaking studies by Ainsworth (1969), Harlow (1958), Robertson (1953), and others (e.g., Main 1995, Spitz 1945) before the conventional scientific establishment of his day completely accepted all of attachment theory's far-reaching implications.

Because attachment theory also fit nicely with Darwin's theory of evolution, this complementary alliance helped persuade many skeptics to accept a great deal of Bowlby's theory. Critics especially found it difficult to refute the idea behind the goal of attachment, which is to provide physical security for an infant, whose helplessness required a nearby protector. Evidence continued to mount, suggesting that natural selection also favored proximity-seeking behavior because it helped ensure the survival of the human species. Gradually, the social sciences came to accept the conclusion that we are social, herd animals that need to stay closely connected to each other. However, as accepted and respected as these views are today, even Bowlby might be surprised to discover the significance of attachment relationships is far greater than he imagined. Advancing technology has helped researchers discover that attachment alters gene expression and modifies biological substrates. More recent investigation into the physiology of relatedness suggests that attachment penetrates to the neural core of what it means to be a human being.

ATTACHMENT AND LOSS

Paradoxically, Bowlby's interest in attachment was initiated by his early investigations into the effects that early separation and loss have on a developing child. He and other investigators discovered that human beings share a collection of responses to loss and separation that crosses all cultural barriers, and these response patterns are strikingly similar for all social mammals. Lewis and colleagues (2000) noted, "The human species exhibits a shared universal mammalian reaction to the rupture of an attachment bond" (p. 87). Short separation provokes an acute response known as protest, while prolonged separation yields the physiological and psychological state of despair and eventual depression.

Lewis and colleagues (2000) state that this universal response is a reflection of the limbic architecture that all social mammals share:

> Human adults exhibit a protest response as much as any other mammal. Anyone who has been jilted in an infatuation (i.e., just about everybody) has experienced the protest firsthand—the inescapable inner restlessness, the powerful urge to contact the person ("just to talk"), mistaken glimpses of the lost figure everywhere (a seething combination of overly vigilant scanning and blind hope). All are part of protest. The drive to reestablish contact is sufficiently formidable that people cannot resist it, even when they understand that the other person doesn't want anything to do with them. Human beings manifest searching and calling in lengthy letters, frantic phone calls, repeated e-mails and telephoning an answering machine just to hear another's voice. [p. 77]

The consequences can be far more ominous for young children. If separation occurs early enough and is prolonged, the infant can in many cases die. If other adequate attachment substitutes aren't provided, the child can become so pathologically detached that they demonstrate an identified syndrome commonly referred to as reactive attachment disorder. The work of Bessel van der Kolk demonstrated that neglect and trauma have far-reaching consequences on a person's memory and psychobiology. More importantly, there is now evidence that even subtle environmental disruptions or failures by poorly attuned caregivers can have a significant impact on the physiological development of the brain.

Evidence from a recent and very public case involving the infamous Unabomber, Ted Kaczynski, demonstrates the possible far-reaching consequences that attachment disruptions can have on a person's life. The popular media tried to answer how a seemingly normal boy, educated at an Ivy League school, could end up brooding alone in a ten-foot by twelve-foot cabin, winter after winter, deep in the Montana woods, plotting to assassinate innocent people he didn't even know. *Newsweek* (1996) re-created how a troubled boy turned into a dangerous man:

> The first clue is something that happened when Kaczynski was only 6 months old. According to federal investigators, little "Teddy John," as his parents called him, was hospitalized for a severe allergic reaction to a medicine he was taking. He had to be isolated—his parents were unable to see or hold him for several weeks. After this separation, family members have told the Feds, the baby's personality, once bubbly and vivacious, seemed to go "flat." [p. 29]

ATTACHMENT IS AN EXPECTED EXPERIENCE OF THE BRAIN

Attachment theory, more than any other theoretical perspective, places particular emphasis on the crucial necessity of early attachment experiences in determining an infant's neurobiological development. All infants enter the world with a given genetic substrate. As their brain develops, there is an early, huge sprouting of synapses and neurons. An experience that the child's brain expects and is waiting for must happen if the structure of the brain is to be developed. Depending on whether that experience happens, the structure of the brain, for better of for worse, is established and set for life. The absence or presence of crucial early experiences either strengthens or weakens certain neuronal substrates of the brain. There are critical developmental stages when certain experiences must be provided or the opportunity for that experience will be forever lost. The absence of critical experiences will shape the structure of the brain for the rest of the child's life and in many cases leave the vulnerable individual with unalterable developmental consequences.

For example, the infant's brain is waiting for the experience of binocular vision. If that experience is not provided by the age of 4 months, the brain will never be able to acquire depth perception after that. The learning of a second language is another good example. Those cultures that provide a multilingual experience for the child's developing brain during the first five years of life are able to take advantage of the brain's receptivity to this opportunity. While second languages can be learned later in life, it is a much more difficult and arduous task. In a similar way, the quality of the early attachment relationship in the first year of life will have a powerful effect on the development of the emotional relational core of a person. The structure of a child's developing brain is more receptive and more likely to be profoundly shaped by the quality of the attachment experience. Once these identifiable patterns or attachment styles are established in the child's brain, they are difficult to extinguish and persist throughout adulthood. While experiences like trauma and other attachment relationships can have an impact on this relational core, alterations in attachment styles are difficult to extinguish and unlearn.

BIOLOGY OF ATTACHMENT AND EMOTION

Recent advances in the study of the biology of emotions have produced a new model of emotion that is more closely aligned with the realities of actual observable behavior. It is more theoretically effective and translates more readily into useful clinical applications. Emotions, from this perspective, cannot be separated from a person's physiological makeup. Not only is this true for humans, but it is the case for most social mammals. Paul Ekman's (1992) classic work is the most recent example of research evidence suggesting that animals and humans share a common physiological link between facial expressions and emotions.

The work of Ekman and others (e.g., Izard 1971) confirmed a central proposition of the survival first put forth by Darwin, who proposed that facial expressions are identical all over the globe, in every culture, and with every human being. Emotional life starts with universal innate functions, which are critically shaped by early experiences and continue on to become a major and unconscious organizing force for all mental activity. Attachment is a specialized example of this. It starts with the natural capacity of the child to send and receive emotional signals from the primary caregiver. The nature of the child's capacity to accurately read emotional signals in self and others is crucially shaped by the mother–infant bond and becomes an unconscious foundation for all subsequent interpersonal relationships. These findings suggest that emotions are universal, closely tied into our physiology, and are central to all human experience and relatedness. Emotions also serve a communitive function, starting first with the mother and infant. The demonstration of affect helps maintain attachment (the separation cry, for instance) and is the earliest and most primitive form of communication. It mediates attachment and serves a basic survival function.

With the mounting evidence that emotions are innate, not learned, and that attachment shapes the structure of the brain and affects our memory, attachment theorists have concluded that all other previous models of psychodynamic theory are lacking in an accurate representation of the correct interplay among the brain, emotion, and attachment. One primary reason for the inadequacies and inaccuracies in other previous theoretical models is that they are hampered by a polarization between psychology and biology, which is the result of medicine's heritage of the mind–body dualism left over from the influence of René Descartes. This polarization is totally incompatible with the position of attachment theory. Emotions, from an attachment perspective, are basic brain functions and not epiphenomenona of psychodynamic conflicts.

Darwin was actually one of the first to propose a theory that was devoid of this polarization. He believed that emotions were behaviors that arose and persisted because of their ability to advance survival and the reproduction of the species. Because of evidence like Ekman's, which suggests that emotions are hard-wired and closely linked to facial expressions, emotions must be considered to be part of our phylogenic past—a past that we genetically share with other mammals. Attachment theory, with its integration of biology and psychology of emotions, assumes the capacity for emotion is innate and not learned. Darwin (1871) addressed this issue over a hundred years ago:

> It has often been assumed that animals were in the first place rendered social, and that they feel as a consequence uncomfortable when separated from each other, and comfortable whilst together: but it is a more probable view that these sensations were first developed, in order that those animals which would profit by living in society, should be induced to live together, for with those animals which were benefited by living in close association, the individuals which took the greatest pleasure in society would best escape various dangers: whilst those that cared least for their comrades and lived solitary would parish in greater numbers.

This capacity for emotion becomes part of a broader function of the brain, which reads the environment and readies the body for an appropriate response (flight or fight) to a given situation. Our emotional responses also affect our memory of these experiences and because of this, emotion is looked upon as an important organizer of mental activity that shapes our priorities, beliefs, and convictions. Thus, the connections between our emotions and our memory have important far-reaching implications in determining and defining us as human beings.

Emotions also play a significant role in our socialization.

The emotional system is particularly aimed at the social part of our environment, reading the emotional signals from others and displaying our own appropriate emotional states (e.g., smiling when our loved one enters the room) for others to read. Infants are born with an innate emotional fluency, and emotions provide an immediate language between mother and infant. Emotions are vehicles of information exchange, which occur in the developing attachment relationship, thus enhancing attachment. This model of the brain holds that emotions are basic brain functions that provide us with our earliest forms of communication, which helps serve and mediate attachment and helps organize memory and all mental activity in general. However, when a person's early emotional climate is lacking or defective (poor attunement and responsiveness), the resulting deficits can seriously impede an individual from correctly reading emotion signals from others, severely impairing the person's capacity for relationships.

> Wilson was brought to therapy by his distraught wife. She was threatening to divorce him unless he "straightened up." The therapist saw them a few times for couple's therapy before referring Wilson to a substance abuse specialist. Five years clean from marijuana, Wilson said he had stopped going to Alcoholics Anonymous and Narcotics Anonymous a couple years ago, "because no one's very friendly there." His wife was also a recovering addict whom he had "met at a meeting, a few months ago." Exploration into his early history revealed a father who suffered from posttraumatic stress disorder and a mother Wilson described as "crazy." His childhood was dominated by a painful history of few friends and continual taunts and teasing by his schoolmates.
>
> After a few sessions with Wilson, it soon became apparent why he suffered as he did in school and why few people were friendly to him at twelve-step meetings. Wilson was pleasant enough, but his social behavior was discordant and jarring. He stood too close when shaking hands. He spoke too loudly and he could not maintain eye contact, giving the impression of someone always watching you out of the corner of his eye. His voice was flat and

his dress atypical and somewhat eccentric for a man of his age. It was apparent that Wilson was an intelligent man who did not know how to read people or interact with them. He was genuinely confused by people's avoidance and rejection of him. Wilson was completely unable to intuit the rules of social exchange; consequently his dress, manner, and style of greeting left others feeling uncomfortable in his presence. Once, in an attempt to show appreciation for some guidance that his very macho boss had given him, Wilson presented him with some flowers and a sentimental card. He explained to the therapist that he had observed that people often give small tokens of appreciation to each other. He was completely baffled by his boss's cold reaction to his gift.

ANATOMY OF ATTACHMENT

Because of recent advances in the science of neurobiology and the neuroanatomy of emotion and memory, attachment theory pays particular attention to the parts of the brain that mediate these components. Attachment theorists see the limbic system as the crucial apparatus of the brain because it is the seat of both emotions and memory. The limbic system is a powerful mediator of attachment, and the intricate interplay between emotion and memory lays a foundation for understanding the impact that separation and loss have on a person's physiological and psychological state.

The limbic system is at an advantage to accomplish its organizing tasks because it is located at a neuroanatomical crossroads that is essential for organizing complex brain functions. All learning and conditioning takes place at the limbic level. Information is encoded and stored here, forming a motivational map indicating the location of emotionally significant objects like food, predators, and sexual partners. This information is so highly processed at this point that the individual can scan his environment and immediately sense secure versus dangerous areas. The rapid firing of neurons at the limbic level will allow a person to tell you there is danger, but unable to tell you why, like the patient who has a gut feeling but cannot explain it.

THE MYTH OF HIGHER BRAIN FUNCTIONS

Because of our society's preoccupation with facts and psychology's obligatory heritage of the "talking cure," science shares the same cultural bias that we all have about the hierarchical structure of the brain. Common teaching implies that the lower areas of the brain, which contain the limbic system, must obviously serve lower brain functions. Since the neocortex is considered the latest developmental achievement of human evolution, it is thus assumed to serve a higher, and thus more important, brain function. Attachment theorists consider this to be a mistake, and suggest that this popular hierarchy may actually be misleading and even a hindrance to the correct understanding of brain functioning. The limbic system in fact provides an important organizing component to our brain that essentially determines how we live and run our lives.

Attachment theory contends that the neocortex actually serves the so-called lower parts of the brain and that it is really at the limbic level that the most crucial levels of communication occur. Consider how words spoken without emotion have little power to persuade. Also consider research that demonstrates the powerful exchange of wordless communication that goes on between a mother and her infant. Lewis and colleagues (2000) discuss the subtleties of this type of communication, reminding us that what is obscure is not always without significance:

> The limbic brain is another delicate physical apparatus that specializes in detecting and analyzing just one part of the physical world—the internal state of other mammals. Emotionality is the social sense organ of limbic creatures. While vision lets us experience the reflected wavelengths of electromagnetic radiation, and hearing gives information about the pressure waves in the surrounding air, emotionality enables a mammal to sense the inner states and the motives of the mammals around him. [pp. 62–63]

THE DEVELOPING BRAIN

All neural development starts with a genetic substrate. In the newborn infant's brain, there is a high initial sprouting of neural synapses. As the child develops, its brain is waiting for an experience. Depending on whether that experience is provided or not, two potential outcomes will occur:

Blooming: As the newborn infant's brain develops, there is an initial sprouting of neural synapses. Due to the infant's limited psychomotor capabilities, the brain at this stage is a passive recipient, waiting for an experience. As experiences and environmental stimulation are provided, these occurrences shape the structure of the brain.

Pruning: If certain experiences and age-appropriate environmental stimulation are not provided, pruning occurs. Pruning is actual neuronal death, resulting in the loss of synaptic potentials and the weakening of neuronal pathways.

To the degree that a particular experience is provided, the developing brain responds with neuronal growth. If these experiences aren't provided, the child goes from a potentially large neural substrate to one shaped by pruning and lack of stimulation, which alters the structure of the brain for life. Synaptic connections that are reinforced by an infant's exposure to language, sounds, facial expressions, and even lessons in cause and effect (e.g., the infant smiles, the mother smiles back) become permanent parts (blooming) of the brain's structure. Tentative connections that are not reinforced by early experience are eliminated (pruning). Examples include binocular vision, the developmental of language, musical competence, and the capacity for attachment. Developing kittens deprived of visual stimulation for the first four months of their life lose the capacity forever to have binocular vision (depth perception). Children exposed to foreign languages and music in the first few years of their life demonstrate a much greater capacity for the enrichment of these skills than those who attempt to learn later in life. If critical periods of stimulation are not provided, the developing brain moves on. The remaining neural structure is hard to alter. A more chilling example of the potentially detrimental impact of failure to provide proper, needed responses to a developing brain is seen in the isolated, affectionless sociopath whose capacity for human warmth and attachment is forever loss.

Healthy development is determined by the infant's ability to attach itself to an external object. Horner (1979) describes the ramifications of the infant's inability to bond with another:

> At the most primitive level, failure of attachment may carry with it severe deficits in the early organization of the self. The failure to develop attachment and to achieve a satisfactory symbiosis because of environmental factors, such as institutionalization, may lead to the development of characteristic disturbances such as the inability to keep rules, lack of capacity to experience guilt, and indiscriminate friendliness with an inordinate craving for affection with no ability to make lasting relationships. The "affectionless psychopath" is also characterized by the failure to develop the affectional bond that goes with attachment. Another form of pathological attachment is attachment through the false-self organization. In this situation the real, core self has remained in a nonattached, non–object-related state. [pp. 28–29]

During the first five or six months of life, in the developmentally healthy child, there is innate attachment-seeking behavior to bring about a normal symbiosis. The earliest mental representations of self and object (the undifferentiated self-object representation) is characteristic of this stage. Mahler (1979) contends that there is neither physical nor psychic differentiation. This brings us to the heart of Mahler's developmental work. She observed that it is crucial during this time that there be mutual selection of cues by mother and infant: "We observed that infants present a larger variety of cues to indicate needs, tension, and pleasure. In a complex manner the mother responds selectively to only certain of these cues" (p. 18). Mahler points out that mutual cuing creates the complex pattern that becomes what Lichtenstein (1961) refers to as "the infant's becoming the child of his particular mother" (p. 19).

Bowlby (1979) emphasizes the degree to which infants themselves play a part in determining their own environment. Certain kinds of babies who tend to be overreactive or unpredictable make it difficult for the mother to provide good-enough mothering. But the mother has a much larger role than the infant by the end of the first year in determining the quantity and quality of the transactions that occur between them.

The failure of attachment carries several deficits in the early organization of the self. There is a delicate and subtle interplay between constitutional and environmental factors that determines how this disturbance will manifest. Mahler outlines this process in clear detail:

1. The affectionless psychopath is characterized by the failure to develop the affectional bonds that go with attachment.
2. Disruption of attachment due to separation and loss may lead to a lifelong schizoid detachment. In this case, detachment is used as a defense against the frightening impact of object relatedness.
3. Another form of pathological attachment is attachment through the false-self organization, leading to narcissistic personality structure.

A few years ago I was recruited to provide a series of training workshops for a number of counselors who were getting ready to lead substance abuse groups in the state prison system. While describing the adaptations in strategies required for leading groups with substance abusers, I spent the time covering the topic of co-occurring personality disorders. A lively discussion soon ensued around the topic of the preoedipal personality and early developmental arrestment.

One of the young counselors, who looked like he was fresh out of graduate school, raised his hand and said, "From what I'm understanding, many of these people we're treating here in the prison have suffered a lot of severe trauma, neglect, and deprivation at a very early age."

I nodded in agreement.

"Well then," the young man continued. "This implies that since the damage occurred so early in their lives, they're going to be very difficult to rehabilitate."

Before I could respond, one of the older counselors who had worked in the state prison system for years shouted, "Rehabilitated, hell! We're talking about *habilitation*. How in the world are you going to rehabilitate someone who's never been *habilitated*?

ATTACHMENT AND DEVELOPMENT

Circuits in the different regions of the brain mature at different times. As a result, different circuits are more sensitive to life's experience at different ages. Consider the typical critical developmental periods of a child's brain:

Birth to one year: Motor development, emotional control, vision, attachment, implicit memory, and vocabulary.

One year to two: Second language, math, logic, and rudimentary signs of explicit memory (e.g., may grasp the meaning of "soon" and "after dinner," but has limited knowledge of days and time).

Two to three: Music, separation and individuation, object constancy, relationships between objects.

The brain is an open system that interacts with and is easily influenced by its environment. The relationship between a child's brain and the environment is reciprocal: brain development affects a child's response to experiences, and a child's experiences influence brain development. Furthermore, interpersonal relations or attachment are necessary for normal brain development. Research has demonstrated that attachment and interpersonal interactions not only influence brain activity but also are crucial for brain development.

For instance, the kind of emotional attunement provided by secure attachment actually increases blood flow to the prefrontal areas of the child's brain, resulting in the growth of neural tissue in the emotional and attention centers of the brain. Without the emotional resonance provided by attunement from an attachment figure, the child's excitement and prefrontal arousal areas of the brain are dampened, and growth in regions of the brain that encourage inhibition is accelerated.

While there is an abundant amount of research that demonstrates that secure attachment stimulates growth in important areas of the brain, the reverse is also true. The absence of stimulation at crucial stages of brain development can inhibit neural growth. In addition, stress can have significant impact on the developing brain through the mechanism of neurochemical activity. Neurochemical stress not only impacts the mature brain, it also adversely impacts the immature or developing brain. Studies have shown that neglected children have brains that are strikingly different from those of children who weren't neglected. Neglect produces children whose head circumferences are measurably smaller, whose brains on magnetic resonance scanning evidence shrinkage from the loss of billions of cells. Similar anatomical changes, related to the parts of the brain that mediate emotions and attachment, were also discovered in children raised by depressed mothers. In all these cases research has convincingly demonstrated that "nurture" not only affects "nature" but also often determines "nature."

REWARD DEFICIENCY SYNDROME

While there is an abundance of research evidence that inadequate attachment can have a profound influence on a child's developing brain, evidence is also accumulating that one common adverse consequence is the brain's increased susceptibility to addictive diseases. Research on the possible relationship between certain genetic anomalies and alcoholism has led to the discovery of a statistically significant incident of a genetic variant (called an *allele,* which is an alternate form of a gene occupying the same position on matching chromosomes) that is related to a number of behavioral syndromes:

Addictive disorders

Smoking

Compulsive overeating

Obesity

Attention deficit disorder

Pathological gambling

Tourette's syndrome

These disorders are linked by a common biological substrate (a hard-wired system consisting of cells and signaling molecules) that leads to either an inborn or induced imbalance in the limbic-diencephalic area of the brain (commonly referred to as the pleasure center of the brain) that leaves a person with feelings of deficits in safety, warmth, and satiety. If these requirements are not responded to, the limbic system signals threat, anxiety, and discomfort. Craving will be triggered, which motivates the individual to take action to eliminate negative emotions.

The reward deficiency syndrome (Blum et al. 1996) just described involves a form of sensory deprivation of brain pleasure mechanisms. The syndrome is believed to be a consequence of an individual's biochemical/neurological inability to derive reward from ordinary everyday activities. It is hypothesized that depletion in dopamine and serotonin levels contributes to this condition. In a normal person, neurotransmitters work together in a cascade of excitement or inhibition—between complex stimuli and complex responses—leading to a state of well-being. In the cascade theory of reward, genetic anomalies, prolonged stress, or long-term abuse can lead to a self-sustaining pattern of abnormal cravings in both animals and human beings. Disruption can be induced by all of the following:

Prolonged stress (Seligman's learned helplessness)

Genetic anomalies

Long-term abuse of alcohol

Prolonged substance abuse

Compulsive binging

Compulsive gambling

The reward deficiency syndrome supports many of the new research findings from the emerging neurobiology of addiction. Prolonged use of substances alter synapses and the endogenous production of certain neurotransmittors. At some point, the addicted brain becomes qualitatively different from the nonaddicted brain.

Alan Leshner (1996), the director of the National Institute of Drug Abuse (NIDA), argues that prolonged use can produce alterations in the neurophysiology of the brain that cannot be reversed. When this "switch" in the brain occurs, the substance user changes from an abuser to an addict or an alcoholic. The addicted brain becomes qualitatively different in its neurobiology from the nonaddicted brain. In a very similar statement, Steve Heyman (1996), director of the National Institute of Mental Health (NIMH), adds that addiction involves biochemical and physiological alterations of brain functioning, resulting in adaptations of the brain's neuropathways. Addicted persons' behavior is no longer under their volitional control, but their actions become determined by induced adaptations of the brain's reward circuitry and conditioned cues. Drug craving and compulsive use is induced in responses to internal affect states and conditioned cues. Prolonged chemical use results in the "commandeering of the motivational centers of the brain."

Alan Leshner (1997a) explains the significance of recognizing the fundamental discontinuity between chemical use and addiction:

> What matters is that while addiction may be the result of a lot of drug use, it is not the same as using drugs a lot. Drug use and drug addiction do not reside together along a continuum of say, drug use, drug abuse, a whole lot of drug abuse, and then addiction. And the user cannot voluntarily move back and forth along such a continuum at will. Addiction is a qualitatively different

> state because the addicted brain is, in fact, different in its neurobiology from the nonaddicted brain. [p. 2]

SECURE ATTACHMENT CREATES NEUROPHYSIOLOGICAL HOMEOSTASIS

The results of the absence of attachment are not limited to physiological disruptions of the brain. Not only are nurturance, social communion, play, and communication based in the limbic area, but other aspects of the body are also severely affected when attachment is disrupted. Abandoned individuals experience multiple disruptions to their entire homeostasis. Lewis and colleagues (2000) give a disturbing account of all that can go wrong when children and adults are forced to deal with loss:

> Prolonged separation affects more than feelings. A number of somatic parameters go haywire in despair. Because separation deranges the body, losing relationships can cause physical illness. Growth hormone levels plunge in despair—the reason why children deprived of love stop growing, lose weight no matter what their caloric intake, and dwindle away. Children confined to a hospital for extended periods of time used to surrender to this syndrome in droves. Rene Spitz called their affliction "hospitalism," a term taken by the politely tautological phrase still employed, "failure to thrive." Once doctors appreciated the physical damage contained in social loss, they increased the survival of these children by allowing them more contact with their parents.
>
> Children aren't the only ones whose bodies respond to the intricacies of loss: cardiovascular function, hormone levels, and immune processes are disturbed in adults subjected to prolonged separation. And so medical illness or death often follows the end of a marriage or the loss of a spouse. One study, for instance, found that social isolation tripled the death rate following a heart attack. Another found that going to group psychotherapy doubled the post-surgical lifespan of women with breast cancer. A third noted that leukemia patients with strong social supports had two-year survival rates more than twice that

> of those who lacked them. In his fascinating book *Love and Survival,* Dean Ornish surveyed the literature on the relationship between isolation and human mortality. His conclusion: dozens of studies demonstrate that solitary people have a vastly increased rate of premature death from all causes—they are three to five times likelier to die early than people with ties to a caring spouse, family, or community. [pp. 79–80]

Accumulating evidence on the impact of loss suggests overwhelmingly that attachment figures (relationships) are powerful regulators of normal physiology. How a person handles separation and loss is determined by the length and quality of their earliest attachment relationships. The quality of this early relationship is encoded in the person's memory and limbic system. Before we discuss the full impact that attachment and separation can have on a person, it is important to explore the biology and neuroanatomy of memory.

To summarize, there are three important points to remember about attachment:

1. Secure attachment creates stable neurophysiological homeostasis.
2. With a secure attachment experience, the person is more able to regulate self.
3. With the absence of a stable attachment experience, the person is more vulnerable to disruption.

IMPLICIT VS. EXPLICIT MEMORY

As stated earlier, there is a close link between memory and emotions because this association helped humans survive as a species. Since all emotional learning takes place at the limbic level, and the limbic system is anatomically interconnected with memory, information that is available for recall has a profound influence on attachment, psychopathology, and learning. Emotionally charged information is stored and encoded here, functioning as a "motivational map." This map serves an important task, indicating emotionally significant objects like food, predators, and sexual partners. Primitive man could immediately scan his environment and sense (e.g., gut feeling, intuition, etc.) secure versus dangerous situations. This information is finely processed and stored so a person could immediately sense danger and react without having to stop and think or explain why.

KNOWLEDGE THAT CANNOT BE EXPLAINED

Many ingenious and creative studies have been designed to show that it is possible for people to acquire knowledge and improve their performance on a task without their understanding why they solved the problem as they did. Subjects in these studies exhibit the acquisition of knowledge by demonstrating an improvement in their performance on a new task. When asked how they solved the problem, they were unable to explain the strategies they applied in their solution. Similar results were discovered with brain-damaged individuals who had lost their hippocampus, the area of the brain required for the storage and recall of explicit memory. Even though individuals without a hippocampus could learn new tasks and demonstrate this ability by completing an assigned task, they were unable to remember learning it. They were also unable to explain how they accomplished or solved the problem.

Knowledge without awareness is a scientifically demonstrated phenomenon. While this capacity to experience comprehension divorced from memory is similar to what psychodynamic theory calls the unconscious, attachment theorists prefer making the distinction between explicit and implicit memory because they believe these terms are more anatomically correct and more in line with what actually occurs in the brain. *Explicit memory* is a small percentage of memory. It is information that is accessible for recall and is more related to the storage and retrieval of facts. *Implicit memory* is knowledge that can't be explained. It is memory divorced from the power of comprehension and thought. The greatest percentage of our knowledge is implicitly stored and more difficult to retrieve. Implicit memory also represents things we have learned (e.g., muscle memory like riding a bike or hitting a ball, etc.). We can't explain how to do them, but still we can do them. While there is some similarity to the unconscious, it is not just repression, active censorship, or dissociation. The information is there and can often be demonstrated by a person's action, but cannot be explained. Implicit memory is distinguished from explicit memory by three important features:

1. *Relational*: This type of memory is more emotionally loaded because it serves survival purposes. It is anatomically driven by powerful affect states like fear, anger, hunger, and sex. Its activation is instantaneous, not requiring the loss of time it might take to process information ("Is that a bear about to jump on me? Am I in danger? What should I do?")
2. *Earliest memory*: This is the kind of memory working most often in childhood before the development of language. It is used when the child is most vulnerable and under the influence of powerful affect states.
3. *Emotional*: Implicit memory is "hard-wired" to emotions and the limbic system. It mediates attachment and is closely aligned with Bowlby's concept of the internal working model.

Implicit memory is a generalization of the rules extracted about the relation of things and how one has to act in relation to the rules in order to survive. Direct experience is much more powerful than direct explanation in shaping or conditioning these learned responses. The child essentially learns how "I have to behave in relation to you in order to survive and not be abandoned." Knowledge without awareness and the rules that govern this process are internalized, becoming a crucial component of a person's internal working model. Once a rule is learned and becomes a basic property of the brain, it becomes part of implicit memory. The rules that determine how I will behave in relation to you are difficult to unlearn because this information is not readily available to explicit memory. Since the rules of relatedness remain out of the person's awareness, the individual's behavior becomes self-perpetuating. Experiences with others remain under the influence of powerful emotions that govern implicit memory and lead to a heightened distortion of others to ensure that their actions do not deviate from the rules. The rules of relatedness continue to be applied without knowledge.

Internal working models ("If I do that, this will happen") have long-term consequences and are difficult to alter. The latest discoveries with implicit memory suggest that our individual patterns of emotional reactions get written into our implicit emotional memories. Therapy, from this perspective, is aimed at the ways these emotional reactions written in memory can be rewritten through the synchronous exchange of emotions that occurs within a therapeutic relationship. The person continues his or her attachment style long after the initial primary attachment experience. These attachment styles are discussed at length in the next chapter.

ATTACHMENT AND ANIMAL RESEARCH

The consequences of a mammal's failure to attach have been widely demonstrated by animal research. Research with monkeys has been particularly useful because of the many important parallels that have been discovered between isolated monkeys and addictive-type behaviors found with addicts and alcoholics. Monkeys raised in isolation from other monkeys in their colonies and deprived of secure attachment have extreme difficulty surviving or fitting in when they are returned to their monkey society. They frequently are loners and have difficulty getting along with other monkeys because they cannot read or express appropriate emotions and signals. Isolated monkeys get into fights more frequently, are often self-injurious and aggressive, and demonstrate inappropriate sexual behavior. They also go on food and water binges, and demonstrate difficulty in unlearning dysfunctional patterns of behavior.

The "isolation syndrome" of Kraemer (1985) has special relevance for addiction. Witness the similarity between isolated monkeys and the practicing alcoholic and addict. The implications for diagnosis and treatment are profound. Isolated monkeys, like addicts and alcoholics, are more likely to demonstrate the following:

Food and water binges.

A propensity to prefer and consume more alcohol than normal monkeys.

Difficulty extinguishing learned patterns of behavior or altering response sets.

Unstable, aggressive relationships.

Self-defeating behavior.

Poor sexual relationships.

Difficulty providing parenting.

A tendency to isolate ("loners").

Peer Monkeys

Research has also shown that when these loner monkeys are placed with peer "therapist monkeys," who have had a healthy attachment relationship, the sick, isolated monkeys start to look normal. Their behavior changes and they begin to fit in with the other monkeys in the colony. However, when they are taken away from their therapist monkeys, their improvement doesn't last. They quickly deteriorate and don't function as well because they still do not demonstrate the capacity to learn and respond to appropriate emotional signals and cues.

Peer monkeys and the attachment to therapist monkeys can offset poor parental attachment experiences. Similar conclusions have been drawn about children who have an absent parent or have been raised by alcoholic parents. Sometimes, the siblings in the family can compensate for the parental failings. However, when therapist monkeys are returned to the larger society after spending prolonged periods of time with the sick monkeys, they show more signs of depression and anxiety. Human counterparts to Kraemer's therapist monkeys who work extensively with difficult populations will no doubt see the parallels in their own experiences. A case can easily be made that both therapist monkeys and human therapists are suffering from a syndrome commonly referred to as therapist burn-out.

Isolated or sick monkeys also demonstrate other signs of impairment in their neurochemistry:

1. Norepinephrine levels are depleted. If levels get too low, the despair response is worse.
2. Disregulation of the dopamine system occurs, resulting in a tendency to be more easily overwhelmed by sensory input.
3. Serotonin levels are adversely impacted. Low levels lead to depression and high levels lead to high dominance ranking in the colony.
4. The body's natural opiate system is adversely impacted.

Nurture vs. Nature

Research with laboratory rats reveals that the quality of an attachment experience is not just limited to behavior but can also impact gene expression (Hofer 1996). Infant rats raised by high-grooming rats are more secure, handle stress better, and have less hormonal disruption. When rats from low-grooming mothers were "put up for adoption" and raised by high-grooming rats, these baby rats handled stress better and eventually demonstrated many of the healthy signs of the highly groomed baby rats. When these strains of "adopted rats" from low-grooming mothers were followed over different generations, there was evidence of genetic/biological transfer of learned behavior. As adults, they were more likely to demonstrate high-grooming behavior than their siblings who were not raised by high-grooming mothers. Secure attachment alters gene expression and the structural maturation of neural pathways.

ATTACHMENT AND OPIATE RECEPTORS

During critical times of development, if children have been provided a poor attachment experience, their brain shows less opiate receptor density. Consequently, it is more difficult for them to regulate their affect and self-soothe. Deprived of an adequate supply of their own body's natural painkillers, they are more vulnerable to painful affect states. When isolated monkeys are given high doses of opiates, it inhibits their separation cry. When given opiate antagonists, their separation cry returns and their separation stress response is enhanced. The situation is very similar with human heroin addicts who just don't react to separation or loss. When they are high, they treat people as if they just don't matter. The heroin in their veins protects them against separation anxiety and the panic of attachment loss.

> Joe was only three weeks into recovery from intravenous heroin use. Because enough time had elapsed since Joe last used, he was no longer caught in the throes of the severe withdrawal symptoms that always accompanied opiate addiction. His thinking had cleared and he was able to engage the substance abuse counselor at the hospital in more genuine dialogue than he had previously. Joe had picked up a white chip (a poker chip given to all new members who announce at a meeting that they are taking the first step in AA or NA's twelve step programs) at a Narcotics Anonymous meeting and spoke of his genuine desire "to stay off drugs and turn my life around."
>
> "I can't believe the shit I was doing while I was high." Joe leaned forward in his chair, rested his face in his hands, and looked down at the floor. "I'm ashamed of myself. The money I wasted, the people I've let down."
>
> "That's one of the worst things about drugs, it leads us to do things that we would never do if we weren't high," the counselor said.
>
> Joe looked up at the counselor; the emotional pain evident in his bloodshot eyes. "I hope you're right. I pray to God it was the drugs that caused me to behave as I've have."
>
> "Stay around AA and NA long enough and you'll learn that all addicts have a long string of people they've hurt because of their addiction." The counselor made a circular motion with his hands. "Making amends to those we've hurt or let down is a crucial part of the recovery program."

"What about those people I don't even know very well? How do I make amends to them?" Joe ran his hand through his hair and shook his head like he was trying to rid himself of some unpleasant memories. "The week just before I came into the hospital, I was shooting up with a bunch of other addicts, half of them I didn't even know or even give a damn about. But there was this one guy who had been especially kind to me, warning me about dirty needles and cautioning me to keep an eye on the other addicts who couldn't be trusted. A couple hours later, after we all had shot up, he was standing by the sink in the kitchen, and suddenly he collapsed and crashed to the floor like a sack of potatoes." Joe looked into the counselor's eyes. "You know what I did? Nothing!" Joe pounded his fist on his leg. "I just shrugged and went back to my drugs. I thought, 'Oh good. This means more heroin for me.'"

6

Avoidant Society: Cultural Roots of Impaired Attachment

On knowing what you are not supposed to know and feeling what you are not supposed to feel.
John Bowlby (1979b)

Western society has been conducting a vast, complex experiment for the last two hundred years. No one knows the exact outcome of this study, although Kohut implied years ago (1984) that the increasing number of personality disorders (and alcoholics and addicts, I might add) showing up at therapists' offices is one result of this experimental inquiry. This investigative research is not a series of well-controlled trials conducted by a group of prestigious universities, but is an evaluation being conducted and carried out by our so-called nuclear families, which now make up the bulk of the holding environments available in our modern-day society. Harried parents—stretched far too thinly by the demands of their two jobs, constant travel to work, and carting their children across town to schools, day-care centers, softball games, and so on—are making a courageous, but often vain attempt to provide the attachment needs for their children. Despite the fact that their efforts fly in the face of nearly two million years of human evolution, they continue to take on this challenge without much support or help from extended families and their community, tribe, or village.

A few years ago I traveled cross-country to visit Scott, an old friend I hadn't seen since graduate school. He had married shortly after receiving his doctoral degree and he

> and his wife now had a 13-year-old son who was very much involved in the kinds of activities that our society demands of young adolescents. I spent the weekend watching them take turns carting him from tennis lessons in the morning to a soccer game in the afternoon and to a school dance that evening. After Scott had gotten off work the next day, he and I drove his son across town for soccer practice after picking him up at school that afternoon. We returned home after dropping his son off. As we sat in his living room waiting for his wife to get home from her job, I watched as he flopped exhausted across the sofa. In a few minutes, she arrived hurriedly through the door, and set the cat food and the kitty litter in the closet before beginning the arduous task of negotiating who was going to run to the grocery store and who was going to pick up the sitter or their son before we hurried out to dinner that evening. Neither had family that lived in the city and both work desperately to keep up with the demands of parenting and their careers. They were doing a courageous job against overwhelming odds.

Ever since the human species crawled down from the trees and scurried along the ground with the rest of the mammals that inhabited the prehistoric world, humans have been forced to band together in herds in order to stay alive. Whether sleeping together in caves or hunting in packs, human survival—especially for the young—required that we keep others close by our side. In the past, many people would turn to their family physicians among others for this kind of stabilization. With the advent of managed care and the increasing emphasis of modern medicine on technology over relationships, conditions have been created that are very similar to the sterile environments that Spitz (1945) found in her studies: infants die or become severely ill when they are provided everything but a secure attachment. The decline of modern medicine is now a more tragic consequence reflected by a society that assigns a low priority or little value to the importance of relationships.

Karen (1994), in his classic book on attachment, eloquently addressed the more recent historical and cultural ramifications of this evolutionary change:

> Before the modern era, most life tended to be family life. In preindustrial Europe, production was carried on in family farms or small shops. Hired laborers lived with the farmer, the baker, or the cobbler and his next of kin and were considered family members themselves. Servants fit into the affectional system. The relationships with their master's children were often like that of an uncle or aunt, and their own children like that of siblings or cousins. Apprentices were treated like sons, obliged to obey the master, and were completely dependent on him until they turned twenty-one. Few people went out to work. The old did not become segregated in retirement villages or institutions, but lived out their days within the family they'd been a part of all their lives. The setting may have been claustrophobic, with intense hatred, resentment, and murderous jealousies that inevitably arise under such conditions; but there was also love, familiarity, and unquestioned belonging. [p. 411]

There was also, I might add, unlimited opportunity for mutual affect regulation. The relief that can come to isolated, dysregulated people who stumble into regulatory group attachments not only explains the popularity of twelve-step programs, but also speaks to the inherent vulnerabilities, especially for the lonely and isolated individual to fall victim to the dangerousness of religious cults. As our society becomes more mobile and fragmentary, it produces more and more people who possess inadequate stabilization and lack adequate stabilizing relationships. Individuals find themselves more and more desperate to encounter something to ease their pain and alleviate their lonely, sometimes meaningless existence. Substances and other addictive behaviors often serve to fill the vacuum created by the lack of stabilizing interpersonal attachments.

As Karen (1994) correctly implied, the close attachment bonds that were provided by premodern society were not without their liabilities. Existence was precarious in many ways, with poor nutrition and primitive medical practice, abhorrent living conditions, and crippling poverty. Psychological disturbance could not be averted any more than it can today, even though the types of disturbances were more likely of the variety (e.g., hysterical conversion, neurosis, etc.) that Freud and the other early psychoanalytic theorists witnessed in their patients. However, individuals in all probability experienced a more stable security, the type that comes from societies guided by tradition and values that are accepted without question. People felt they belonged, even though that sense of belonging carried its own special price. The change that the Industrial Revolution and the more recent technological revolution have forced upon us has its special cost. Karen describes it:

> No longer cradled by unchanging, familiar connections, by home surroundings, and by the known rhythms of nature, men went out to work in impersonal, often crushing environments. Frequently, they had to steel themselves and swallow their emotional needs. "Dependency," an unnecessary concept before, became an undesirable quality in men and much later, in women. Meanwhile, as old bonds dissolved or became less central to one's life, the sphere of intimacy that surrounded each person shrank. [p. 413]

Not only do Karen's observations have important implications for how our society raises its children, but his commentary also has important relevance for the treatment of individuals suffering from attachment disorders. Because of our culture's investment in autonomy at all costs and its accompanying fear of dependency, security has been sacrificed for independence. Our society's preoccupation with the avoidance of dependency may be one possible reason for its preoccupation with drugs. Consequently, it has become a drug-oriented society. Whether the drug is illicit, such as heroin, or licit "nondrug" drugs such as nicotine and caffeine, the theme is similar. We take drugs to perk up, and we take drugs to calm down. Beginning with the morning cup of coffee, through the midday cola, and ending with the evening martini, we have learned more and more to rely on drugs as effective means of helping us cope with the everyday stress of living. The current increase in drug taking reflects a general cultural change in the way our society sees drug use as an acceptable way to regulate our affect (Johnson 1973, Ray 1983).

Besides our culture's inability to provide adequate attachment needs, there are other reasons for the increased use of drugs in our society. In our generally affluent society, each individual learns early to depend on science and technology to supply answers to problems once they are identified. Because of the present rate of social and technological change, the expectation of quick solutions to problems is now well ingrained in our culture. Drugs provide these quick solutions. The increase in drug use and misuse is a consequence of this rapidly developing biological revolution. One aspect of this awakening is the pharmacological revolution. One of the most interesting but least studied cultural change is the use of psychoactive drugs for their effect on the mind, rather than on the body. We have moved from drugs to cure the body to drugs to cure the mind. For the first time, potent chemicals clearly labeled as drugs are being widely used by healthy individuals because of their social convenience.

This societal expectation of an instant pharmacological answer to all ills has been facilitated by the promise of drugs to solve all of our personal problems. Television and newspaper advertising is replete with exhortations to use drugs to remedy a variety of uncomfortable situations. Such advertisements are not false, just misleading. Adding to these misconceptions of unrealistic expectations has been the medical profession's enthusiastic encouragement for the consumption, prescription, and use of drugs. The physician's support has helped legitimize drug use in our culture by individuals who might not, under normal circumstances, tolerate its use. The issue becomes one of illusion, false assumptions, and a failure to view drugs beyond culturally defined terms.

Our culture has become more lackadaisical about acknowledging some drugs as drugs while at the same time reacting with increased alarm over the recreational use of other drugs. The discrepancy, in part, is an indication of whether a drug's use becomes an accepted and ingrained part of society. Many individuals fail to see how the need for a cup of coffee, a cigarette, a cola, or a beer is in any way related to drug use and abuse. The recent flow of antipsychotic, antidepressant, and antianxiety drugs from the hospital pharmacy to the home medicine cabinet is but a modern version of the acceptance of caffeine, nicotine, and distilled spirits as an intricate part of the American way of life.

Societal attitudes toward drug use as an acceptable and

easy way to solve our interpersonal difficulties are also reflected in attitudes toward definitions of and the treatment of addiction. What may be normal or acceptable use in one case may reflect misuse, abuse, or even addiction in another. The attitude toward drug use and the criteria one uses to define addiction dictate how, when, and in what way addiction will be treated. Certainly, the criterion confusion is a primary reason why there are so many conflicting recommendations and definitions of addiction.

> Ken scheduled an appointment with a therapist following a recent DUI arrest. An immaculately dressed, handsome man of 42, Ken looked like he had just stepped out of *Esquire* magazine. He spoke hesitantly about his concerns about his drinking, explaining that his associates, family, and friends assured him that he couldn't possibly be an alcoholic. A successful philanthropist, Ken explained that his thriving consulting firm had left him with more money than he knew what to do with. A well-respected patron of the arts and recognized pillar of the community, Ken casually mentioned that he was also currently ranked as the top amateur tennis player in the city. The repercussions from the DUI arrest did not concern him because he had friends in the city government who had already taken care of "that little problem." He had taken his concerns about his drinking to his analyst years ago, who assured him that there was no possible way he could be an alcoholic. His wife supported the analyst's opinion, as did the members of the therapy group he had been in for a number of years. At the therapist's request, Ken proceeded to describe occasional blackouts and a few embarrassing incidents that had occurred when he had a "little too much to drink." No other outstanding evidence of alcoholic drinking was uncovered.
>
> When he had finished with his history, Ken ran his hands slowly down his neatly pressed trousers and spoke in his perfectly articulated English. "Doctor, what do you think? I would so much appreciate hearing your opinion."
>
> The therapist leaned back in his chair and pondered Ken's question. He preferred to overdiagnose rather than

> underdiagnose alcoholism. If he incorrectly diagnosed someone as an alcoholic, the worst that could happen was that the person would give up an unhealthy habit, join a program that demanded complete self-honesty, and live a life devoted to helping others and developing a richer spiritual life. But if he incorrectly *failed* to diagnose someone as an alcoholic, the consequences would be far more dire and even life threatening. As AA has taught him, the therapist knew from experience that if a person thought he was an alcoholic, more likely than not he was.
>
> The therapist carefully worded his reply. "It's a tough call to make, but I think there's enough evidence to suggest that you're an alcoholic."
>
> Ken's face showed a sign of immediate relief. He smiled and cleared his throat. "Thank you, doctor. I've been trying for years to get someone to confirm what I've always known. What would you recommend I do?"
>
> "I'd suggest you go to an AA meeting and see if you identify with the members there."
>
> Ken followed the therapist's instructions and returned for a second appointment later in the week. As soon as he sat down, Ken smiled gratefully at the therapist. "I've found a home where I belong. Thank you for the referral."

While some researchers (usually those associated within academic settings) view addiction as a bad habit that must be altered, such as biting one's nails, others (usually practitioners who work with addiction in treatment settings) view it as a life-or-death disorder that has a multitude of spiritual, physical, and psychological ramifications. The former group often speaks of behavioral contingencies and cognitive reframing as treatment alternatives. Research is undertaken and articles are published addressing the importance of matching patient characteristics and attitudes with treatment methods. It is often recommended that brain-impaired addicts and alcoholics (see Chapter 4) be asked to choose whether they prefer moderate use of chemicals or abstinence as treatment alternatives, much like someone who is asked whether they prefer their steak cooked medium-rare or well-done.

This is not to imply that alternative approaches to addiction treatment should not be explored. Rather, the suggestion is that the different societal and cultural attitudes toward drug and alcohol use reflect a similarity in attitudes toward treatment options and definitions of what constitutes an addiction. Certainly individuals who drink moderately, who have no prior history of social, legal, spiritual, marital, physical, psychological, or economic consequences as a result of drinking, and who ask for guidance or directions concerning their drinking should be presented other options. But how many of these individuals show up voluntarily seeking treatment? Not only does the issue of criterion differential have to be carefully evaluated, but also the ethical consequences of applying treatment alternatives that have little practical value or have the potential for negative ramifications for an individual must be given cautious consideration. The picture becomes a little clearer if the implications that attachment theory has for the etiology and treatment of addiction are given serious consideration.

It is important to remember that attachment theory is not so much a single theory as an overall framework for thinking about relationships, particularly the way that the lack of secure attachment influences early patterns of relatedness that are internalized (internal working models) and perpetuated throughout adulthood. Until these patterns of relatedness and insecure attachment are altered, the addicted individual will remain vulnerable to the substitution of one addiction for another. To understand how to modify these dysfunctional patterns of relatedness in adulthood, it is important to review some of the more significant research on attachment styles and the evidence that shows how they continue to manifest through adulthood. Understanding the ways that parents rear their children has important implications for how therapists need to treat their patients.

SECURE ATTACHMENT

Secure attachment is a central and crucial concept in Bowbly's model. His psychology is based on the opposing themes of attachment and separation/loss. To appreciate the significance of his theory's implications for treatment, it is important to list the three key features of Bowlby's orginal formulation:

1. *Biological function*: The biological function of attachment is protection from predation. Thus the principal role of attachment is to provide a safe haven.
2. *Attachment and play*: There is a reciprocal relationship between secure attachment and creative or explorative play. Only when children are securely attached to the attachment figure can they turn away from him or her. This principle has important implications for treatment. Just as securely attached children will move farther away from the attachment figure and take more risks in exploring their external world, so too will securely attached patients take more risks in their exploration of their inner world. The same is true for securely attached group members, who will take more risks in group and go farther in their exploration with other group members.
3. *Attachment persists throughout life*: Bowlby believed that attachment is not a childish need and that the styles of attachment initiated in childhood persist throughout life. Adult relationships and their associated pathology can be understood in attachment terms no less than those of children.

ATTACHMENT, LOSS, AND EMOTIONS

Bowlby (1979a) stated, "The psychology and psychopathology of emotion is . . . in part the psychology and pathology of affectional bonds" (p. 130). There is a powerful emotional relationship between attachments and their disruption. Attachment theory goes as far as to suggest that all affect is in some way related to attachment seeking or attachment disruption. Attachment theory provides a relational context in which all troubling feelings—fear, sadness, anger, terror, and even envy—can be explained in relation to loss. However, as important as loss is in Bowlby's model, he did not believe that continuous uninterrupted maternal care during the first five years of a child's life was either possible or a required precondition for psychological health. Since separation or more subtle forms of loss (e.g., loss of omnipotence, loss of perfect attunement, etc.) are inevitable, the way that loss and disappointment are handled within the family is far more important. The capacity of the caregiver to recognize and accept protest is as much a foundation of psychological health as is the absence of a major separation. The denial of trauma and the suppression of protest are major contributors to psychopathology.

> Nowhere was this struggle played out more dramatically than with Paul, a 55-year-old alcoholic physician with nearly twenty years of recovery. He initially sought psychotherapy because of debilitating bouts of depression, which were not alleviated by continuous sobriety or regular attendance at AA meetings. Over the course of more than a year of therapy, Paul felt securely enough attached to the therapist to reveal a secret that he could not even risk telling his wife or sponsor. Paul led a secret life of frequenting massage parlors and prostitutes, both male and female. Tremendously ashamed of his compulsive, secretive behavior, Paul felt hopeless to stop his sex addiction. Over the course of the next few months his therapist helped Paul identify a pattern to his acting-out behavior that shared many parallels with his childhood experiences with his parents.
>
> Even though his parents were financially well off, they neglected both Paul's emotional and material needs. His mother would often send him to school poorly dressed, not properly bathed or groomed, leaving him open to ridicule from the other children. His poor eyesight was not properly taken care of, and when his parents did finally furnish him with glasses, they were ill fitting and unfashionable. Whenever Paul would protest about his treatment, asking for better clothes or new glasses, his parents would ridicule him, calling him "ungrateful" or admonish him by saying, "You are never satisfied. You have it so good and you still complain all the time." Paul

adapted to this shaming of his protest by becoming a very good and polite little boy, who would secretly gather evidence to justify his right to clandestinely gratify his denied emotional and material needs. Masturbation as a teenager and hiding his excessive drinking as a young adult became his means for relieving the shame he experienced because of what he believed was an insatiable neediness.

As an adult, he became a polite, nice man who secretly watched for others' mistreatment of him, collecting evidence of others' abuse and neglect so he could prove that he was right; "See, they are depriving me!" Paul would gather injustices like a beggar gathering alms, refusing to directly oppose anyone, but taking secret pleasure in their mistakes and mistreatment of him. When he had gathered enough proof, he would feel justified in secretly seeking ways to take what he felt he rightfully deserved. At times like this, his repressed anger would come out with a ruthless demanding vengeance. However, after the discretion was acted out and the denied need gratified, tremendous shame would always follow, with a determined vow to never do it again.

As in Bowlby's (1979b) article, "On Knowing What You Are Not Supposed to Know and Feeling What You Are Not Supposed to Feel," Paul compounded his dilemma by trying to keep his own feelings and knowledge secret even from himself.

Despite the insight that Paul gathered from his therapy, understanding did little to alter his behavior at first. The reparative experience came out of his relationship with his therapist. Paul no longer felt that he had to deny the injustices done to him, both in the past and in his current relationships. Old, destructive relationships were gradually eliminated, and new, healthier ones were established in their place. He slowly but surely came to accept that his need for gratification in a relationship was not reflective of his insatiable neediness, and that he could trade his archaic ways of getting his needs met for more mature gratification in satisfying adult relationships. Most importantly, Paul did not feel he had to "behave and act good" with the therapist who encouraged, but did not demand, that Paul give up his sexual compulsivity until he could relinquish it on its own accord. Gradually, over time, the energy that drove his compulsive acting out subsided on its own.

AINSWORTH AND THE STRANGE SITUATION

Bowlby's theory of attachment would not enjoy the acceptance it does today if it weren't for the work of Mary Ainsworth. Her simple, but easily replicated test enabled researchers to classify infants as either securely or insecurely attached to an attachment figure (Ainsworth 1969). The strange-situation test assesses the infant's response to being separated from the primary caregiver and left alone or with a stranger for three-minute periods in a strange room. There are four identified patterns of responses:

1. Securely attached infants protest on separation and can be pacified on reunion with the primary caregiver, after which the child will return to exploratory play. Two-thirds of normal children respond in this way. However, children of mothers who were abused as children and children from lower socioeconomically disadvantaged groups display the following insecurely attached patterns.
2. Insecure-avoidant infants protest little at separation. On reunion with the primary caregiver, they show indifference, but linger nervously nearby.
3. Insecure-ambivalent infants protest when the primary caregiver leaves the room, but cannot be pacified when they are reunited. Insecure-ambivalent children tend to either bury their heads in the caregiver's lap or cling furiously to him or her.
4. Insecure-disorganized infants display no coherent pattern of response. They either freeze, or collapse and fall to the ground upon separation. Upon reunion, they often lean vacantly against the wall.

ATTACHMENT STYLES

Research conducted after Ainsworth's initial findings has generally confirmed her results, suggesting that insecure attachment styles fall into distinct predictable categories. In normal populations, insecure-avoidant makes up about one-fifth of the infants tested, insecure-ambivalent makes up one-sixth, and insecure-disorganized makes up about one in twenty.

TABLE 6–1.

ATTACHMENT STYLES
Identified through home and laboratory observation of children with their parents
Secure Anxious-Ambivalent Anxious-Avoidant Disorganized

Ainsworth and her followers did not limit their investigations on attachment to only the infant's response patterns to strange situations. Because attachment theorists viewed the infant–caregiver bond systemically, Ainsworth made a second significant contribution to the understanding of attachment. Her research focused on how parental responses to children, or the lack of response, impacted secure and insecure attachment styles. Securely attached children were not necessarily the infants who were taken up into their mother's arms most frequently or held the longest. Rather, the securely attached children had mothers who would consistently pick them up and hug them when they wanted to be picked up and hugged, and put them down when they were ready to be put down. When they were hungry, their mothers fed them. If they began to tire, their mothers would sense this and place them in their bassinet. Ainsworth found no simple correlation between the length of time a mother spent attending to her child and the child's ultimate emotional health. Four identified parental response patterns were found to be key determinants of attachment:

1. Consistently responsive and secure mothers of securely attached infants picked them up during signs of stress, played with them, and were more in tune with their unspoken needs.

2. Consistently unresponsive and ambivalent-insecure mothers of ambivalently insecure infants were more likely to ignore their children when they were stressed. They would often intrude when the child was playing happily and were generally much less attuned to the child's emotional states and unspoken needs.

3. Inconsistently responsive and avoidant-insecure mothers of avoidant-insecure infants were more brusque or gruff

TABLE 6–2.

SECURE ATTACHMENT STYLE	
Child's Behavior	Parent's Behavior
Distressed when parent leaves	Aware of child's emotions
Seeks comfort when parent returns	Attends to child quickly when distressed
Easily reassured by words and touch	Consistently available and reassuring
Explores when parent is present	

TABLE 6–3.

AVOIDANT ATTACHMENT STYLE	
Child's Behavior	Parent's Behavior
Shows no distress at separation from parent	Rebuffs or deflects child's bids for comfort
Avoids contact with parent upon return	Avoids close bodily contact
	Appears unaware of child's emotions
Attention focused on toys and activities but with little enthusiasm	Emphasizes achievement

when handling their children. While they appeared functional in their responses, they often demonstrated a lack of warmth, attunement, or emotional responsiveness to the child's needs or emotional states.

4. Disorganized responsive and insecure-disorganized mothers tend to be greatly distressed and have a high incidence of abuse in their own childhood. Like the infants they rear, they show no consistent pattern in responses to emotional states and attachment.

Tables 6–2 through 6–5 summarize the relationships between parents' and infants' attachment styles.

TABLE 6–4.

AMBIVALENT ATTACHMENT STYLE	
Child's Behavior	Parent's Behavior
Very distressed when parent absent Both angry and anxious at parent's return Clingy with parent and unable to explore	Inconsistent response to infant emotions Unavailable/intrusive Mismatch between child's emotion and parent's response May seek out and praise child's attention and support

TABLE 6–5.

DISORGANIZED ATTACHMENT STYLE	
Child's Behavior	Parent's Behavior
Shows both avoidant and ambivalent behavior No strategy for managing anxiety Responses are often extreme	Major disturbances in attachment system Caregiver depression Emotional neglect Physical and/or sexual abuse

ATTACHMENT AND SELF

Continued data gathered through the observations of children's response to their parents with the strange-situation test conducted in both the home and the laboratory suggest that the functions of attachment fall into three distinct categories: proximity maintenance, safe haven, and secure base (Table 6–6).

TABLE 6–6.

FUNCTIONS OF ATTACHMENT
Proximity maintenance—it is easier to keep children safe when they are physically close to the parent
Safe haven—everyone needs comfort in times of distress
Secure base—if we have people to lean on, we can move forward much easier
Recent critique suggests that the secure base phenomenon may apply only to cultures that stress independence and autonomy

If these important functions of attachment aren't provided, serious long-term ramifications for the child's developing sense of self can occur. Bowlby and Ainsworth state that insecure attachments are really defensive strategies designed to maintain contact with rejecting or inconsistent caregivers. Insecurely attached children are much more likely to sacrifice exploration for the sake of security. As Holmes (1996, p. 8) states, avoidant, ambivalent, and disorganized children are more likely to "cling to things because they find people too threatening." Needless to say, this is one reason why insecurely attached children will be vulnerable to addictive behavior. A securely attached child demonstrates the "fluid attentional gaze" of Main (1995) and "can move from things to people and back to herself with confidence and poise" (p. 8).

Parental figures must provide two key elements to enable the child to develop a secure sense of self and the capacity to achieve adult intimacy. Holmes (1996) describes what these are:

> Parental attunement on the one hand and the ability to accept protest without retaliation or excessive anxiety on the other

> form the basis for secure attachment. In Winnicott's terminology the parental environment must be sufficiently responsive to give a child a sense of both healthy omnipotence and vulnerability. First, through parental attunement, the child must be able to feel she has "created" the object, that the world is her oyster. This is the basis of healthy narcissism and self-esteem. Second, the child needs to be able to feel that her parents can survive her rage, and so be able, after an angry outburst, to say, "Hello object, I destroyed you!" As we shall see, these primary attachment and separation experiences provide a nucleus for the development of the capacities for intimacy and autonomy, respectively. [pp. 9–10]

SECURE ATTACHMENT, PLAY, AND SELF-AWARENESS

Enough data have been accumulated for attachment theorists to identify demonstrated patterns of behavior that indicate a secure sense of self has been developed. Winnicott (1965) starts with the notion of the child's ability to play alone in the presence of mother if a stable "true self" is to emerge. The ability to play alone in the presence of the mother indicates that the child is securely attached because he/she can forget about mother and concentrate on self-exploration. With a poorly attuned, unavailable mother, the child is forced to think about his attachment haven and forgets about self.

Internalization of interactions shaped by the attachment dynamic leads to an internal working model that accommodates three important functions:

1. The vigilant, yet nonintrusive maternal function, which becomes part of the child's psychic apparatus.
2. The capacity to initiate playful generative functions.
3. The capacity to put feelings into words.

Tape recordings made of children engaged in solitary play reveal that the securely attached child is more likely to develop the capacity for inner speech (Holmes 1996). As we will soon discover, acquiring inner speech has important implications for later development. Inner speech means the child has established the rudimentary steps of becoming intimate with oneself. Knowledge of self goes hand in hand with knowledge of others. The cornerstone for the capacity for mutuality and intimacy—crucial for developing healthy adult attachments later in one's life—is established at this crucial developmental stage. Continuing research that follows infants into adulthood has demonstrated the far-reaching consequences of the different attachment styles.

LONGITUDINAL STUDIES OF ATTACHMENT

Research has demonstrated the predictive power of attachment status in infancy for subsequent behavior. Long-term follow-up studies have shown that infants identified as securely attached at 1 year of age will, on the whole, still be demonstrating signs of security at school entry, such as interacting with peers and teachers. Holmes (1996) discusses the long-term impact for insecurely attached infants:

> By contrast, the insecure-avoidant children are more likely to be loners, given to unprovoked aggression, while those classified as insecure-ambivilent tend to be potential victims, unable to ask for help appropriately and clinging to their teachers. Attachment patterns are self-perpetuating developmental tracks that maintain some predictability in an uncertain interpersonal world.
>
> However, despite the stability of attachment patterns, attachment status can change over time. Children classified as insecure may become secure if their mother's circumstances improve, or if she receives successful psychotherapy. [p. 11]

Mary Main (1995), using a narrative interview (Adult Attachment Interview) she developed to assess adult attachment styles, found striking similarities between adult and infant attachment styles, suggesting that patterns learned as children persist throughout adulthood. Paralleling Ainsworth's strange-situation classification, narratives are categorized as follows:

Secure-autonomous

Insecure-enmeshed (or preoccupied)

Insecure-dismissive

Insecure-disorganized (or unresolved)

Table 6–7 lists some of the parallels between with adult and infant attachment styles based on narratives that Main put together from the data she gathered from the Adult Attachment Interview.

TABLE 6–7.

ATTACHMENT NARRATIVES
Secure infant-autonomous adult: It is safe to express my attachment needs. I expect that I will get these needs met.
Insecure, resistant infant-preoccupied adult: Sometimes I am responded to, but most of the time I am not. So I must keep trying for more. Responses are never satisfying.
Insecure, avoidant infant-dismissing adult: I won't allow myself to need others (although I do) or I'll believe that I'm getting all I want from others (even though I'm not).
Disorganized, disoriented infant-unresolved adults: Attachment need leads to loss and/or fear. It is not safe to experience attachment feeling (but I do) or think about attachment feelings and past loss (but this happens) because this awakens need and pain. And if I feel attachment need and grief, this only means more loss and fear. There is no resolution to this cycle.

Currently, some controversy exists among researchers on whether adult attachment styles fit into four (Bartholomew 1990) or three (Main 1995) categories. Most of the controversy is related to disagreement about the types of avoidant attachment styles. Bartholomew and his supporters say there are two types of avoidant styles, each with different defenses. The avoidant-fearful type wants relationships, but is afraid he or she will never be loved. The avoidant-dismissing type avoids relationships by taking the position that the other person is always at fault and not worthy of trust. Both camps agree that the insecure-preoccupied individuals rely overwhelmingly on others for their value and self-worth. Tables 6–8, 6–9, and 6–10 illustrate the ramifications of these different attachment styles.

TABLE 6–8.

ATTACHMENT MODEL		
Anxiety		
Preoccupied	Fearful	
		Avoidance
Secure	Dismissing	

TABLE 6–9.

ADULT ATTACHMENT STYLES
How many styles?
Secure, preoccupied, dismissing (Main)
Secure, preoccupied, fearful, dismissing (Bartholomew)
Research suggest that the four-style model is most accurate
Underlying dimensions
Anxiety, avoidance

ATTACHMENT PATTERNS IN ADULT RELATIONSHIPS

Research using the attachment typology of infant–parent relationships has found some interesting correlations with intimate attachments between adults. Hazan and Shaver (1994) have found that Bowlby's two key elements (proximity and responsiveness) of secure parenting are equally applicable to successful adult relationships. The need for responsiveness and proximity is more easily achieved and assumed to be readily available for secure adults. Ambivalently attached adults fall in love too easily, reveal themselves too quickly and too early in relationships, and can be excessively jealous and possessive. They frequently view their partners as fickle and undependable. Avoidant individuals, in contrast, experience close relationships as too much trouble. They tend to dissociate sexual from emotional commitment, and are uncomfortable with intimate self-revelation. Secure individuals are more likely to see themselves and their partners in a more favorable light. (Fig. 6–1).

Within the attachment model, the goal of successful adult development is the achievement of the capacity for both intimacy and autonomy. The securely attached infant has been provided a foundation for both intimacy and autonomy. The apparent paradox—autonomy based on intimacy and intimacy as a prerequisite for autonomy—is a developmental task that not all adults achieve. Most, if not all, of the patients that show up at a therapist's office will enter complaining of symptoms (e.g., depression, anxiety, alcoholism, addiction, etc.) related to difficulties resulting from an impaired ability to establish and maintain satisfying, affect-regulating relationships. Bowlby saw all affect as being related to attachment and separation. Others

Model of other (Avoidance)	Model of self (Dependence): Positive (Low)	Model of self (Dependence): Negative (High)
Positive (Low)	CELL I SECURE Comfortable with intimacy and autonomy	CELL II PREOCCUPIED Preoccupied with relationships
Negative (High)	CELL III DISMISSING Dismissing of intimacy Counterdependent	CELL IV FEARFUL Fearful of intimacy Socially avoidant

Figure 6–1. Model of self and model of other.

(Hamiliton 1985, Holmes 1996) took this further and suggested that all defenses are designed to maintain contact with objects at all costs. Infant research suggests that the modulation of infant affect by an attuned and responsive mother is an essential precursor of secure attachment. The patterns of insecure attachment represent compromises that infants must make to find some balance in modulating their emotional discomfort with the threat of object loss. Holmes (1996) describes the ramifications this dilemma has on many adults:

> If intimacy and autonomy, like attachment and exploration, are reciprocally related, insecure attachment can be seen as an unbalancing of this reciprocity. The avoidant person—and this is a pathology particularly of men—is detached but not autonomous. He longs for intimacy, but fears he will be rejected; he hovers on the shores of intimacy, ever fearful to take the plunge. The ambivalent individual—this is typical of insecure women—is attached but cannot be intimate. She longs for autonomy, assertion, and independence, but is fearful that if she strikes out on her own she will lose her secure base forever. In psychiatric terms the avoidant is the obsessional or the schzoid individual, the ambivalent is the anxiety-driven or hysterical type. [p. 20]

Substance abusers and their spouses display strikingly similar patterns to those that Holmes describes. The co-alcoholic is attached but not intimate. The alcoholic can be neither, since his attachment relationship remains to his substances. Each does not possess the capacity to feel good about either oneself or the other. Until this model of self and other is altered, difficulties will continue to plague their life and their relationship.

TABLE 6–10.

SELF/OTHER MODEL
Secure—positive self/positive other
Preoccupied—negative self/positive other
Dismissing—positive self/negative other
Fearful—negative self/negative other

IMPLICATIONS FOR ADDICTION TREATMENT

Examining addiction from an attachment perspective has led Karen Walant (1995) to explore the way our culture abuses its children without knowing or acknowledging it as abuse. She believes that "the twentieth-century emphasis on self reliance and individuation has greatly affected the psychological conditions most frequently requiring psychotherapeutic treatment later in life, including personality disorders and addiction" (p. 1). Furthermore, Walant contends that a primary reason for the increase of addictions in our society is that the normal attachment needs of our children are being sacrificed for cultural norms that emphasize separation and individuation. Normative abuse occurs when parental instinct and empathy are replaced by cultural norms, which shame needing and pathologize dependency.

Addiction treatment, from Walant's perspective, needs to be geared toward helping the alcoholic and addict develop the capacity for attachment. Like most addiction specialists, she views alcoholism as a disease of isolation. Addiction treatment, therefore, needs to be geared toward breaking through this seclusion and detachment from others. Wallant says one method for accomplishing this task is to provide an "oceanic" immersion experience—moments of oneness that are important to deepening the sense of connectedness and closeness between two people. One reason why Alcoholics Anonymous works so well with these patients is that, unlike many psychotherapists, it is not afraid to explore emotions like love or spirituality. Our alienated society has created a population that is not only alienated from others, but also in many cases alienated from self. The need to be part of something larger, greater, and more than ourselves forms the basis of the spiritual needs that our society lacks and that AA provides. Spirituality, from AA's perspective, is an immersion experience—a brief moment of feeling connected to a higher power or something larger and superior. It is the antithesis of feeling alienated, cut off, and isolated.

ADDICTION AND TREATMENT

Walant's recommendations follow a theme that has run through this chapter. It is the need for good treatment, like good parenting, to provide a holding environment that promotes an atmosphere of connectedness without interfering with the child's or patient's autonomy and sense of self. The research on attachment styles reviewed here has important implications for treatment. Examining the aspects of what determines secure attachment can inform and guide therapists in a number of ways:

1. Attachment theory provides a theoretical basis for the plethora of research evidence indicating that a good therapeutic alliance is the best predictor of successful therapy outcome.
2. Attachment theory, with its emphasis on the importance of a secure base, helps explain an important paradox about treatment: secure attachment liberates. Just as securely attached children take more risks in exploring their environment, securely attached patients take more risks in exploring their inner world. Similar to Winnicott's (1965) recommendation that the child must be able to play "alone in the presence of the mother," good psychotherapy provides an opportunity not just for secure attachment—to overcome clinging or avoidance—but also for detachment to take place.
3. As infant–caregiver attachment research has shown, the regulation of affect in the parent–child relationship is a crucial determinate of secure or insecure attachment. Mothers who can regulate their infant's excitement, rage, disappointment, and so on, and enable the infant to integrate emotion into the developing self serve an important organizing function for the child. Applying this principle to psychotherapy suggests that the regulation of affect and emotional attunement needs to become a central aim of good treatment.
4. Since no parent, no matter how caring and attentive, can protect the child from loss and disappointment, the capacity

> to recognize and accept protest without retaliation or abandonment is crucial for both development and attachment in adult life. Therapists who provide this capacity for their patients serve a crucial function in the repair of the person's developmental arrest.

The remaining chapters of this book discuss how these principles should be applied in the treatment of the addicted patient.

7

Rules for Effective Treatment: An Attachment Perspective

> If one lives the second half of his or her life by the same rules as the first half there will be inevitable problems.
>
> *Carl Jung*

Bowlby (1980) wrote convincingly about the special advantages that the attachment paradigm has for understanding and explaining human behavior. It might also be added that his paradigm has special advantages for understanding and providing direction for more effective psychotherapy and addiction treatment. Bowlby's theory facilitates a new and illuminating way to understanding why human beings are biologically driven to form powerful emotional bonds to others. Consequently, it also explains the many forms of emotional distress (e.g., anxiety, depression, detachment, addictions, and personality disorders) that are provoked by unwanted separation and loss. To take full advantage of the attachment paradigm's implications for repairing and treating the various disorders just mentioned, it will prove helpful to review Bowlby's (1980) own concise outline of his theory:

> (a) Attachment behavior is conceived as any form of behavior that results in a person attaining or retaining proximity to some other differentiated and preferred individual. So long as the attachment figure remains accessible and responsive the behaviour may consist of little more than checking by eye or ear on the where-abouts of the figure and exchanging occasional glances and greetings. In certain circumstances, however, following or

clinging to attachment figures may occur and also calling or crying, which are likely to elicit his or her caregiving.

(b) As a class of behaviour with its own dynamic, attachment behaviour is conceived as distinct from feeding behaviour and sexual behaviour and of at least an equal significance in human life.

(c) During the course of healthy development attachment behaviour leads to the development of affectional bonds or attachments, initially between child and parent and later between adult and adult. The forms of behaviour and the bonds to which they lead are present and active throughout the life cycle (and by no means confined to childhood as other theories assume).

(d) Attachment behaviour, like other forms of instinctive behaviour, is mediated by behavioural systems which early in development become goal-corrected. Homeostatic systems of this type are so structured that, by means of feedback, continuous account is taken of any discrepancies there may be between initial instruction and current performance so that behaviour becomes modified accordingly. In planning and guiding goal-corrected behaviour use is made of representational models both of the self's capabilities and of relevant features of the environment. The goal of attachment behaviour is to maintain certain degrees of proximity to, or of communication with, the discriminated attachment figure(s).

(e) Whereas an attachment bond endures, the various forms of attachment behaviour that contribute to it are active when required. Thus the systems mediating attachment behaviour are activated only by certain conditions, for example strangeness, fatigue, anything frightening, and unavailability or unresponsiveness of attachment figure, and are terminated only by certain other conditions, for example a familiar environment and the ready availability and responsiveness of an attachment figure. When attachment behaviour is strongly aroused, however, termination may require touching, or clinging, or the actively reassuring behaviour of the attachment figure.

(f) Many of the most intense emotions arise during the formation, the maintenance, the disruption and the renewal of attachment relationships. The formation of a bond is described as falling in love, maintaining a bond as loving someone, and losing a partner as grieving over someone. Similarly, threat of loss arouses anxiety and actual loss gives rise to sorrow; while each of these situations is likely to arouse anger. The unchallenged maintenance of a bond is experienced as a source of security and the renewal of a bond as a source of joy. Because such emotions are usually a reflection of the state of a person's affectional bonds, the psychology and pathology of emotion is found to be in large part the psychology and psychopathology of affectional bonds.

(g) Attachment behaviour has become a characteristic of many species during the course of their evolution because it contributes to the individual's survival by keeping him in touch with his caregiver(s), thereby reducing the risk of his coming to harm, for example from cold, hunger or drowning and, in man's environment of evolutionary adaptedness, especially from predators.

(h) Behaviour complementary to attachment behaviour and serving a complementary function, that of protecting the attached individual, is caregiving. This is commonly shown by a parent, or other adult, towards a child or adolescent, but is also shown towards another, especially in times of ill health, stress or old age.

(i) In view of attachment behaviour being potentially active throughout life and also of its having the vital biological function proposed, it is held a grave error to suppose that, when adult, attachment behaviour is indicative either of pathology or of regression to immature behaviour. The latter view, which is characteristic of almost all other versions of psychoanalytic theory, results from conceptualizations derived from theories of orality and dependency which are rejected here as out of keeping with the evidence.

(j) Psychopathology is regarded as due to a person's development having followed a deviant pathway, and not as due to his suffering a fixation at, or a regression to, some early stage of development.

(k) Disturbed patterns of attachment behaviour can be present at any age due to development having followed a deviant pathway.

One of the commonest forms of disturbance is the over-ready elicitation of attachment behaviour, resulting in anxious attachment. Another, to which special attention is given in this volume, is a partial or complete deactivation of attachment behaviour.

(l) Principal determinants of the pathway along which an individual's attachment behaviour develops, and of the pattern in which it becomes organized, are the experiences he has with his attachment figures during his years of immaturity—infancy, childhood and adolescence.

(m) On the way in which an individual's attachment behaviour becomes organized within his personality turns the pattern of affectional bonds he makes during his life.

Within this framework it is not difficult to indicate how the effects of loss, and the states of stress and distress to which they lead, can be conceived." [pp. 39–41]

HOW AND WHY THERAPY WORKS

Examining the possible implications Bowlby's theory has for treatment suggests that therapy works because of one simple principle: exposure to people changes people—or more correctly, a powerful attachment experience alters a person's nervous system. Individuals in an attachment relationship are provided help in regulating their nervous system, and they unconsciously acquire implicit knowledge about the rules that govern healthy interpersonal relationships. Attachment stabilizes individuals, and long-term exposure to powerful attachment environments can shape the pattern of relatedness, which becomes ingrained in implicit memory. The patients' internal working model is eventually altered and the old rules that guide their behavior in relationships are reconfigured.

Amini (1996) convincingly argued that a proper attachment environment not only has the power to alter old patterns of relatedness, but also can establish lasting memory for new and healthier representations. When patients enter a therapy relationship and engage in a transferential relationship, they exhibit the outward manifestation of the knowledge structure inside of them. This knowledge structure of the rules that govern relatedness is not a discrete record of any particular event, and the structure that dictates its repetition cannot be accessed consciously. Therapy, because it activates patients' attachment system, provides the opportunity for patients to reflect on their actions and behavior. They are also provided the chance to experience and witness what they intuitively know about how attachment works (e.g., What happens when I do this? What do I expect? etc.). Even though many individuals' behavior may seem baffling to an outside observer, their actions follow naturally from the rules that their implicit memory compels them to perform.

> Adam called to schedule an appointment "because I need to see someone and my last therapist just fired me." At the initial interview, this 35-year-old investment banker described a volatile history of multiple relapses and failed treatments for crack cocaine use. A brilliant money manager with an MBA from a prestigious Ivy League school, Adam had been able, until recently, to keep his frequent weekend binges from affecting his work performance. His employer was expressing growing concern about Adams increased absences and lapses in judgment. When asked why his previous therapist had fired him, Adam explained, "I kept relapsing and he told me if I didn't agree to enter a treatment program or go into a halfway house, he would refuse to see me."
>
> "How do you feel about that?" the therapist asked.
>
> "Oh, I'm used to it," Adam shrugged and grimaced. "See, that's my problem. Everyone abandons me sooner or later."
>
> By the end of the session, the therapist discovered that starting with his birth, Adam had indeed been abandoned repeatedly throughout his life. He was put up for adoption at birth and never knew his biological parents. The initial exploration into this topic was met by indifference from Adam. "I never think about it. So I don't think it's such a big deal. I'm more concerned about now. Why is it that everyone I care about doesn't care about me?"

Adam proceeded to describe a series of failed relationships, both in and out of therapy. He revealed that in the last three years, he had been through four different therapists and five different sponsors. A troubling pattern emerged of being abandoned and abandoning others because of his erratic behavior when on drugs. Never married and currently still living at home with his adopted parents, Adam described a relationship with his parents dominated by extreme ambivalence and passive hostility. His adopted mother clung to him, refusing to encourage his separation, while at the same time demeaning him for "not settling down and marrying a good woman." He hated living at home, but was terrified to leave. "The thought of me alone in an apartment is just overwhelming. I can't imagine staying clean or sober if I lived alone." His mother "refused" to let him move until he could prove to her that he could live on his own first by staying off of drugs. She had paid for his first inpatient alcohol and drug hospitalization when he was a teenager, an event that Adam was still furious over. "Those assholes abandoned me and shipped me off for someone else to take care of, rather than help me themselves."

Over the course of the next few months, a disturbing pattern emerged in Adam's relationships. Even though he regularly attended twelve-step meetings, he haunted nightclubs and Internet dating services. Relationships were sporadic and typically short lived. If a woman showed an interest in him, she quickly lost any appeal for him. He explained, "The emotional excitement just wasn't there." However, if a woman were emotionally distant or unavailable, he would become obsessed with her attention and would pursue her affection. During these periods he would use the entire therapy session obsessing about her comments, trying to figure out what she meant by this action or that statement.

Despite the instability of his personal life, he was able to put together a string of four months of abstinence. As his attachment with the therapist deepened, he began to experience an increased frequency of weekend relapses, usually triggered by some interaction with his mother or a rejection from a woman he had just met. Over the course of the next six months, it became apparent that Adam was testing his new therapist to see if he would be abandoned if he misbehaved. The rules that governed all his relationships were triggered and enacted in the therapy sessions. Despite Adams provocative behavior, he remained thankful and appreciative of the therapist's consistency with him.

Since successful treatment requires the alteration of these implicit memories that are encoded in the person's nervous system, the patient must be emotionally engaged or these old patterns will not be activated, and subsequently little will change. If the therapist just acts nicer and nicer, nothing much will happen or be accomplished. The patient, with his old pattern of relatedness, will not recognize the therapist's efforts because they are not attuned with his emotional melody. Consequently, the relationship will remain weak and little affect tuning will occur. Consequently, therapy will have an inadequate impact on him. The memory patterns will be sidestepped and not activated, giving the therapist little chance to relive the old rules in their relationship, so they can be changed and altered.

If there is an authentic, genuine attachment relationship established, the patient's behavior and attachment style should trigger in the therapist a genuine emotional response that matches the "tune" the patient is playing. The therapist's job is not to deny the emotional responses evoked in him, nor is it his job to allow himself to be induced to repeat the old patterns. Rather, his task is to alter his responses so that a new and different outcome can be achieved.

IMPLICIT MEMORY

When patients become attached in therapy, not only is their implicit memory engaged, but they also engage the biological mechanisms that permit implicit memory to be modified. If the therapeutic relationship is powerfully established, patients will eventually begin to extract the new rules that govern the relationship with the therapist, and the modification of their nervous system has begun. From a psychobiological standpoint, psychotherapy is a delicate establishment of a regulatory attachment relationship aimed at stabilizing physiology and emotions, and revising their emotional memory of attachment patterns.

The answer to the question of why so much emotional and relational knowledge is unconscious is a topic that has plagued psychology since the time of Freud. The answer from the earlier Freudian model was that much of what remains out of conscious awareness is because of active censorship. Emotional and relational exchanges are assumed to be often conflict ridden, containing an unpleasant, forbidden knowledge, which requires that the material be repressed and censored out of awareness. In contrast, the implicit/explicit model of memory holds the position that all that is called unconscious is the result of the basic properties of the brain system that encodes different types of memory. Because of the structure of the brain, emotional knowledge and recollection about the rules that govern patterns of relationships are divorced from the power of comprehension and thinking (explicit knowledge). Transference from this perspective is viewed as the outward behavioral manifestation of unconscious (implicit) knowledge of the rules that govern relationships—how relationships work (what to expect in them, what's coming next, etc.).

Evidence suggests that the language of emotional life and relatedness is implicitly learned and encoded out of a person's conscious awareness. Lewis (1996), at a professional conference, described a series of studies that captured this process. In one study, Lewis explained, subjects were shown pictures of individuals' faces, which were matched with stories such that the physical characteristics of faces were coordinated to correlate with the emotional qualities of the person described in the story. For instance, how likable the person was in the story was correlated with the length of a person's face—an arbitrary and artificial variable that nevertheless influenced the outcome of the story.

After showing subjects a series of faces and their accompanying stories, the researchers then showed subjects a series of pictures of new faces that they've never seen before and asked them to rate the new faces for likability or dislikability. Subjects rated long-faced people as more likable. Surprisingly, they had extracted the rule they had been exposed to on the first trial and proceeded to apply the rule to the second set of pictures. The subjects were then asked if they thought there was any relationship between how long a person's face was and how likable they were. All the subjects of course said, "No, that's a ridiculous idea." But at the very moment the subjects were disavowling this knowledge, they were demonstrating it, indicating that because there are different ways of acquiring knowledge, a person can actually become confused. As Lewis explained, "It's as if the right hand doesn't know what the left hand is doing." Lewis cited further evidence that once a rule is learned, it is difficult to extinguish and it perpetuates itself, distorting the perception of subjects so that any further experience in the real world doesn't help them unlearn the rule, but actually confirms the rule even more.

Research evidence supports the type of memories that attachment theory says is operative early in a person's life (Schacter 1990, Squire et al. 1993), suggesting that explicit memory increases with age in the developing child (Pinker 1997). Children do not demonstrate much evidence of explicit memory before the age of 3. Study after study (e.g., Lewis et al. 2000) show that humans do not have autobiographical memory before the ages of 2 to 3. Explicit memory is largely inoperative before 2½ in most children. This is not the case for implicit memory. Studies demonstrate that the skill level of implicit memory stays about the same from the earliest point that it can be tested (DeCasper and Fifer 1980).

In adulthood, explicit memory decreases with age as demonstrated by the increased difficulty of remembering people's names, dates, or where the car keys have been left. However, deterioration in implicit memory (e.g., how to tie a shoe or ride a bike) is much less evident. Because implicit memory is more likely to be operative during one's early attachment experience, the rules for relatedness are difficult to forget or undo. Since these memories are implicit and do not pertain to specific events (like what happened at age 1), they are not swayed by explicit memory. The implicit rules of relatedness are generalizations extracted from the experience of attachment, which leaves the person with implicit knowledge of how relationships work. Therefore, implicit memory operates to influence perceptions and actions in a reflexive manner. Because the behavior is reflexive, it is impossible for people to have conscious knowledge or awareness about what they are doing. Later in life, people enact attachments and have relationships in accordance to the rules they have been exposed to and extracted in their early attachment experiences. If a person's attachment style is aberrant, the individual doesn't have any conscious choice other than to extract aberrant rules and generalizations. Because the knowledge of these rules is implicit, individuals would apply these rules without conscious awareness of what they are doing. People carry them and perpetuate these maladaptive patterns of relatedness. Because individuals have limited insight into the nature of what or why they behave as they do, their attachment styles are difficult to modify.

The following facts about implicit knowledge have important implications for therapy:

People possess knowledge without awareness.

In this kind of knowledge the person extracts a rule exemplified in a given situation, even when that rule is complex.

People can demonstrate the knowledge they have through their actions, but can't describe it, understand it, and in many cases don't have an awareness that they possess it or that they have learned anything at all.

Direct experience and not explanations are influential in altering or modifying this type of memory. Furthermore, explanations sometimes create more confusion and make things worse, not better.

Implicit knowledge can also distort later perceptions, and once acquired, the knowledge is self-perpetuating and confirming of what people know but are unaware that they know.

People can acquire an implicit bias that is out of their consciousness. They can't explain what they know, but can demonstrate it in their behavior.

In relationships, implicit knowledge is demonstrated in a behavioral pattern more commonly called transference.

RULES FOR EFFECTIVE THERAPY: KENDALL'S PRINCIPLES OF PSYCHOTHERAPY

The false separation that exists between biology and psychology is gradually diminishing. Research has revealed that a number of erroneous conclusions have to be changed. The following six factors have been demonstrated by recent scientific discoveries:

1. Attachment can alter gene expression.
2. Attachment and psychotherapy can alter brain chemistry.
3. Learning-based experiences alter neuronal connectivity.
4. Potentiation requires activation (environmental stimulation), which alters the strength and autonomous patterns of brain functioning.
5. Synaptic strength is an experience-dependent phenomenon.
6. Talking in a meaningful way, paying attention, and attachment alter brain biochemistry and lead to changes in synaptic transmission, strength, and number of synapses.

Viewing therapy from an attachment perspective has specific implications for applications in psychotherapy. The following ten rules represent an attempt to organize and present attachment-driven guidelines for providing effective therapy.

1. *Psychotherapy alters the structure of the brain.* Changes in behavior and changes in people's lives mean there have been accompanying changes in their neurophysiology.
2. *Psychotherapy, even good psychotherapy, has its limits.* If the structure of the brain has already been set at a physiological level, certain things cannot be changed—especially if the damage occurred very early in the person's life. However, some disturbances (e.g., schizophrenia)

can be moderated with medication, so that individuals can function the best they can with their limitations.

If the trauma, neglect, injury, or deprivation is extreme and occurred very early in a person's developmental life, attachment relationships—even powerful ones—cannot always alter a person's damaged neurophysiology. Like the isolated monkeys in Kraemer's (1985) studies who function or look normal as long as they are continually provided for by peer monkey "therapists," once the emotional regulating attachment figure (peer therapist monkey) is removed, the isolated monkeys quickly deteriorate. The attachment experience that their brains were waiting for, but was never provided, has forever changed the structure of their brain. There are certain changes in the brain that cannot be redressed anymore. Because certain individuals' nervous systems have failed to be exposed to the experience that was supposed to happen, but never did, they will forever require someone else to help keep their nervous system up and running for them. They will always require an abundant amount of external affect regulation. With certain individuals, a long-term therapeutic holding environment, like the one that AA provides the alcoholic, will always be necessary.

3. *Psychotherapy is not an intellectual exchange of words.* Good therapy is more than a casual conversation. The therapist and the patient are not just having an exchange of ideas or a casual discussion about hypothetical ideas. They are having a mutually regulating attachment relationship, which is a potent biological force for change and one that has existed for millions of years. People are social mammals, and therapy is fundamentally a social system that is the source of powerful influences. The effective therapist understands the nature of that power and guides it with maximal efficiency.

4. *Experience—not explanations or ideas—effects change.* Consequently, the attachment model emphasizes experience over insight—implicit learning over explicit learning. This is the reason why explanations and self-help

books rarely change anything. Experience over time works in therapy in producing change. Insight has little effect as an agent of change. In fact, insight is usually the result of change.

5. *Emotional neutrality doesn't work, and attachment theory does not recommend that the therapist strive to obtain it.* Because therapy is an attachment relationship based on an emotional exchange, remaining emotionally neutral is equivalent to not having a relationship with the other person at all. Attempts to achieve emotional neutrality deprive therapists of the main mechanism they have at their disposal to effect change.

6. *The worst therapists are those who are either out of touch with their emotions or in bondage to them to the degree that their feelings dictate their actions.* Attachment theory expects a re-creation of the emotional life of the patient in the relationship with the therapist. Such a position requires an active evocation of the therapist's real emotional responses, which match and are attuned with the pattern that the patient displays. Knowing when and how to respond in tune with the patient's emotional signals is a crucial aspect of attachment-guided psychotherapy. Emotional tuning in and real emotional responses that spontaneously match the patient are a critical component of any therapy that works.

7. *Contriving emotional experiences doesn't work.* Emotions come from phylogenic, ancient times, and the ability to read and display them is an inborn given that is honed by millions of years of evolution. Because of this, contrived feelings, mimicking emotional states, and inauthenticity on the therapist's part, no matter how well intended, are worse than useless. The patient's inborn ability to read emotions correctly far exceeds the therapist's ability to deceive the patient. While the patient may participate in an in-authentic relationship that is determined by the falsehood inherent in the old rules of interaction the desired effect of change will not occur. To the contrary, the old patterns of relatedness will only be strengthened.

8. *Just being nice doesn't work.* An authentic relationship must be established. A strong attachment bond should not be confused with complete gratification. Just as infant research demonstrated, mothers who cling to their children and remain enmeshed with them do not provide the optimal attachment relationship required by the developing brain. Mothers who held their child the longest or picked them up in their arms more frequently were not the optimal mothers. Optimal mothers were attuned to their child's needs to be picked up and held when he/she wanted to be picked up and to be set down when the child wanted to be set down. When the child was hungry, the mother knew and fed the infant. When the child was tired, the mother felt it and eased the child's transition into sleep by tucking him/her into bed.

9. *Rotating therapists and specialists in treatment approaches works against the requirements that secure attachment demands.* Medicine and psychotherapy have lost sight of the importance of *specificity* in treatment—especially insofar as *specificity* applies to the attachment relationship. The members of a therapy relationship are not interchangeable. Specificity in therapy applies to the specific atmosphere that the dyadic pair or the group establishes in therapy. Therapy is like any other attachment relationship—its power to persuade and change is intricately aligned with the specific people in the relationship. After a duck has been imprinted to Konrad Lorenz, it can't be told to follow another ethnologist. Therapy that works is not interchangeable. The patient becomes healthier within the specific context of the relationship with the attachment figure. The outcome of therapy is generally determined by who does it.

10. *Therapy that works is intersubjective and mutually regulating.* A working therapy is a two-way street. The aim is to have the patient change, but the therapist cannot help but be impacted. While this implies that patients need to choose their therapists carefully, it also means that therapists need to choose their patients wisely.

ADDICTION TREATMENT AND ATTACHMENT

The rules for effective therapy have important implications for the effective treatment of addiction. How these rules need to be applied and modified for the recovering addict and alcoholic is explored in the following three chapters. First, a clinical vignette is presented to demonstrate how maintaining the attachment bond and an authentic relationship over the course of therapy, especially when therapy is difficult and unsteady, can have a crucial impact on successful treatment.

> Allison was brought into therapy by her angry, disgruntled husband who demanded that "my wife get treated for her alcoholism." As her husband brutally berated her for her "sloppy, disgusting behavior," Allison sat quietly, staring vacantly at the floor. Although distraught and without make up, she was an attractive woman in her mid-thirties. In contrast to her husband, who was immaculately dressed in an expensive, well-tailored suit, Allison wore a rather old and shabby looking dress. Despite her obvious discomfort, the frightened, meek woman managed to portray a simple kindness in her eyes while her husband's face remained fixed in a perpetual sneer.
>
> After fifteen minutes of listening to Allison's husband describe his disgust with her drinking, the therapist asked Allison—who had not yet uttered a word—if she agreed with her husband's assessment of her alcoholism.
>
> Allison looked up and whispered, "I guess so."
>
> "Guess so? Hell!" her husband bellowed. "I grew up with an alcoholic father and I'll be damned if I'll continue to live with an alcoholic wife." He shoved his finger in front of Allison's face and glared at her. "You either get treatment or I'm divorcing you, and believe me, you'll never see the kids again if I have anything to say about it."
>
> Before the session ended, the therapist explained the options before them. "You can either go into a structured outpatient or inpatient program. Or we can see if we can do this on an outpatient basis in my office. If you choose the last option, I would require you to go to AA meetings on a regular basis."

Allison looked at the therapist for a moment before turning toward her husband. "What do you think?"

He ignored her question and faced the therapist. "If she goes into a structured treatment program, who will watch the kids while I'm at work?" Not waiting for an answer, he shook his head. "What about the last alternative? Can you see her in your office?"

"Of course," the therapist answered. "I often suggest that as the first option; it's sometimes preferable to start off with the least intrusive and least expensive treatment first to see if it works. If there's a relapse and it doesn't work, we can always try the more structured approach later."

"Good, let's do that then." Her husband gave the therapist a crooked smile. "Don't worry about the expense. That's not the problem. I need someone at home to run my house. I've got too much responsibility as it is to have to also worry about her and the kids." He turned toward his wife. "You'll come twice a week and find some AA meetings that won't interfere with my schedule."

Allison set up an appointment and showed up for the second meeting with a completely different demeanor and attitude. She was much more engaging and communicative. Over the course of the next few weeks, she began to paint a distressing picture of an emotionally, physically, and sexually abusive relationship with a man who completely dominated every aspect of her life. However, as she gained abstinence and confidence in herself, it became painfully clear that she could not continue to stay in the marriage with someone she "never loved." Whenever she would broach the subject of divorce, Allison would panic at thc thought of lcaving him.

The therapist encouraged her not to take any action until she felt strong enough to face her fears, and suggested that she instead continue to stay focused on her sobriety. The therapist reminded her that as long as she drank alcoholically, she remained more vulnerable to his control and domination.

Allison continued to progress in therapy over the next year, but the course of treatment was difficult and not without its setbacks. The therapist discovered a disturbing pattern with her treatment. She would relapse every three to four months. Each relapse followed a similar pattern. As she would gain confidence with her increased sobriety, Allison would become more vocal with her protests. Her husband, threatened by her emerging strength, became more intimidating and abusive. Relapses would follow. After a few months, the husband realized that increased sobriety made her more difficult to control, so he made countless efforts to stop her therapy, complaining that it wasn't helping her.

Allison resisted his efforts to control her treatment, telling the therapist that this was the first time in her life she felt she had an ally. Despite a series of more than seven relapses over the next fourteen months, the therapist held firm with his original treatment plan. He kept insisting that Allison carefully explore the reasons for her relapses, reminding her each time that this was an opportunity to learn something about what she was failing to do to ensure her recovery. They methodically explored each relapse to identify the contributing factors. Finally, an explanation emerged after the seventh relapse.

"I think I know what's going on with the relapses," Allison explained. "He tries to control every aspect of my life. I realize the thing he wants most is for me to stay sober. I get so furious at him at times and strike back in the only way I know how. I deprive him of what he wants most: my not drinking."

Over the course of the next six months, Allison was able to put a stop to his physical intimidation by calling the police. Since her husband was a prominent attorney in town, her threat of exposure to the legal community was enough to hinder any more physical assaults. Eventually, Allison made the break, knowing that unless she did, sobriety and recovery would not be possible. A long and vicious court battle followed, but armed with her newfound sobriety and increased self-esteem, Allison prevailed.

8

Early Treatment: Creating the Capacity for Attachment

Nothing is so bad that a few drinks won't make it worse.
Alcoholics Anonymous

Successful addiction treatment is dose-related; the more treatment the substance abuser gets, the better the results.
Alan Leshner, (1997b, p. 212)

A well-known axiom in the addiction treatment community is that addicts or alcoholics will usually not give up their chemical use until the pain and dysphoria they experience from its continual use exceed the pleasure or euphoria they derive from its present use. Conversely, the possibility of successful long-term recovery is greatly reduced unless the alcoholic's newfound life of abstinence is more rewarding than the previous one that was centered around alcohol use. This reflects an important principle of recovery: alcoholics and addicts will not remain abstinent unless they derive more pleasure from a chemically free life than they did from their substance abuse. Since attachment theory holds the position that addiction is a compensatory, driven compulsion because of the lack of satisfactory attachment experiences, long-term recovery is not possible until the capacity to achieve satisfaction from interpersonal attachments is achieved.

Consequently, a great deal of early addiction treatment is aimed at monitoring the delicate balance between pleasure and dysphoria. Since most addicts and alcoholics are exceedingly intolerant of delaying gratification, they usually choose a certain source of immediate gratification (e.g., drugs and alcohol) over an uncertain source of probable satisfaction in the distant future. To alter this ingrained attitudinal and habitual characterological pattern of behavior, they must first accept the premise that their solution is the problem.

Convincing addicts and alcoholics that it is in their best interest *not* to return to drugs and alcohol is an arduous task. Logic and reason alone do not accomplish this end. The limits of reason and logic were eloquently captured by the German philosopher Schopenhauer: "Hence the uselessness of logic; no one ever convinced anybody by logic; and even logicians use logic only as a source of income. To convince a man, you must appeal his self interest, his desires, his will" (Durant 1926). Spinoza addressed this issue nearly two hundred years prior to Schopenhauer when he wrote of the importance of substituting one strong emotion for another in bringing about change. Spinoza knew that passion always wins over reason: "Unless we use reason to help steer our passions to a less destructive action, we will forever remain in 'human bondage.' An emotion can neither be hindered nor removed except by a contrary and stronger emotion" (Durant 1926).

EARLY TREATMENT STRATEGIES

Keeping alcoholics sober and addicts clean requires an entirely different set of strategies than getting them to initially stop their chemical use. The expectation that addicts or alcoholics will stay off of drugs and alcohol requires that they come to realize, accept, and experience the benefit of abstinence. Addicts and alcoholics cannot just be convinced that it is advantageous for them to stay abstinent and sober by persuasive reasoning; they must be provided with something else that will sustain them until they achieve enough sobriety to experience this for themselves. One source of something that can sustain them is the regulating power of a strong attachment relationship.

Breaking an ingrained and powerfully conditioned addiction, however, usually requires more than the regulatory power of a single relationship and therapeutic alliance. AA and other twelve-step programs are sources of powerful persuasion that do more than just appeal to the addicts and alcoholics to give up alcohol and drugs. AA knows that recovery requires that the substance abuser must also relinquish old sets of attitudes, behaviors, and even friends associated with the addictive lifestyle. As AA members tell new members who enter into the twelve-step program, "If you want to avoid a slip, don't go where it's slippery," and "If you're serious about your recovery, you have to change your playmates and your playgrounds." To maintain sobriety, the addict and alcoholic must relinquish the regulatory function that their drug or alcohol use previously provided and substitute the fellowship of the AA program as an alternative attachment object.

ADDICTION TREATMENT AS A TIME-DEPENDENT PROCESS

What differentiates early treatment goals from later treatment requirements is the stance taken toward abstinence. Alcoholism treatment is basically a simple two-step process involving strategic shifts related to abstinence. Early in treatment, the task is to get alcoholics to stop their use of substances. Later in treatment, they must be prevented from starting again. Closely related to the "Keep it simple stupid" (KISS) approach of AA is the need to adapt strategies that match the special circumstances of the newly abstinent alcoholic and addict.

Addiction specialists have been advocating for years the need to differentiate early treatment strategies from later treatment requirements (Brown 1985, Flores 1982, Wallace 1978). Effective addiction treatment requires an alteration in treatment strategy when moving from early to later stages of treatment. This represents one of the important paradoxes of successful addiction treatment. Clinical interventions that are often successful and necessary in early treatment will prove ineffective if applied unmodified in late-stage treatment, and they can contribute to a relapse rather than enhance continued abstinence.

Most of his adult life, Bob had consumed alcohol regularly without much difficulty. However, soon after his fortieth birthday, Bob's drinking escalated and he began to experience blackouts and job-related difficulties. His family became more alarmed and encouraged him to seek help. He reluctantly agreed to try therapy and attempted to control his drinking for the next two years, with disastrous results. He saw three different therapists during this time, terminating therapy each time after a few sessions, complaining, "I just don't feel connected to them and I don't like them fawning over me." Eventually, he lost his job and his wife threatened divorce. Bob reluctantly agreed to try group therapy but quickly gave up on the sessions complaining, "I'm not like them, I can't stand their self-pity." Following a severe drunken binge that left him devastated and defeated, Bob readily agreed to seek treatment. During the initial interview and his first group session, Bob showed a dramatic shift in his willingness to "let others help me with my problem." He told the group "I have to swallow my pride, admit I am like you, and stop acting like I don't need anyone." Over the next six weeks, he proceeded to become very attached to the group and after treatment stayed active in aftercare and AA.

John Wallace (1978) was one of the first to write about alcoholism treatment as a *time-dependent process*. Currently, most addiction treatment specialists (Kaufman and Reoux 1988, Washton 1992) hold to some variation of the recommendation that treatment strategies be adapted to fit at least three distinct phases of treatment: (1) achieving sobriety, (2) early recovery or abstinence, and (3) advanced or late-stage recovery. Applying these recommendations to attachment theory, three primary stages of treatment need to be addressed:

1. Since substance abuse is an attempt at self-repair, which exacerbates the individual's already impaired capacity for attachment and intimacy, abstinence and detachment from the object of addiction are required before the

individual can make an attachment to group or establish a therapeutic alliance.

2. Early treatment strategies require adaptation in technique so that gratification, support, and containment are given priority because these strategies maximally enhance attachment possibilities.

3. Once abstinence and attachment to the recovery process are established, deficits in self and character pathology must be modified. An essential part of this stage of treatment requires the patient to develop the capacity for conflict resolution in a nondestructive manner while becoming familiar with mature mutuality and the intricacies that define healthy interdependence and intimacy.

EARLY TREATMENT ISSUES

An approach that is very effective with a nonaddicted patient might be totally inappropriate for someone who is addicted, especially in the early stages of recovery. Many alcoholics and addicts have rather sophisticated defenses that serve the primary purpose of protecting their attachment to substances. Unlike nonaddictive patients who pursue treatment of their own free will and are actively seeking help for their symptoms, most addicted patients come to treatment under pressure or duress and want to convince the therapist that there has been a horrible mistake made with their referral for treatment. They might well try to steer the therapist toward the "real problem"—a wife or boss who's always hounding them about one thing or another. This problem may well be sincerely formulated in substance abusers' minds as the root cause of their excessive use of substances. Secretly, substance abusers hope that once this root cause is discovered, they will be able to return to the normal use of chemicals. Because drinking or drug use is frequently the only pleasure they derive out of life, it is an attachment relationship that must be protected at all costs.

Most approaches to early-stage addiction treatment take the position that the primary emphasis must be on abstinence, relapse prevention, and managing the cravings stirred up by conditioned responses to external cues (Brown 1985, Brown and Yalom 1977, Flores 1997, Kemker et al. 1993, Khantzian et al. 1990, Matano and Yalom 1991, Vannicelli 1992) Flores and Mahon, 1993: These approaches recognize the fragility of the addict's early recovery, and adaptations in technique must be made to address these vulnerabilities. Careful consideration is also given to providing enough emotional gratification to keep alcoholics and addicts in therapy while helping them accept their diagnosis and "acculturating them into the culture of recovery" (Kemker et al. 1993), p. 286.

The significance of the acceptance of the diagnosis and the acculturation into AA is an issue often ignored by those whose interest in addiction is only passing or purely academic. Addicts and alcoholics struggling with their disease don't have the luxury of taking this matter lightly because for them it is a matter of life or death. For instance, Wallace (1984) sees the ideological base of AA providing a crucial component in the alcoholic's and addict's recovery process. In fact, he contends that the alcoholic and addict need AA's biased view of reality. "The alcoholic can ill afford the dispassionate, disinterested, and indeed, almost casual play upon words and ideas of the inquiring academic intellectual" (1975, p. 7). Wallace strongly feels that chemically dependent individuals recognize intuitively the need for a stable and enduring belief system if they are to stay clean and sober. Wallace has more difficulty in comprehending and discerning the equally biased view of reality of the academician:

> Hidden neatly beneath the rhetoric of science and scientism are the actualities of dreadfully inadequate personality measuring instruments, inappropriate sampling procedures, inadequate measuring operations, improper choice of variables for study, grossly violated statistical assumptions, data gathering, recording and analyzing errors, and so on and so forth. Is it any wonder then that the most outstanding quality of most academic research is now you see it, now you don't? Are we really amazed to find sober alcoholics clinging to their belief systems like drowning poets to their metaphors in a sea of confusion? [p. 7]

The art of treating addiction is to overcome the enormous denial and resistance—whether it be passive or active—that most alcoholics and addicts present. Such a stance in treatment raises many important ethical and therapeutic issues. However, a therapist cannot afford to stand back and take a stance of therapeutic neutrality, because time, the severity of chemically dependent patients' condition, and their lack of motivation interfere with the typical evolution of psychotherapy that usually takes place with most nonaddicted patients. Treating the chemically dependent patient requires therapists to make a dramatic shift in focus and utilize techniques that are new to them.

Working with alcoholics and addicts therefore requires a therapist to reevaluate many of the conventional and unquestioned assumptions about psychotherapy. While therapists know that it is important *not* to make decisions for patients and that a therapeutic alliance should never be compromised at any cost, it is crucial to evaluate this stance when working with an alcoholic or addict who is struggling with decisions about abstinence in the early stages of recovery. As Shore (1981) states, "Therapists who remain inflexibly supportive while alcoholics continue to kill themselves by drinking need to reconsider the moral repercussions of their position" (p. 13).

Wallace also recognizes the importance of helping individuals achieve a self-attribution of alcoholic and, hence, an explanatory system for their behavior. Treatment from this standpoint is very much the teaching of an "exotic belief" whose true value of actually describing what has occurred to individuals because of their addiction is held as irrelevant. Its true value is determined by the fact that it:

1. Helps explain the past in a way that gives hope for the future
2. Provides a way for alcoholics and addicts to cope with their anxiety, remorse, and confusion
3. Helps them with a specific behavior—staying sober or clean and working the twelve steps of the program—that will change their lives in a desired direction.

As Wallace says, alcoholics and addicts have a lifetime of sobriety in which to recognize and figure out that not all of their personal and social difficulties are the result of their substance use.

> The chief of police and the mayor of a small rural community stopped by to pay an impromptu visit to the director of the local mental health center, asking, "Can you do us a big favor?"
>
> "We have," they explained, "this little problem with one of our more loved, but troublesome citizens." They proceeded to tell the director about Andy, a 32-year-old local hero of sorts, who kept creating a number of embarrassing situations in their quiet rural community. Andy, they explained, was a lifelong member of the community and had always been revered and loved by the townsfolk, ever since he was the starting quarterback on the local high school team that won the state championship fifteen years ago. In high school, he had been elected prom king and senior class president, and everyone in the community looked up to Andy. On top of all that, he had married the daughter of the town's only Baptist minister. After graduation, Andy received a full football scholarship to the state university, but kept getting into trouble at college and eventually got kicked off the football team and expelled from school. He returned to plenty of job offers from his grateful community, but squandered or wasted every opportunity given him. Lately, things have gotten much worse. Andy was constantly getting himself arrested for "fighting and general hell raising." The mayor and chief of police were worried that "something is just not right in Andy's head."
>
> "I'll assign one of my best therapists to see Andy. Do you think he'll come in for an appointment?" the director asked.
>
> "Oh, he'll be here," the police chief responded. "That's the only way I'll let him out of jail."
>
> Andy came for his appointment the next day. Less than a half-hour into the session, the therapist had gathered

enough evidence to suggest that Andy had never been arrested or gotten into any kind of trouble when he *hadn't* been drinking. All his fights occurred at the local bar on Friday or Saturday nights. His other arrests had been for DUIs, disorderly conduct, or public intoxication. When asked about his experience in college, Andy admitted his football coach threw him off the team for repeatedly missing curfews and team practices, and for excessive "partying." Before the session ended, the therapist presented Andy with evidence supporting a possible diagnosis of alcoholism.

Andy shrugged. "I guess it's possible."

The therapist recommended some AA meetings.

"I guess it couldn't hurt," Andy readily agreed.

The change in Andy's behavior over the next few weeks was dramatic. Three months into treatment, the grateful chief of police and the mayor took the director of the mental health center out for lunch in a show of their appreciation for "straightening out Andy's thinking."

The biggest confirmation came from Andy a few weeks later when he gratefully thanked the therapist for steering him to AA. "Until I got into AA, I thought I was just crazy," Andy said. "I was worried something real bad was wrong with me. I was never so relieved when I found out I was just an alcoholic and that I was acting crazy because of that."

GRATIFICATION VS. FRUSTRATION

The degree to which the therapist frustrates or gratifies the patient is one of the most consistent dominating themes in the treatment of addition. Alcoholics and addicts demand and require certain levels of gratification if they are going to tolerate the relinquishing of their primary source of gratification—namely, alcohol and drugs. Self psychology's perspective on this issue is most useful in helping the therapist determine when and how much gratification is necessary when treating the addicted patient. Addiction, as self psychology defines it, is the result of deprivation of developmentally appropriate needs for gratification. Alcohol, drugs, food, sex, and other forms of potentially addictive behavior are attempts at self-repair. The addict and alcoholic try to acquire externally what cannot be provided internally because of defects in psychic structure. This is not to imply that therapists should "love their addict or alcoholic into health." Not only is this impossible, it is countertherapeutic since this is what the addict or alcoholic has been trying to do symbolically with chemicals. Rather, the addicted individual needs to learn how to tolerate frustration without immediate gratification since it is through managing tolerable levels of frustration that psychic structure is laid.

It is here that the concept of *optimal frustration* captures the necessary stance of the therapist when working with alcoholics and addicts. Too much anxiety interferes with the necessary trust and safety required for openness, exploration, and the revealing of one's self to occur. *Optimal gratification* means that the therapist will provide enough nurturing or emotional responsiveness until addicts or alcoholics are able to provide it to themselves without returning to old methods of gaining immediate gratification. Early-stage treatment with substance abusers requires more gratification than later-stage treatment.

The disease concept and abstinence-based treatment strategies that dominate the addiction treatment field often seem at odds with many psychodynamic approaches to therapy. Most substance abusers cannot tolerate the frustration and regression that is induced by the more classically influenced psychodynamic approaches to psychotherapy. Addicts and alcoholics, especially those in the early stages of their recovery, respond more favorably to a direct, practical, no-nonsense approach than they do to a therapeutic stance that waits for dynamics to gradually develop in therapy. Substance abusers typically do not tolerate passivity or the absence of gratification very well. If therapy is to reach its full potential with this population, it requires active emotional engagement.

EMOTIONAL AVAILABILTY OF THE THERAPIST

The beginning phase of early therapy needs to be structured, supportive, and directive. To help the alcoholic or addict accomplish the task of recovery most effectively, therapists must gear most of their efforts toward creating an attachment bond or developing a therapeutic alliance. Therapy works best when it is a vitalizing experience. Substance abusers usually respond more favorably to a therapist who is spontaneous, alive, and engaging than they do to the therapist who adopts the more reserved stance of technical neutrality associated with these more classic approaches to therapy. The more available and engaging therapist can counter the characterlogical deficits of these patients who constantly have to battle the feelings of boredom, deadness, meaninglessness, and inner emptiness that threaten to overtake them. The more passive and unresponsive therapist is likely to be experienced by the substance abuser as withholding, timid, dull, or dead. This stirs up unconscious fears of annihilation and nothingness, which are associated with primitive identifications. Transference distortions are thus heightened, which in turn increases resistance.

However, an increased activity level does not mean that the therapist should be overly charismatic, because this can induce fears of engulfment, destructive idealization, competitive distractions, and archaic mergers in the patient. Also, this does not imply that the therapist gratify the patient in an infantile manner. Not only is this unrealistic, antitherapeutic, and ultimately impossible, but it also feeds the substance abuser's infantile narcissistic grandiosity and demands for immediate gratification. Establishing a climate of optimal frustration meets patients' dependency needs until they are able to internalize control over their own destructive impulses and emotions.

CREATING THE CAPACITY FOR ATTACHMENT

There is a very subtle interplay among attachment, safe haven, and proximity-seeking behavior. Attachment theorists have long recognized an important paradox about attachment: secure attachment liberates (Holmes 1996). This is as true for the securely attached child as it is for the securely attached patient who has a firm therapeutic alliance with the therapist. Just as the securely attached child will move greater distances away from the caregiver, taking more risks exploring the surrounding environment, securely attached patients will take more risks in therapy, exploring their inner world more readily.

During the later stages of early recovery, helping the addict and alcoholic learn how to negotiate the demands of attachment and mutuality becomes important for another reason. Relapses are always of primary concern during this stage of treatment and are often related to difficulties with affect regulation. Substance abusers are usually unable to use their feelings as signals and guides in managing or protecting themselves against the instability and chaos of their internal world. This disturbance in the regulation of affect manifests as "an inability to identify and verbalize feelings, an intolerance of incapacity for anxiety and depression, an inability to modulate feelings . . . and extreme manifestations of affect, such as hypomania, phobic-anxious states, panic, and lability" (Khantzian 1982, p. 590). If they should return to using substances, it will only reduce their existing capacity for self-regulation even further.

ALEXITHYMIA

Much of the early efforts in treatment need to be directed toward the rudimentary process of helping the substance abuser facilitate affect regulation by labeling and mirroring feelings when they occur in treatment. The novice therapist will soon learn that substance abusers require help with becoming acquainted with their feelings. Not only will they have difficulty identifying their feelings, they are notoriously inadequate in communicating them to others. The larger lesson the substance abuser has to learn is that emotions are not only vital to self-understanding, but also crucial to the understanding of others' feelings and the negotiation of all forms of intimacy in interpersonal relationships.

Alexithymia has been identified as a characteristic pattern indicating an inability to name and use one's emotions. Alcoholics' and addicts' inability to verbalize feelings leads to the somatization of affect responses. Consequently, the substance abuser is confronted with sensations rather than feelings. Such physiological sensations are not useful as signals, but remain painfully overwhelming. Painful affective states call attention only to their discomfort rather than to the story behind the feelings. Substance abusers possess a striking inability to articulate their most bothersome and important feelings. Many if not all of their feelings translate into somatic complaints about physical discomfort and craving. Alcohol and drugs are used to block the affect, preventing the substance abuser from interpreting and attending to the signal. Krystal (1982) says this results in "a diminution in the capacity for drive-fantasy. Thinking becomes operative, mundane and boring. The capacity for empathy with development of utilizable transference is seriously diminished" (p. 614).

The recent work of attachment theory and self psychology has taught addictions specialists that dysfunctional attachment styles interfere with the ability to derive satisfaction from interpersonal relationships and contribute to internal working models that perpetuate this difficulty. Experiences related to early developmental failures leave certain individuals with vulnerabilities that enhance addictive-type behaviors, and these behaviors are misguided attempts at self-repair. Deprivation of age-appropriate developmental needs leaves the substance abuser constantly searching for something "out there" that can be substituted for what is missing "in here."

The following vignette illustrates the futility of attempting therapy with a practicing alcoholic. Their attachment to substances interferes with their capacity to establish or maintain a therapeutic alliance.

> Alex, a 52-year-old addict and sexual abuse survivor, had been in and out of treatment and Alcoholics Anonymous for nearly thirty years with little improvement or success. The only long-term relationship he had maintained during this period was a 25-year marriage to a suffering wife who derived great pleasure in reminding him how miserable he made her life. Despite frequent recommendations that they seek couples therapy, she refused, saying that she was not the problem—he was. A severe and persistent introject of self-blame resulting from his sexual abuse prevented him from establishing anything other than sadomasochistic relationships. Following a severe weekend

binge that nearly killed him, Alex was eventually persuaded to enter a therapy group. After putting together three months of abstinence, Alex began to gradually become more attached to the group. With the help of the other group members, he began to explore the destructive nature of all his relationships, especially the one with his wife. It soon became apparent that "Saint Sally" could only contain her position of goodness as long as Alex held on to his position of the "bad one." As Alex became more attached to the group and developed new relational configurations, his wife became more depressed and eventually sought individual therapy. During the next three months Alex continued to show marked improvement, staying sober and developing a new and important role in the group. Anytime the group would drift into superficiality or evasiveness, he would assume responsibility for keeping the group on task and encouraging the members to stay serious about recovery and remaining honest with each other.

All this abruptly changed one night when Alex, distressed and devastated, announced to the group that his wife just had been diagnosed with breast cancer. In the middle of an angry confrontation, she blamed him for her condition and screamed at him, "Your drinking caused me so much stress that I got cancer. This is all your fault!" Despite the absurdity of her accusations, Alex's nascent developing "good self" could not tolerate her verbal onslaught. Within two weeks, he relapsed. Following the relapse, his demeanor and relationship with the group and its members changed dramatically. He became more withdrawn and emotionally detached from the group, missing more and more sessions. Whenever he did show up, he either was bored or surly, and frequently critical of group members, telling them to stop whining and feeling sorry for themselves. The exuberant and involved individual had now been replaced by a detached, disparaging man who was self-absorbed and showed complete disregard for others' feelings or difficulties. The group tried unsuccessfully for the next two months to restore their relationship with him and encouraged his return to AA and abstinence. He gradually drifted out of the group and returned to his old relationship with his wife, who also had stopped individual therapy.

TRAUMA BONDING

As long as the alcoholic remains attached to alcohol, he will not be able to establish a therapeutic alliance. Sometimes creating the capacity for attachment requires nothing more than taking advantage of a well-known fact about attachment: an individual's attachment system opens up during a crisis. Substance abuse and urgent circumstances usually go hand in hand. If the therapist is patient and does nothing to interfere with this process, the consequences of a substance abuser's drinking and drug use eventually will provide them with a favorable therapeutic opportunity. AA refers to this as hitting bottom. The art of successful early treatment with the addicts who refuse to accept their diagnosis or the alcoholics who remain in denial is to gently encourage them to look at the consequences of their substance use without damaging the therapeutic alliance. The therapist must take every opportunity to "reframe" the problem patients present to help them see that most of their difficulties are the result of their chemical use. The basic thrust of addiction treatment is to get substance abusers to perceive and understand the relationship between their present difficulties in their life and their drug or alcohol use.

James was a 28-year-old computer programmer who was encouraged to see a therapist because of his family's concern about his depression and increasing isolation. He came for his first appointment looking somewhat unkempt and disheveled. His eyes were bloodshot, and his sunken cheeks made the ashen color of his skin more pronounced and unappealing. All of this was in striking contrast to his facial features, which were pleasant and potentially attractive. The first few sessions were spent focused on the symptoms of his depression, which he felt were all directly related to his difficulties at work and his lifelong history of unsatisfactory relationships with women.

"For some reason, women just seem to shy away from me after they get to know me or they just want to be buddies," James lamented.

As he spoke of his difficulties, it became apparent that all his male friends were heavy drug users, and although James smoked pot daily, he defended his pot smoking by adding, "I don't do the heavy stuff like they do. I don't mess with the needles or do cocaine and Ecstasy every day."

When James was asked if he thought he might be addicted, he adamantly rejected the possibility. "I can't be an addict. I don't use nearly as many drugs as all the other people I know."

James's continued drug use was spinning a distorting web of self-deception in James's clouded mind, preventing him from accurately perceiving what he and his isolated circle of drug-using buddies were doing. The therapist carefully assessed all sides of the present dilemma. The therapist knew that James's attachment to his peer group and his attachment to his drugs was far stronger than any attachment that James currently had to him or their therapy relationship. Rather than risk rupturing the rudimentary beginnings of their therapeutic alliance, the therapist gently encouraged James to talk about his concerns, "but keep a careful watch on your drug use and see what happens when you don't smoke pot or use Ecstasy."

Since James did derive a great deal of satisfaction from talking about his struggles at work and his difficulties with women, he agreed to "try an experiment and see what happens when I cut down on my pot smoking."

Over the course of the next few weeks, James reported an improvement with his performance at work, which reversed a growing acrimonious trend that had been established with his boss.

At this point, the therapist seized the opportunity to say, "I can understand why your relationship with your boss has gotten better. Not only has your work performance improved since you've cut down on your pot smoking, you're probably easier to engage and more responsive to her just as you are more responsive and easier to engage here in therapy."

James initially looked surprised. A smile gradually spread over his face. "Yeah, I guess I am more responsive and alert since I've cut down smoking."

The next session, James volunteered that he had decided to stop all other drug use "for a while and only smoke a little pot now and then."

"Why?" the therapist asked.

"I've been feeling a lot less depressed lately. Maybe you're right. The drug use and the depression might be connected."

The therapist nodded. "I agree. The evidence suggests the two are related. The less drugs you use, the less depressed you are. Your performance at work also improves, which also helps your self-esteem." The therapist pointed at James's appearance. "Look, even your skin tone and eyes appear brighter."

James laughed. "You know, I've noticed that too when I looked in the mirror. I just thought it was my imagination. You think this is also related?"

"I'm sure of it," the therapist replied.

Over the course of the next few weeks, James announced that he had started running and working out at the gym again. "I don't know why I stopped in the first place. I always feel better when I exercise regularly."

"Don't you think it has something to do with your drug use?" the therapist asked. "It's pretty hard to run when you're high on Ecstasy or hung over from partying the night before."

James nodded in agreement. "You know, you might be right. I'm beginning to notice how much all my friends' lives are centered around drugs and getting high."

A couple weeks later, James showed up feeling depressed and discouraged. Halfway through the session, the therapist learned that James had stayed out all night with some old buddies smoking pot and doing cocaine.

"Think there's any connection between how bad you feel about yourself and your drug use?" the therapist asked.

"Huh?" James looked up in surprise. "I don't think so. Do you?"

"I sure do. Look at the picture." The therapist held up his hand and began counting on his fingers. "First, your mood and outlook on life have steadily changed since you cut way back on your pot smoking and stopped all your other drug use. Second, your work has improved tremendously. And lastly, one weekend binge and you're practically feeling as bad as you were when you first showed up here in my office three months ago."

James did not protest or object to the therapist's observations and left the session thoughtful and with a fresh determination.

The course of his treatment and abstinence took on a new commitment over the next few weeks. At his most recent session, James showed up beaming. "I met this girl the other night. She came up and talked to me at this party. A lot of my old drug-using buddies were there, and as usual, they were really stoned, gathered together off to one corner of the house. A number of us were on the periphery watching them make fools of themselves." James smiled appreciatively at the therapist. "A couple months ago, I probably would have been right in there with them. I'm sure this woman wouldn't have bothered to initiate anything with me if I had been stoned. I'm beginning to see how so many of my problems were related to my drug use."

NEUROPSYCHOLOGICAL IMPAIRMENT

Another important and often ignored variable in the diagnosis and treatment process is the effect that drugs and alcohol have on the brain. This has important implications for a number of reasons. Most simply put, all forms of psychotherapy (individual, group, family, cognitive, psychodynamic, etc.) rest on the assumption that patients will be rational enough to make decisions based on accurate insight and understanding of themselves and their situation. It is impossible to conduct traditional forms of therapy with addicted patients who are actively using substances or are in the very early stages of recovery. While most therapists would agree with such a position, few fail to understand the significance of substance abusers' cognitive impairment three, six, or even nine months into their recovery because these symptoms are often very subtle and specific. Because most alcoholics and addicts do not demonstrate significant difficulties in their verbal intelligence, they often sound better than they really are. An awareness and understanding of these cognitive deficits is necessary so that adaptations can be made in treatment that match the needs and capabilities of the patient.

Within the last twenty years there has been a vast accumulation of evidence related to the neurological functioning and neuropsychological deficits associated with alcoholism. Review of the literature reveals that the pattern of impairment associated with chronic alcohol abuse is identifiable and even predictable (Flores 1997, Grant et al. 1980, Parsons and Farr 1981, Ryan and Butters 1980, Wells 1982, Wilkinson and Carlen 1981). Most important, the pattern of deficits noted in cortical compromise and cognitive deficiencies has important implications for treatment.

On neuropsychological tests sensitive to abstract reasoning, flexible thinking, fluid intelligence, and new learning, alcoholics and addicts consistently score in the brain-impaired range. Yet their verbal intelligence and old learning remain pretty much intact. Consequently, they often appear unimpaired to the unsuspecting observer. Their level of impairment is usually not permanent and does not involve cortical structural damage. Rather, their brain dysfunction is of a diffuse nature, usually the result of an alcohol-induced encephalopathy exacerbated by nutritional and vitamin deficiencies. Most alcoholics and addicts experience spontaneous recovery from the loss of cortical functioning if they remain alcohol and drug free and improve their vitamin and nutritional intake. This recovery of cognitive functioning is gradual and steady. The greatest improvement is usually experienced in the first months, with total recovery achieved after one to two years of abstinence.

MOTIVATION AND STAGES OF CHANGE

Therapists soon discover that few substance abusers are completely willing to do everything necessary to ensure the successful treatment of their addiction. Most alcoholics and addicts possess varying levels of motivation to abstain from alcohol and drug use. This is especially true during the early initial stages of treatment when their level of alcohol- and drug-induced cognitive impairment is most severe and they are more rigid and limited in their ability to explore alternative solutions to old problems. Even when addicts and alcoholics enter treatment completely of their own free will and possess a strong innate desire to stop their use of chemicals, many of these patients have difficulty doing the things necessary to ensure their recovery because of their character pathology or neurological impairment. This condition is also made more severe by their recent use of chemicals, which usually leaves them more rebellious, suspicious, and manipulative.

The neuropsychological research also sheds some light on the importance of providing alcoholics and addicts with a clear, structured program that they must follow during their first months of abstinence. New members of twelve-step programs are told not to make any major decisions during the first year of recovery. They are instructed not to analyze the program. They are told, "The program works because it works! Go to ninety meetings in ninety days! Take the body, and the mind will follow!" Each of these suggestions is based on AA's and other twelve-step programs' intuitive understanding that alcoholics and addicts, during the early stages of abstinence, are incapable of thinking clearly and do not possess the intellectual capabilities necessary for rational, intelligent decisions. The program provides them with twelve clear steps that they must follow. New members are told to "keep it simple." After they finish the first step, they are told to complete the second step and then proceed on to the third step, and so on.

Such a stance is crucial for individuals suffering from an impaired ability to think abstractly. It gives them what they desperately need at the beginning of treatment—direction, structure, and guidance. As alcoholics gradually recover their lost cognitive functioning, alternative treatment strategies can be implemented once their capacity for new learning, consolidation of information, abstract thought, creative thinking, and motivation have all returned to their premorbid level of functioning. At that point, alcoholics can utilize insight, self-understanding, and autonomous decision-making. A therapist can then start to employ more traditional modes of treatment in their therapy.

Matching interventions to stages of neurological readiness has important implications for treatment. Complicating the degree of neurological impairment is the motivational level and degree of readiness for behavioral change that will vary from alcoholic to alcoholic. While there is a strong correlation between psychological readiness and neurological readiness, not all individuals present with the same levels of motivation or denial. Personality variables interact with the specific properties of specific drugs. Some addictions have a much more powerful impact on the brain than other addictive behaviors do. While many cognitive and behaviorally oriented researchers tend to classify all addictions under the general heading of addictive behaviors, they run the risk of overgeneralizing the addictive process. Addiction to nicotine, for instance, even though it is life-threatening and bears many similarities to the addictive process with alcohol and drugs, poses none of the immediate impairment and behavioral consequences that the abuse of substances does. Few will argue that nicotine abuse needs to be addressed with the same aggressiveness or immediacy that addiction to alcohol or drugs does. In a similar view, substance addictions are often compared to the addictions that involve compulsive activities such as gambling, sex, and spending. Outcome studies that generalize the results of smoking cessation or reduced caffeine intake to those of drug or alcohol treatment are guilty of seriously misreading the usefulness of such approaches. Despite these shortcomings, there is much to be gained from examining how motivational levels and stages of readiness to change can have important implications for treating the alcoholic or addict.

Within the last ten years, behaviorally oriented researchers have attempted to quantify how it is that individuals change. Much of their work has been adapted to addiction and the identification of variables that influence a person's decision to stop alcohol or drug use. One popular conceptual model identifies five stages of the change process that have significant relationships with the motivational levels of the individual and require intervention strategies of the therapist (Prochaska and DiClemente 1992). Applying this conceptual framework to addictive disorders, it is suggested that motivation enhancement, or what some call "motivational interviewing," is of primary importance only in the very early stages of addiction treatment when individuals are ambivalent about or have no interest in stopping their chemical use. Motivating individuals for treatment essentially consists of getting them to believe strongly in both the desirability and likelihood of change. Someone already convinced of this needs little help in this area, but needs more guidance in the latter stages of change where activities like preparation, action relapse prevention, and maintenance of recovery become the necessary priorities. In contrast to this position, others believe that early-stage motivational interventions are all the assistance that some individuals will require in addressing their addiction. Once individuals are able to get past the precontemplative and contemplative stages, they will take the actions necessary to remain abstinent.

RELAPSE PREVENTION

The road to recovery requires a careful balance between affect release and affect containment. Since rapid switches in affect states can be potentially destructive, the substance abuser's feelings must be delicately managed until they have enough sobriety and emotional stability to tolerate a closer look at themselves. The potential for a relapse is heightened anytime the substance abuser feels too good or too bad too quickly, which is often a signal that the old narcissistic defenses have returned and the substance abuser will soon be thinking, "I got this thing licked, I'm special. I'm different." On the other hand, feeling too bad too quickly leads to "I don't give a damn. I might as well be using; this is no fun," indicating that abstinence has become intolerable and substance use is the only refuge from the intense discomfort that dominates recovery.

While relapse prevention is a crucial part of the maintenance stage of change, it is a continual focus after action is initiated to stop using alcohol and drugs. Relapses are inevitable for most, if not all, alcoholics and addicts. They can be invaluable learning experiences if properly examined and integrated. Staying closely connected to other recovering addicts and alcoholics in the twelve-step recovery programs will ensure that learning from relapses does not always have to come at individuals' personal expense since they have the opportunity to learn from one another by witnessing one anothers' relapses. They soon learn that relapses follow a predictable and recognizable pattern. This is vitally important since relapses can often be fatal. The therapist can provide information and direction and explain the typical warning signs of relapse, thus helping prevent or minimize its impact and occurrence. As important as this information is, it does not carry anything close to the impact and emotional learning that comes from witnessing a fellow addict or alcoholic in the early throes of a relapse.

> Sam had a little more than three months' sobriety and had been doing "ninety-in-ninety" (ninety meetings in ninety days) as his sponsor had suggested. Faithfully following all the recommendations of AA, Sam was actively working the steps of the program, taking it one day at a time, and reading the Big Book of AA. Despite his best efforts, Sam had come off the "pink cloud" high that many alcoholics experience during the early stages of recovery and was experiencing more intrusive thoughts about drinking. He confessed these difficulties one afternoon to his sponsor, who replied, "Well, maybe it's time you did a little twelve-step work. I just got a call a little while ago and I'm going

to see someone who's in a bad relapse. Why don't you come along?"

"Twelve-step?" Sam's voice was full of surprise and concern. "You think I'm ready to help someone else?"

His sponsor laughed. "I think you got this helping stuff turned around. Remember, twelve-step work is about keeping *you* sober, not the other person."

"What?" Sam stammered. "I don't get it. How's doing a twelve-step call going to help me? I . . ."

"Come along," his sponsor interrupted. "Maybe you'll find out."

They drove to a seedy part of town and parked in front of the dingiest flophouse that Sam had ever seen. Sam followed his sponsor up a creaky set of stairs and down a dimly lit hallway until they found the room he was searching for.

The sponsor knocked on the door.

"Who's the hell's there?" a slurred voice croaked.

"It's me, Pete. Bob Cramer."

"The door's not locked," the voice responded.

The stench of the room invaded Sam's nostrils as soon as his sponsor opened the door. Once inside the room, Sam stood transfixed by the sight before him.

There on the edge of the dirty bed, dressed only in his urine-stained underwear, sat the disheveled, inebriated, sorriest example of a man that Sam had seen in years. The poor creature had thrown up all over the front of his stained tee shirt, and dry vomit was caked all over his teeth and unshaven face. Cigarette butts and empty wine bottles were scattered around the room. Before Sam's sponsor or the drunk on the bed could respond, Sam was overcome by a spontaneous response.

Sam pushed past his sponsor, charged across the room, and grabbed the man's hand, pumping his arm in a vigorous handshake. "I want to thank you. Seeing you like this, I know for *damn* sure I won't have a drink for at least the next twenty-four hours."

THE LIFE HISTORY: NARRATIVES AND AA FROM A PHENOMENOLOGICAL PERSPECTIVE

Carl Thune (1977) took the phenomenological method and applied it in a penetrating investigation and interpretation of AA. From Thune's perspective, AA works because of its emphasis on members' recounting their life histories at AA meetings. It is through the telling of their life histories that they are taught how to interpret their past in a way that gives meaning to the past and hope for the future. Thune, operating from a pure phenomenological framework, holds a position very similar to the narrative constructionist's model that contends that the past never merely exists for anyone, alcoholic or not. Instead, the past is interpreted and created through the use of conceptual models. More significantly, "These models become models of and for the creation of the future, a future that is no more automatically 'given' than is the past" (p. 83).

One of the major tenets of the narrative model is the demonstration that the world and the self, rather than being automatically given in the order of things, are being constantly created as individuals proceed through life. Insight into individuals' lives then comes from an analysis of the world as they construct it, in which they must live. It is suggested by Thune that the nature, meaning, and experience of these constructions of the self and the world by alcoholics are subject to an ongoing process of reconstitution and redefinition, both in the process of becoming alcoholics and in the course of any successful treatment and recovery program. Central to this process is the redefinition of the meaning and experience of alcoholism. Complementing this is the suggestion that alcoholism is better understood as in the terminology of AA: a defective mode of life (Madsen 1974). A treatment regimen directed at reconstitution and redefinition of self and world provides a better way to deal with alcoholism than a model holding it analogous to a physical disease or a bad habit subject to modification. This is AA's claim, and Thune feels this position lies at the heart of the success that AA has enjoyed.

Unlike most medically oriented therapeutic systems, the

real problem as AA analyzes it centers around helping alcoholics understand their basic being as alcoholic rather than as normal and nonalcoholic. It is AA's emphasis on the spiritually defective mode of being rather than a physical disability that provides the clearest expression of the belief that alcoholism is a defect of being. In many respects, AA invokes a spiritual or religious vocabulary in the absence of perhaps a more accurate but inaccessible philosophical-ontological terminology.

A clinical vignette helps illustrate this point:

> Paula called her therapist, distraught by her latest relapse, despite going to some of the best treatment programs in the country. When she and her concerned husband showed up at the therapist's office together, the husband described his wife's ten-year struggle to obtain abstinence. "It is painfully difficult to watch someone I love try so desperately to stop drinking, but be unable to do so even though we've tried everything that the doctors at two treatment programs had recommended."
>
> When asked what treatment programs they had tried, Paula described two well-known behavioral and aversion therapy hospitals in the northwest United States.
>
> "Have you tried AA?" the therapist asked.
>
> The husband rolled his eyes and Paula sat up in her chair and clenched her jaw. "No way," Paula insisted. "I hate that rigid, dogmatic, religious crap." Her husband patted her on the knee to calm her, and explained to the therapist, "You'll learn that Paula has a real aversion to organized religion of any kind. She is intolerant of any kind of religious dogma. She's tried a few of those meetings, but got so angry at them that she went out and drank afterward."
>
> The therapist nodded and sighed. "Well, that makes it a little harder, but let's see what we can do. Let's meet twice a week, and if you can get a month or two of abstinence under your belt, I'll put you in a therapy group with other recovering alcoholics."
>
> Paula and her husband readily agreed. "Thank you,"

Paula said. "I'm at the end of my rope. I'll do whatever you tell me as long as I don't have to go to AA." Therapy progressed rapidly over the next six months. Paula joined a group and quickly became a dedicated member. As her abstinence increased, the therapist learned more about her aversion to organized religion. She grew up in a home with very repressive and controlling Baptist fundamentalist parents. Paula had to fight desperately to escape their clutches and the indoctrination of the church. Once free of their influences, she vowed never to allow herself to be subjected to control by any organized religious doctrine again. Her treatment experiences at the two hospitals had been very positive. She had enjoyed the feeling of camaraderie while there, but the sense of belonging could not be sustained after she was discharged. Each time, her conviction not to drink eroded after a few months, and she once again felt isolated, alienated, and alone.

After nearly two years of uninterrupted therapy, Paula's sobriety gained momentum, as did her alliance with her therapist. With increased abstinence, she was able to better understand the strength of her reaction to AA and organized religion, even though this realization did nothing to moderate her unwillingness to go to AA.

During one session Paula had an awareness that she spontaneously shared with her therapist. "You know, I think I just realized something," Paula laughed. "I think you've been my higher power. I've used you, the group, and these sessions as my AA program. I was so desperate when I came here, I surrendered to you and decided to accept the fact that I was an alcoholic, and would do whatever you recommended."

Like most therapeutic systems, AA faces the twin problems of diagnosis and treatment. However, the program's analysis of these facets of the therapeutic process bears little relation to those of more orthodox Western medical systems (Thune 1977). It is in the diagnosis and definition of *alcoholism* that AA parts company with many of the psychological definitions of *alcoholism*. Thune states:

> Consequently, it is no accident that the therapeutic program of Alcoholics Anonymous challenges the conventional medical, psychological, and sociological concepts of causation and that it ignores the findings and questions of specialists in these fields. Its roots lie less in the sciences than in such nonpositivist, quasirevivalistic, transcendental efforts of the Oxford Group Movement. To attempt to understand AA on an analytic and positivist model obscures its uniqueness. [p. 75]

Objective diagnosis (an important and necessary component of scientific assessment in psychology) from a source other than alcoholics themselves is held irrelevant to the program. The success or failure of the program depends on whether individuals can diagnose themselves as alcoholics. It is this self-diagnosis that is the essence of AA's twelve steps to recovery. To paraphrase Laing (1969), alcoholics must come to understand that one does not have alcoholism; rather, one is alcoholic.

A case vignette illustrates this point:

> Steve, a 22-year-old college senior at a local university, sought an initial consultation with a therapist because of concerns about his anger and depression. During the course of the initial interview, the therapist learned that Steve's anger and verbal conflicts always manifested when he was either high on marijuana or out drinking with his buddies. The young man's depression always followed his weekend episodes of "heavy partying." When questioned about the extent of his drug use, he denied it was "any more or less than my friends I party with." There were no other alarming signs of other substance-related problems like DUI, or a poor academic performance that might strongly support a diagnosis of addiction, dependence, or even abuse. He readily admitted, though, that his father, a very successful physician, was a recovering alcoholic who regularly attended AA meetings. When asked by the therapist if he had ever wondered if he too might be an alcoholic like his father, the young man admitted that "the thought had crossed my mind." The therapist then suggested he might go to a few AA meetings and check to see

if he identified with the others or discovered for himself that he might indeed be an alcoholic like his father. Steve readily agreed.

When he returned for his next appointment later in the week, his mood had drastically changed. Steve had been to AA meetings every night since his appointment and had decided to telephone his father and speak to him about his drug use. His father, who had achieved sobriety through AA, was very supportive of him. The young man continued his weekly sessions and daily attendance at AA meetings until he graduated from college four months later. After graduation, Steve left the city to pursue a job outside the state.

Nearly three years later, after moving back to the city, he telephoned the therapist to set up an appointment. Upon entering the office, Steve quickly acknowledged that he was doing well and had successfully started a new job. Still sober and active in AA, he admitted that he had some gnawing doubts about his diagnosis and said the primary reason he set up this appointment was to question why the therapist had diagnosed him as an addict and alcoholic. He wondered if he should "try drinking alcohol again." Steve was somewhat alarmed and taken aback by the therapist's reply.

"I never diagnosed you as an alcoholic or addict; you did."

"What?" Steve stammered.

"I had only asked the question if it had ever crossed your mind that you might be an alcoholic," the therapist reminded him. "I only suggested you 'check it out' by attending a few AA meetings."

The young man sat back in his chair, speechless.

"In actuality, you had made a self-diagnosis," the therapist said.

It took a few minutes for Steve to absorb this realization. Eventually, he sat up and announced, "I don't think I'm an alcoholic anymore. What do you think I should do?"

Without batting an eye the therapist replied, "Well, you could always check it out."

Steve arched his eyebrow. "Check it out? How?"

"By drinking. I don't know any other way to be absolutely sure if someone is an alcoholic or not."

"Drinking?" Steve shook his head. "I don't know. What if I'm wrong?"

The therapist shrugged and gave him a wry, crooked smile.

Steve gradually acknowledged that the risk to discover if he was really an alcoholic by drinking again was too great. He had seen literally hundreds of people in the program return to the street or to drinking, and in every case the result was disastrous. By the end of the session, he concluded that the question of whether or not he was an alcoholic was not one he was willing to test empirically. "I can live with the doubt and uncertainty of whether my diagnosis was a correct one."

CHARACTER DEFECTS

In addition to the physical allergy to alcohol suggested by the disease model of alcoholism, alcoholics are held to possess an alcoholic personality described as immature and self-centered. They are spiritually sick, their naively egotistical and self-centered personalities preventing any but the most artificial and superficial relation to others or to a "higher power." Whereas society has irrevocably linked alcohol to the alcoholic, AA insists upon their separation. AA argues that individuals are alcoholics whether or not they drink and that their behavior may be that of a typical alcoholic even if they have not had a drink for years. AA is therefore aware that many drinkers, even heavy drinkers, are not necessarily alcoholics. Alcoholism from the program's perspective is a total lifestyle or mode of being and action in the world within which misuse of alcohol is but one component, albeit the most important component. Eliminating drinking is an indispensable first concern, but it is just the first step before altering other important aspects of the overall defective lifestyle. It is not uncommon to hear AA members refer to someone who has stopped drinking but still maintains the defective mode of life as being a "dry drunk."

From this perspective, alcoholism is viewed as more than

just excessive drinking. This is why AA believes that alcohol consumption cannot be curtailed without addressing and treating the rest of the alcoholic's personality disturbance. The difficulty that many have with AA's treatment approach centers around the issue of the necessity of total abstinence. While many therapists continue to view alcoholism as a focal disturbance that could be eliminated or cut out as you would cut out a bad spot in an otherwise good apple, AA views it as the primary issue that must be dealt with first. Abstinence from alcohol is the first step required for breaking the alcoholic style of living. Only after abstinence has been assured can alcoholics learn to focus on changing their characterological personality style.

Within this system, at any given moment, individuals are either healthy or unhealthy depending on which system is dominant. Drinking only encourages the unhealthy lifestyle to dominate the healthy potential within the alcoholic. As AA recognizes, alcoholics are isolated spiritually and can relate to others on only a superficial level. They cannot define themselves because their being is controlled and clouded by their drinking. Their alcoholism makes it impossible to relate to anyone or anything in a meaningful way.

NARRATIVES AND THE LIFE STORY

Within AA's therapy, the change needed to eliminate this mental and spiritual disequilibrium, which the program identifies as the heart of alcoholism, is more than just a shift in understanding the essence of the self. It requires a sharing with others of one's past. From its founding, the life story has been a key element of AA practice and theory. In the life story, the members recount their experience and eventual control of alcoholism. In most cases, if members were not physical derelicts at the time of their active alcoholism, the attempt is made to demonstrate that they were at least in a derelict frame of mind when drinking. And after accepting the program, many claim to have experienced personality changes, which accompany a new understanding of themselves and their world.

The life stories are typically stereotyped and lead to the conclusion of the proper way to analyze and construct one's past. Individuals' pasts are the means through which they attain control over their alcoholism. Through the stories, alcoholics come to understand their life as more intelligible; they view it within a different structure and logic than they had previously.

NARRATIVES AND ATTACHMENT

Thune's perspective on the telling of one's story has special relevance for the work on attachment and narrative styles. The work of Mary Main (1991) on attachment narratives has helped give new impetus to attachment research, moving it away from the exclusivity of children and applying it to the clinical realities of adult psychopathology. The Adult Attachment Interview (AAI) developed by Main and her colleagues is based not so much on content as on the form and structure of a subject's narrative style. The AAI was developed within a theoretical framework that predicts there would be similarity between attachment styles in childhood and narrative styles in adulthood. Main collected and measured narratives related to a person's relationship with parents and significant others, and to the person's history of losses and separation.

Four types of narrative styles have been identified:

1. *Secure-autonomous:* Subjects speak coherently, logically, and concisely about their past and its vicissitudes, however problematic or conflicted their history may be.
2. *Insecure-dismissive:* Subjects' narratives are unelaborated and unrevealing. They may deny any memories of childhood, or they will consistently claim that their parents were "wonderful" or "perfect" without producing relevant examples.
3. *Insecure-enmeshed:* Subjects are often bogged down with their history, telling rambling and inconclusive stories that sound as if their past difficulties are currently happening.
4. *Insecure-unresolved:* Subjects' descriptions are usually interrupted, fragmented, or fractured. They often contain elements of both of the other insecure narrative styles.

Fonagy and colleagues (1994) extended Main's work and found a strong relationship between attachment styles and a person's capacity to think about oneself in relation to others. They called this ability the reflexive self function (RSF), which reflects a person's capacity for inner speech and insight. The acquiring of inner speech means that a person is able to be intimate with oneself. Knowledge of self goes hand in hand with the development of empathy and knowledge of others. Evidence suggests that the capacity for RSF can develop only in a secure attachment relationship where the child does not have to be preoccupied with the availability or well-being of the mother. Fonagy and colleagues cite the child's ability to play alone in the mother's presence as one indication of secure attachment and competence. In a similar fashion, the developmentally arrested and insecurely attached patient who does not have to be preoccupied with the therapist is more likely to develop the capacity to be oneself in the presence of another. This reflects an important principle of development and emotional health: one cannot know oneself until one feels understood and known by another. Like Thune, Fonagy and colleagues are suggesting that all forms of good therapy (AA and psychodynamic theory) are more concerned with meaning rather than mechanism, coherence rather than correspondence, narrative rather than historical truth, and constructions rather than reconstructions.

Narratives generated in both therapy and in AA meetings serve intrapsychic as well as interpersonal functions. In particular, narratives often represent alcoholics' and addicts' attempt to establish a sense of coherence in their lived experience. It is important to think of narratives that the substance abuser presents as a representation in which events are organized in meaningful sequence. However, the interpersonal context of narrative stories can serve other purposes; they can be told to instruct, impress, implore, invite, test, or even distance the therapist. Thus it is useful to focus on the definition of the purpose of the narrative by considering what is included and what is left out. Kelly (1963) in his "fixed role enactment" postulated that any meaningful concept must have a contrast and that therapeutic narratives are no exceptions. His stance has particular importance when understanding the importance of the self-attribution of "alcoholic" or "addict."

SELF-ATTRIBUTION OF ALCOHOLISM

Next to the importance Thune places on the telling of one's life at an AA meeting, he views the constant introduction of oneself as an alcoholic as the next most essential component of the recovery program. Each self-proclamation of "I am an alcoholic" is a constant reminder to AA members that they are just a drink away from being the person they once were. This is a very confusing state of affairs to those whose interest in AA is only passing, superficial, or purely academic. They fail to understand the important significance of this ritual. Critics of AA often take special issue with the insistence that all AA members introduce themselves as alcoholics. Individuals outside of the AA program interpret this as degrading, serving only as a constant negative reminder of the alcoholic's shortcomings. They do not understand how such a requirement by the AA program can do anything but leave alcoholics feeling a sense of continual debasement and loss of self-respect. To the contrary, AA members who introduce themselves as alcoholics do so for they are conveying an important message to themselves each time they stand up and make such a proclamation. The self-attribution of alcoholic conveys far more information for the alcoholic in AA than it does for the individual outside the program who defines him- or herself as someone who once drank too much. The term *alcoholic* signifies everything (self-centered behavior, negative attitude, corrupt values) that sober AA members must guard against if they are to maintain a healthy sobriety. By constantly utilizing the self-definition of alcoholic, AA members automatically imply the opposite, which is everything a healthy, recovering, and sober member of AA must attain. AA members are thus reminded with each pronouncement of themselves as an alcoholic that they are just a drink away from losing what they have become, which is a person whose values, attitudes, and behavior is the direct opposite of that of an alcoholic.

From this perspective, the discovery of personal meaning and the experience of shared narratives between fellow alcoholics serve to firm up the attachment bond. As with good therapy, newly recovering alcoholics and addicts learn how to make better sense of themselves and their substance use. Narratives provide a containing boundary and a sense of continuity across time—a movement from the past, however painful, through the present toward the future. As sobriety is solidified over time, alcoholics and addicts are better able to look at not only how their substance use exacerbated the difficulties in their lives, but also how their difficulties with attachment contributed to their substance use.

9

Late-Stage Treatment Issues

> I began to think we can only get better having people around us who raise our good feelings.
>
> *George Eliot (1894)*

There is a big difference between *getting* sober or clean and *staying* sober or clean. Strategies for helping the alcoholic and addict maintain a lasting and satisfying recovery are far different from the strategies for initially achieving abstinence. Consequently, what substance abusers need from therapy during the first few weeks of treatment is far different from what they require three, six, or twelve months into recovery. If the way substance abusers establish and manage their interpersonal attachments is to be transformed, it is essential they learn new behaviors, values, and attitudes that are incompatible with the old drinking and drug-taking behaviors, values, and attitudes. Integration and assimilation into the twelve-step program and philosophy are crucial components of this process. Learning how to effectively use psychotherapy over the long term is another crucial component of their recovery process.

EMOTIONS: SELF-DISCOVERY AND SELF-CARE

The entire course of late-stage treatment can be defined as the successful establishment of empathic attachment relationships, while at the same time helping substance abusers become acquainted with their emotional selves. Until alcoholics and addicts develop the capacity to use their feelings as signals and to become emotionally intimate with themselves, they will continue to engage in their self-destructive and self-defeating behavior. Substance abusers typically lack the ability to take care of themselves or protect themselves from their own self-defeating actions. Because chemically dependent individuals have a deficient or underdeveloped capacity for identifying their feelings, they are often unable to tell when they feel tired, sick, hungry, anxious, or depressed. Along with their history of substance abuse, they usually have numerous other poor health habits; many smoke incessantly, do not exercise or over-exercise, have poor dietary regimens, and demonstrate an almost complete inability to relax and enjoy themselves. Such disturbances in self-care also lead individuals to fail to be aware, cautious, worried, or frightened enough to resist or avoid behavior that is self-injurious or damaging.

Ed Khantzian (1999), in an interview, described his initial discovery of the poor self-care habits of substance abusers:

> When I first began working with heroin-dependent patients coming to our methadone maintenance program at The Cambridge Hospital, I subjectively recoiled and at the same time was curious about patients' history of transitioning from smoking or swallowing their drugs to using them intravenously; the phenomenon was referred to as "crossing the needle barrier." Sitting with such patients, I would privately be thinking and feeling, "I am a physician and am used to administering drugs or drawing blood, but the idea of putting a needle in my own veins feels repugnant and dangerous." . . . I began to present variations of this reaction to patients, asking one patient after another how they felt or thought about using a needle for the first time. . . . Namely, they neither thought much about nor experienced any emotional reaction that remotely approached my level of concern about the significance of using a needle for the first time. While extreme, this failure to be aware of the danger is an example of what I witness over and over again with my patients. Even when [patients are] abstinent, it is essential to repeatedly review the consequences of both the lack of anticipatory apprehension and the failure to think through or be mindful of their actions when their well-being depends on it. [pp. 11–12]

Because they were often poorly parented as children and since many come from alcoholic or dysfunctional families, they are inadequately prepared to properly evaluate the consequences of risky or self-defeating behavior. They are constantly placing themselves in potentially destructive and dangerous circumstances. Unsatisfying and dysfunctional interpersonal relationships are the norm for them. Khantzian (1982) sees this inability for self-care as developmentally determined. Referring to the work of Mahler (1968) and other developmental theorists, he contends, "They emphasize the importance developmentally of optimal parental nurturances and protection early in children's development for the establishment of this function, and how extremes of deprivation or indulgence have devastating consequences for the development of this capacity" (p. 589).

Lucy had more than ten years of sobriety and was actively involved in AA when she sought psychotherapy because of a recent sexual assault. The referring intake counselor at the rape-counseling center was concerned about the absence of the typical response patterns seen in most rape victims and recommended she see a therapist who specialized in both alcoholism and trauma survivors.

When the therapist opened the door to his waiting room, he was surprised to discover a young attractive woman in her late twenties. He had expected someone with ten plus years of recovery to be much older. Lucy presented in a polite and pleasant manner, speaking softly and coherently. Her affect, though somewhat subdued for someone who had recently been assaulted, was appropriate and consistent with her circumstances. When asked how she was feeling, Lucy shrugged her shoulders and forced a weak smile. "Oh, I've been through a lot worse."

Seeing the therapist's reaction, Lucy leaned forward to assure him. "Oh, don't worry about me. What happened the other night was terrible, but you'll find that I'm a very strong person. It takes a lot to destroy me."

Lucy proceeded to describe a series of events throughout her life that did verify she had indeed "been through a lot worse." She confessed that she had been considering psychotherapy for a couple of years because of the prolonged unhappiness in her life. "Maybe this rape will turn out to be a good thing if it ends up pushing me into therapy to deal with my past."

Over the course of the next few months, her therapist learned that Lucy had grown up with a violent alcoholic mother and a sexually seductive father who provided her with drugs when she was a young adolescent in return for her sexual favors. "My dad was at least kind and paid attention to me even though he used me sexually. My mother was just awful, beating me and my sister during her drunken rages."

Although the circumstances in Lucy's life were horrific, she always relayed their occurrences with a sense of pride. She spoke admiringly of her strength when, at the age of 16, she threatened her father with exposure to the police if he didn't stop abusing her, and she promptly entered AA, never using drugs again. However, a series of abusive relationships with men followed her throughout her young adult life. "But each time," Lucy proudly proclaimed, "I was able to handle whatever they had to dish out and always got out of the relationship, eventually."

As therapy progressed, her therapist helped Lucy identify a destructive pattern to her relationships and the "rules" that governed her attachment style. Lucy's poor self-care abilities were reflective of the neglect, abuse, and exploitation she experienced repeatedly at the hands of her parents. Lucy's passivity and lack of alarm with dangerous people or perilous situations were indications of a defensive position that reflected the attitude that "since no one cares what happens to me or wants to help or protect me, it (substitute "I don't matter") doesn't matter; it's (I'm) no big deal. Her tendency to let others' needs be more important than her own served to reinforce Lucy's investment in an identity that took pride in not needing anyone's protection or help. Consequently, Lucy often failed to keep herself out of harm's way, frequently ignoring signals that certain people and situations might be dangerous.

> Getting Lucy to surrender what Aledort (2002) calls the "heroic position" required years of therapy. Before she could give up the "bad fit" (e.g., like someone wearing a pair of ill-fitting shoes or tight jacket, the person forces his or her body to adapt to the "bad fit." While the individual's body adjusts to the adaptation that he or she is forced to make, it comes at a price. Because of the adjustment to the "bad fit," the individual will likely avoid a "good fit" [e.g., someone who is responsive, loving, and caring] because it doesn't feel normal). Lucy needed to develop a new identity that did not require self-sacrifice or the capacity for endurance of trauma as the primary source of her self-esteem.

During the later stages of recovery, helping the addict and alcoholic with self-care deficiencies becomes important for a number of reasons. Relapses are always of primary concern during treatment and are often related to difficulties with self-care. Substance abusers are usually unable to use their feelings as signals and guides in managing their internal world or protecting themselves against its instability and chaos. This disturbance in the regulation of affect manifests as "an inability to identify and verbalize feelings, an intolerance or incapacity for anxiety and depression, an inability to modulate feelings . . . and extreme manifestations of affect, such as hypomania, phobic-anxious states, panic and lability" (Khantzian 1982, p. 590). If they should return to using substances, it will only deteriorate their existing capacity for self-regulation even further.

LATER-STAGE RELAPSES

The road to recovery requires a careful balance between affect release and affect containment. Since rapid switches in affect states can be potentially destructive, substance abusers' feelings must be delicately managed until they have enough sobriety and emotional stability to tolerate a closer look at their defective attachment styles. While there are a myriad of factors that contribute to the early-stage relapses, late-stage relapses are primarily dominated by two related variables: the potential for a relapse is increased whenever the substance abuser feels *too good* or *too bad* too quickly.

Feeling too good too quickly can be a signal that the old narcissistic defenses have returned. If these feelings are left unchecked, the substance abuser will soon be thinking, "I got this thing licked, I'm special. I'm different." Grandiosity and a sense of specialness have the corrosive capacity to erode the humility that keeps alcoholics' and addicts' substance use in check. As sobriety provides them with the opportunity to marshal the creative forces and energies that were sedated into submission, they rediscover their lost capacity for achievement and success. It is as easy for alcoholics and addicts to attribute all their success to their own special uniqueness as it is for them to harshly attribute and blame themselves completely for any failure or mistake. As their accomplishments accumulate, they become just as vulnerable to the intoxication of success as they were to the intoxication of drugs and alcohol. It is a short step from being too busy with "important things," to skipping meetings, to "I can't be one of them" or "I have this thing licked." A few successes with controlled drinking or recreational substance use helps solidify the new appraisal of themselves as "unique and different." The inevitable relapse is slowly but methodically set in motion.

At the other end of the spectrum is the recovering addict or alcoholic who feels too bad for too long. Even though substance abusers are able to maintain abstinence, they do it without experiencing relief from the dysphoria that continued sobriety usually brings to many alcoholics or addicts. Serenity and contentment eludes them even if they work the steps of the program. A careful assessment is often necessary to ensure that they are not just "white knuckling" it. Are they really into recovery? Specifically, are they working the steps and attending meetings? Do they have a sponsor? Are they practicing honest self-exploration and actively participating in a home group? Sometimes, despite all these efforts, many twelve-step members continue to feel worse. Sobriety and AA does not bring them any long-standing benefit. They feel only the deprivation of relief provided by self-medication (drugs and alcohol). Slowly but steadily, the steadfast resolve that they would never drink or do drugs again is gradually eroded by the gnawing desperation and hopelessness that dominates their existence. Eventually, they cease to care about their sobriety because their life ceases to have any meaningful purpose. Apathy in the form of "I don't give a damn" is a dangerous position for a recovering addict or alcoholic to reach. It is a short distance from "I don't give a damn" to "I might as well be drinking; it can't be any worse than this."

ANHEDONIA AND ADDICTION

By the time alcoholics and addicts have entered treatment, their substance abuse history has robbed them of any capacity for enjoyment, other than the momentary reprieve that alcohol or drugs provide them. The novice therapist will soon discover that alcoholics and addicts do not possess the capacity to experience joy, pleasure, or happiness. Drugs are virtually the only way they can obtain gratification and relief from distressful affective states. Krystal (1982) views this as a consequence of infantile traumatization resulting in a "doomsday" orientation, involving a constant dreaded expectation of the return of the unbearable traumatic state. Such individuals will then keep themselves very active for they fear slowing down, lest their expected catastrophe occur. Krystal (1982) discusses the importance of this in treatment:

> There is hardly any knowledge about how to help the patients to cultivate their capacity for pleasure and joy. This problem is an especially serious one in dealing with the alcoholic professional, such as the alcoholic physician. These individuals tend to present a combination of severe compulsiveness, "work addiction," and anhedonia underlying their problem drinking. The drug is often used to maintain a severe machine-like self-control regime. Many of these patients maintain for a long time a very high degree of success in their professional and business careers. Their "superb" adjustment to reality is actually part of the "operative" life style. [p. 615]

LATE-STAGE TREATMENT CONCERNS

Once the therapist has used the power and the leverage of the attachment relationship to help substance abusers internalize their responsibility for abstinence from alcohol and drugs, the therapist must then help them come to terms with the internal deficits that contribute to their substance abuse. This is not usually possible until substance abusers have had enough time and distance from their use of substances to allow their cognitive processes to stabilize and their emotional lability to be contained. It is during this stage of treatment that they can more readily explore and understand the relationship between their use of substances to regulate their affect and their difficulty with attachment.

This understanding, however, does not come through explanations or even insight; it evolves out of the regulatory power of the attachment relationship. Talking, of course, is an important component of the attachment experience. But explanations alone aren't enough to propel the attachment process to its necessary heights. "Speech is a fancy neocortical skill," Lewis and colleagues (2000) state, "but therapy belongs to the older realm of the emotional mind, the limbic brain. Patients are often hungry for *explanations*, because they are used to thinking that neocortical contraptions like explication will help them. But insight is the popcorn of therapy. Where patient and therapist *go* together, the irreducible totality of their mutual journey is the movie" (p. 179).

THE IMPORTANCE OF THE THERAPEUTIC ALLIANCE

There are a myriad of approaches to treatment for nonaddicted as well as addicted patients. Research is conducted and volumes are written suggesting why one method of treatment is preferable to another. The Project MATCH study (1997) was the latest large-scale venture that sought to identify what variables best contributed to successful treatment of substance abusers. Rigorous applications of procedures were carefully monitored to ensure that therapist activity was standardized and some measure of adherence was maintained across different procedures. One unavoidable pitfall is that researchers in their zeal to standardize treatment sometimes go to considerable lengths to eliminate the therapist as a person and central agent of change. In the process, the therapist variable can be compromised, even though this variable accounts for the greatest outcome variance in successful treatment. Unfortunately many empirically validated therapies suffer from a propensity to depict therapists as disembodied individuals who perform procedures only on axis I disorders. This stands in marked contrast to the seasoned clinician's experience of psychotherapy as an intensely interpersonal and affective pursuit with another person whose diagnostic category is often shifting as treatment evolves. The inescapable fact is that the therapist and the relationship can be as empirically validated as the standardized applications of psychotherapy treatments.

Robust research findings suggest repeatedly that a positive therapeutic alliance, which can be viewed as secure attachment, is the best overall predictor of good outcome in all forms of psychotherapy. The emphasis on the significance of the attachment bond is another way to speak of the strength of the therapeutic alliance. Nowhere is this truer than with the addicted patient, and nowhere is this more difficult to maintain than with the substance-using individual. Stone (1996) states that many clients are compelled to "test" the therapist to ascertain whether they will be traumatized in the present (usually abandoned or punished for not behaving) as they were in the past by their earliest caregivers.

The therapeutic alliance is an especially slippery slope to manage when the compromising effect that substance use has on the attachment relationship is carefully considered. Not only does the use of neurotoxic chemicals erode a person's capacity to bond and manage the give and take required in relationships, but the dangerous and potentially lethal consequences of an addict's or alcoholic's behavior can sometimes require a therapist to take actions that may irreparably alter the strength of the therapeutic alliance.

Hank was a married, 32-year-old father of two small children whose wife sought couple's therapy because of his escalating alcohol use and series of job losses. At the first session she announced that she had been going to Al-Anon for six months and was ready to "bail out of this marriage unless he does something about his drinking." Hank readily admitted his alcoholism, adding, "My father has been in AA for years. I've known for a long while that I'm one just like him. I just haven't wanted to do anything about it."

Hank readily complied to go to AA if his wife didn't leave him. She consented not to file for divorce if he also sought therapy. They agreed that it would be better if he continued individual therapy rather than they both continue seeing the therapist for couple's counseling.

The next six months produced a dramatic shift in Hank's depression, marriage, and job situation. His wife's uncle found him a job in his company, and within three months Hank's performance won him a quick promotion to a sales manager position. Weekly therapy sessions and daily AA meetings became a staple of Hank's newly built life. However, Hank gradually began to miss his weekly therapy sessions, frequently calling at the last minute or failing to give any notice. When Hank did show for appointments, he was usually late and evasive during the session. Questions about his sobriety were met with confirmations that he was sober and still actively going to meetings. He assured the therapist that "I never felt better in my life."

The missed sessions increased in frequency and after not hearing from Hank in nearly a month, the therapist received a call one evening from his distraught wife.

"Listen, I know because of patient confidentiality, you can't tell me anything about my husband's therapy. But you can at least listen to what I have to say. Hank is sitting here on the couch, drunk as a skunk. He gave me permission to call you. His drinking is completely out of control, he's been having hallucinations, and I'm afraid he's going to go into DTs. He refuses to go to the hospital and I don't know what to do."

"Will Hank talk to me?" the therapist asked.

After a short silence his wife returned to the phone.

"No, he's in no shape to talk with anyone. He said you can talk with me, though."

"Can you both come in to see me first thing in the morning?"

"He's shaking his head no, says he doesn't want to talk with anyone." Her voice took on a panic sense of urgency. "Can I come in to see you with my uncle and Hank's parents tomorrow. His father's in the program and he says Hank's going to kill himself drinking if we don't do something soon. We're all at our wits' end and scared as hell."

The therapist hesitated before answering, weighing the delicate ethical dilemma before him. "Can you ask Hank if he has any objections if I meet you with all tomorrow?"

Hank picked up the phone and slurred into the receiver. "Sure, Doc, it don't make no goddamn to me who you talk to." The phone crashed to the floor.

"Sorry," his wife announced. "He just dropped the phone on the floor. We'll see you in the morning and bring Hank if he's in any shape to come."

The therapist met with them in the morning. Descriptions of Hank's behavior convinced the therapist that Hank's drinking had reached frightening and life-threatening proportions. The therapist quickly educated the family members, including the wife's uncle, who was also Hank's boss, about their options. The therapist walked them through the steps involved in an intervention at an out-of-state treatment program. They all agreed that that sounded like their best option. Assured that all the booze had been removed from the house and that the car keys were locked safely away, Hanks' parents and wife felt confident that they could get Hank to the next session without him drinking for the next twenty-four hours.

They brought Hank to the emergency session on Saturday morning. As planned, suitcases were packed, air tickets were purchased, and admission and insurance forms were filled out and ready to go. Hank's wife threatened immediate divorce and the uncle warned of instantaneous termination of the job unless Hank went directly

> from the therapist's office and voluntarily signed himself into treatment. A tearful, remorseful, and inebriated Hank readily agreed.
>
> Hank returned from the program five weeks later. He called the therapist, as he had been instructed to do by the hospital. They conversed uncomfortably on the phone for a few minutes before Hank said he would call back and schedule an appointment in a few days.
>
> Two weeks passed before Hank scheduled a meeting. At the session, Hank remained guarded and withholding. He did, however, schedule another appointment. Gradually, over the course of the next two months the therapist worked hard to repair the damage done by his participation in the intervention. As Hank's sobriety and attendance at AA strengthened, he was able to work through his anger and feeling of betrayal. His injury was lessened by the realization that the therapist's actions probably saved his life. It took months of hard work, but the rupture in the therapeutic alliance was eventually mended.

The inability to establish long-lasting gratifying relationships is directly related to the quality of early attachment experiences (Main 1996). Attachment-oriented therapy can be defined as a way of eliciting, exploring, integrating, and modifying attachment styles represented within a person's internal working model. Object relations theory has taught us that introjected self and object representations carry within them intense affect and that these internalized introjects contribute to people's propensity to project their internal experience onto the external world (Ogden 1982). Through the power of projective identification, we can coerce, induce, and provoke others in our external world to fit our internal expectations. This becomes a "life script," a self-fulfilling prophecy that drives the person's interpersonal interactions in such a way that his external world begins to conform or fit his internal expectations and experiences. Paradoxically, a perverse sense of comfort results from the familiarity of the experience, which serves to satisfy the need or drive for consistency, thus reducing anxiety temporarily.

Eventually substance abusers must come to terms with

their character pathology and their inability to establish and maintain healthy intimate relationships. The therapist must remain aware of the dysfunctional care-eliciting strategies that substance abusers developed early in life and assimilated into their character structure. This becomes an important focus in the later stages of treatment because the inability to establish healthy relationships is a major contributing factor to relapses and the return to substance use. As Khantzian and colleagues (1990) stated, "While it is the drug-taking that initially brings the person to treatment, it is the treatment of character that leads not only to giving up drugs, but also to profound change in one's experience of self and world. . . . Ultimately we view the treatment of character disorder as the royal road to recovery from addiction."

MUTUALITY AND DEPENDENCE

In a mature developing attachment relationship, one in which the substance abuser has had the opportunity to achieve some degree of sobriety and abstinence, a strategy that focuses on the here-and-now relationship is likely to be beneficial. Since increased abstinence will free substance abusers from their preoccupation with withdrawal and craving, they will be able to tolerate an approach that is less gratifying and more demanding than one used earlier in treatment. The ultimate aim of treatment at this stage is to help the addict or alcoholic develop the capacity for interpersonal intimacy, so the skills associated with this capacity can be generalized and applied outside the therapy session in the real world.

Developing the capacity for interpersonal intimacy is no spectator sport. It requires, as Lewis and colleagues (2000) state, "the messy experience of yanking and tinkering that comes from a limbic bond." They describe what is required of an attuned therapist:

> An attuned therapist feels the lure of a patient's limbic Attractors. He doesn't just hear about an emotional life—the two of them *live* it. The gravitational tug of this patient's emotional world draws him away from his own, just as it should. A determined

> therapist does not strive to have a good relationship with his patient—it can't be done. If a patient's emotional mind would support good relationships, he or she would be out having them. Instead a therapist loosens his grip on his own world and drifts, eyes open, into whatever relationship the patient has in mind—even a connection so dark that it touches the worst in him. He has no alternative. When he stays outside the other's world, he cannot affect it; when he steps within its range, he feels the force of alien Attractors. He takes up temporary residence in another's world not just to observe but to alter, and in the end, to overthrow. Through the intimacy a limbic exchange affords, therapy becomes the ultimate inside job. [p. 178]

Competent therapists can engage their patients on an emotional level without getting completely swept away by the emotional current of the patient's projective identification. "The therapist who cannot engage in this open adventure of exploration will fail to grasp the other's essence. His very preconception about how a person *should* feel risks misleading him as to how that person *does* feel. When he stops sensing with his limbic brain, a therapist is fatally apt to substitute inference for resonance" (Lewis et al. 2000, p. 183).

During this final stage of treatment, the therapist functions as a *transformational object*—a source for continual interactive relationships that provide the environmental backdrop onto which the old self can be transformed into a new self. *Old self* and *new self* are concepts put forth by Shane and colleagues (1997) to refer to *relational configurations* that are internalized representational models that influence old constricting patterns of relating.

A new sense of self must be established if the substance abuser's typical cycle of ineffective attachment, conflict, alienation, and isolation is to be altered. The substance abuser's sense of self must not remain tied to "the old self in relation to the old other." It must be transformed, through the attachment experience, to reflect a new and different way of being in relationship with another. Shane and colleagues (1997) describe the three different relational configurations involved in the transformational experience:

1. *Old self with old other:* Self and other are experienced in a repetition of patterns categorized on the basis of past traumatic relationships—the old traumatized self with the old traumatizing other. This configuration represents transference in their model.
2. *Old self with the new other:* The old self continues to categorize the self predominately in old, familiar traumatized ways, but begins to experience the other as a transforming object. The new other is experienced, as much as possible, as someone who operates primarily in the service of the self's well-being and is not based on templates from the past. Secure attachment, affect regulation, emotional resonance, attunement, and empathy are all used to accomplish this end. One primary task of the transformational object is to avoid falling victim to the old self's projective identification, therefore resisting the pull to treat the old self in ways that repeats past trauma.
3. *New self with the new other:* The new self experiences the self and other in novel ways that are not based on the traumatogenic past. As the new self consolidates, it develops the capacity to experience the new other as an *interpersonal-sharing other,* which is the final stage in the development of mature mutuality.

The self evolves and consolidates in development through the dimensions of intimacy made available through attachment. Creating the capacity for attachment by reaching the alienated self is crucial because it reactivates the developmental course toward self and self-with-other consolidation that trauma has disrupted. Once the self has been activated through an attachment relationship, the emergence, evolution, and consolidation of a new self can be completed if the environmental responses remain consistently nurturing and reparative. Gradually, the old self consolidation, established out of necessity through self-protective strategies, can be relinquished as the old relational configuration is exchanged for a new one.

The required transformation of the self is a theme that AA

has long recognized. The program knows that most alcoholics commonly stop consuming alcohol from time to time. Their real problem has always been staying off alcohol, while at the same time finding meaning and contentment in life. Many addicts, recovering from all types of addictive diseases, described their lives as being meaningless and hollow. Until Alcoholics Anonymous was founded in the 1930s, the gnawing problem for abstinent alcoholics was that their lives felt empty when alcohol was removed. The stories of the first alcoholics in AA demonstrated that to truly recover from addiction, one must undergo a transformation. Transformations are the most complex type of change—a radical reorientation of what the person believes and how he lives his life. Because Alcoholics Anonymous and other early treatment programs had the aura of a religious sect, its devotees sometimes appear to be "saved" from their alcoholism. This aura was a product of the transformations that most alcoholics must make to maintain their recovery.

SUMMARY OF TREATING ADDICTION AS AN ATTACHMENT DISORDER

Looking at addiction from an attachment disorder perspective has important implications for treatment. Here is a summary of the principles that guide attachment-oriented addiction treatment:

1. Attachment theory challenges the myth that human beings can regulate their own emotions. People, for better or for worse, are emotional regulators of each other.
2. Attachment cannot be reduced to a secondary drive. Human beings, like all social mammals, are biologically hard-wired to need people. Natural selection favored mechanisms that promoted parent–offspring proximity in an environment of evolutionary adaptation. Because of their ability to keep caregivers in close proximity during times of threat and stress, human beings survived as a species.

3. Secure attachment liberates. The stronger the earliest attachment experience, the less a person will require excessive sources of external affect regulation. Mental health is a substance that attracts itself as readily as money or power: the more of it people have, the more they can acquire what they need in their adult life. Human beings who are loved and responded to by good-enough parenting acquire a consolidated self over the course of their development. If children have been the recipient of another person's consistent interest and love, the more skills and confidence they will have in their capacity to evoke responsiveness from others. Consequently, adult relationships will be more satisfying and rewarding, decreasing the likelihood that a person will be compelled to turn to substances for this regulatory function.
4. Those who develop dysfunctional or insecure attachment styles will be more vulnerable and more likely to turn to other sources of external regulation like substances or other obsessive-compulsive behaviors. Intimate long-standing relationships are an integral part of human nature, and the inability to establish long-lasting, gratifying relationships is directly related to the quality of the earliest attachment experience.
5. Because prolonged substance abuse can produce alterations in a vulnerable person's brain, addiction can be viewed as a misguided attempt at self-repair. The toxic consequences of chemical use exacerbate existing attachment and interpersonal difficulties, further compromising any interpersonal skills the person may have possessed early in one's substance using career.
6. Until healthy forms of affect regulation are developed, the addicted individual will always be vulnerable to substitute one addiction for another. Paradoxically, addicted individuals will never be unable to discover other forms of affect regulation as long as they stay attached to substances.
7. Early treatment first requires that addicts or alcoholics detach from the object of their addiction (i.e., substances). Since relationships can also become addictive,

the substance abuser must learn how to choose better lovers and friends. They must also learn how, through the power of projective identification and the repetition compulsion, they train people to treat them as they were treated in the past.

8. Long-term treatment requires that patients' internal working model be altered in a way that transforms the implicit rules that guide all their intimate relationships. Therapy from this standpoint becomes a reparative experience geared toward addressing the vulnerable individual's developmental arrestment. Character pathology is treated and the capacity for mutuality and conflict resolution is established. Since the need for attachment and selfobject responsiveness is not phase specific but a lifelong process, the ultimate aim of treatment is intended to accomplish the following goals:

    a. Archaic needs are met in a way that fosters the building of psychic structure.

    b. Once archaic needs are relinquished for more mature ways of getting healthy needs met, patients accept their need for selfobjects to keep the self functioning at an optimal level.

    c. Mental health is recognized as the ability to use available selfobjects to fulfill the needs of the self.

    d. The person eventually develops the capacity to recover quickly from small injuries, slights, and other narcissistic injuries or empathic failures.

10

Attachment and Group Therapy

We can do what I couldn't.
Alcoholic Anonymous

Attachment theory applied to addiction and group therapy has important implications for people who strive for independence, autonomy, and self-sufficiency, but all too often at the cost of alienation from self and others. Nowhere is this difficulty played out with more consistency than with substance abusers. Addicts and alcoholics are notoriously counterdependent individuals, living their lives in the extreme ends of the attachment–individuation continuum. Autonomy is purchased at the price of alienation and the absence of mutuality in their relationships. As Nicola Diamond (1996) points out, group therapy not only represents a movement away from one-person psychology, but also contains a fundamental interpersonal conception of human beings as always being situated in relations with others. Group therapy, like attachment theory, is based on the implied notion that the essence of being human is social, not individual.

GROUP TREATMENT OF SUBSTANCE ABUSE

Substance abuse treatment and group therapy have shared two separate but similar developments over the past forty years. First is the rapid increase in the use of drugs and alcohol in our society and the subsequent influence this has had on the rising number of individuals requiring treatment for addiction and substance abuse–related disorders. Second, as this phenomenon of escalating alcohol and drug use in our culture has evolved, so too has there been an evolution in the acceptance and recognition of group therapy as a viable, and often preferred, method of treatment for a growing number of psychological problems and emotional difficulties. Much in the same way that the medical delivery system in our society has come to recognize the alarming increase of substance abuse–related disorders, treatment specialists have come to recognize the unique benefits that can be derived from employing group therapy in a variety of settings with a wide diversity of patients. Complementing these separate but parallel developments is the growing acceptance of group therapy as the treatment of choice for substance abuse and addiction. Besides the countless number of private practice outpatient therapy groups offering treatment for this population, there are an abundance of therapy groups operating within a prodigious number of treatment facilities. It is rare, if not impossible, to find any inpatient or outpatient substance abuse treatment program that does not employ group therapy as an essential component of its treatment regimen.

AA AND GROUP THERAPY

Addiction treatment has been intricately associated with group therapy for more than sixty years. Ever since alcoholism was first recognized as a diagnostic entity, its treatment has been provided in groups. Starting with Alcoholics Anonymous' establishment of the twelve-step group movement in the 1930s, addiction treatment has shared a synchronicity and compatibility with group therapy. Unlike the situation with many other diagnostic categories, group therapy has never had to fight to prove its legitimacy as a viable treatment modality. Addiction treatment specialists usually have embraced group therapy with open arms and historically have welcomed group therapy as an intricate and valuable part of their treatment regimen.

Group therapy and addiction treatment have been drawn to each other because of a very simple principle: substance abusers usually respond favorably to group treatment and are more likely to stay sober and committed to abstinence when treatment is provided in groups. Any treatment modality that facilitates detachment from chemicals and attachment to abstinence will enhance treatment success. Remaining attached to therapy underlies a singularly influential principle of addiction treatment: successful addiction treatment is dose related—the longer the treatment, the better the prognosis. Group therapy, through the curative forces of affiliation, confrontation, support, gratification, and identification, promotes attachment more favorably than do other forms of treatment.

Despite group therapy's wide popularity in addiction treatment, the reasons for its preference have not always been clearly articulated or presented within a clear, comprehensive theoretical formula. A theoretical perspective is needed that explains why the inherent dynamics of the addiction process lends itself in a complementary fashion to the innate qualities of the therapeutic factors operating in a group. Such an explanation is important, because the same forces that contribute to the addictive process can be harnessed to provide its resolution if one is aware of the reasons why addiction manifests itself as it does. Attachment theory provides a theoretical foundation for such an understanding.

INDIVIDUAL VS. GROUP THERAPY

Group therapy is often the preferred mode of treatment because individual therapy can sometimes be too threatening for addicts or alcoholics. They cannot tolerate the stimulation of their dependency yearnings, nor can they handle the hostility that will inevitably surface and threaten the continuity of the relationships. Nevertheless, alcoholics and addicts must establish a capacity to relate to others on a meaningful level. They must be helped to achieve an appropriate dependent relationship without the crippling interference of their own hostility and fear of closeness. Only under the sway of their wish to please others and be with others can they identify and achieve a more stable, internalized set of values patterned after the model set by those trying to help them.

> Jim, an alcoholic with over three years of sobriety, had been in an outpatient group for nearly ten months.

Despite his involvement in AA and the group, Jim continued to live alone and showed little progress in establishing relationships with anyone in or out of the program. It was only within the last two months that he had begun to demonstrate a willingness to engage the group and its members, even though his engagement stayed limited to talking about himself instead of talking with others. During the course of the evening he began to speak to the group about his isolation and history of being ignored by his parents as a child. After Jim stated bitterly, "I don't think anyone in my family ever gave a damn about me," the group leader asked Jim if he was feeling ignored in group right now and if he thought anybody in here "gave a damn about you." Jim said he didn't expect anyone in the group to care about him anymore than anyone else in his life did. A number of group members responded to Jim at this point to say they had grown fond of Jim over the last few months and that they were touched by his story and what his home must have been like for him as a child. Ignoring their responses, Jim proceeded to return to the subject of his past isolation. The group leader stopped him and asked Sally, one of the group members who had tried to respond to Jim, if she thought he had noticed her efforts to relate to him. Sally replied, "No, I don't think he did." Another group member agreed with Sally and said that he felt the same way. "In fact," he added, "I'm feeling ignored by you right now, Jim. It's as if my efforts to relate to you don't matter to you."

Jim protested before adding, "You don't understand. If I let you matter to me, I can't take you home with me when I leave here. I still have to go home alone to an empty house. It's like you're offering me one potato chip, when I want the whole bag. All one potato chip will do is make me hungry for more and remind me of what I don't have in my life."

The group leader then encouraged Jim to take advantage of the opportunity not to be alone here in group right now and to look at ways that he may be contributing to his isolation. At this point, the group leader asked another group member, who had been quietly nodding her head in agreement as Jim spoke, if she wanted to tell Jim what she

> was agreeing with. With a little encouragement, she quickly added, "I think I know exactly how you must feel, Jim. I have this huge empty cavern inside of me that feels like a bottomless pit. One show of warmth or compassion will just ricochet off the empty walls and does little to make the emptiness go away. Consequently, I can do exactly what I see you doing in here. I push people away who are trying to relate to me."

The group approach and Alcoholics Anonymous are effective for a number of reasons. First, by virtue of the number of group and AA members, it dilutes the intensity of feelings that otherwise inundates the patient in a one-to-one setting. Thus, alcoholics or addicts can spread their attachments to several people. The group offers alcoholics and addicts a way of dealing with the intense hostility and ambivalence in their relationships by supplying them with a number of figures on whom they can depend or direct their anger. Their fear of closeness, hostility, and dependence is therefore not as severely threatened.

Thus, the structure of the group and its relationship to AA permit maintenance of the splitting defense as long as needed. Of similar impact is the response of the group leader, who, by his or her firm yet nonhostile ability to absorb anger, can lay the foundation for later identifications. The group and AA can also provide an alternative to the alcoholic's and addict's lifestyle in the bars and on the streets. This is an alternative that can supply the need for a transitional object and thereby pave the way for the development of a more stable and adequate sense of object constancy.

This is where the group and the AA program can become the opportune agent of change in the chemically dependent individual's life. Much as the scrap of blanket or teddy bear serves the infant, the group and AA program allow the individual to begin the strenuous business of movement toward autonomy and separation. The group can become the transitional object for addicts and alcoholics who are seeking to emancipate themselves from their symbiotic tie to their drugs and alcohol as well as their selfobject.

Kosseff (1975) outlines the transitional qualities of the group in this process of internalization:

1. The group is a tangible representation of the relationship between the patient and the therapist. However, the patient is protected from the intensity of the dependency on the therapist because it is transferred to the group.
2. The group carries a degree of separation from the therapist and allows the patient a combination of support and freedom that the dyadic relationship does not provide.
3. The group is a bulwark against too great feelings of frustration and fear of punishment if the patient should function autonomously. The group offers its support of other members as an alternative to dependence on one object.
4. The group provides a "space between" the therapist and patients and allows an area of freedom for patients to fill creatively. They can use the group as they choose, relaxing or tightening their relationships with the therapist and splitting their transferential identification as they need.
5. The group serves as a convoy in patients' efforts to deal with their internalized bad objects.
6. The group as a "good-enough facilitating environment" substitutes for and also denies the possibility of being controlled by or controlling the therapist.
7. As patients give up their internal distortions of the therapist, with the help of the group they become more able to differentiate reality from distortion. Boundaries between group leader and patient become firmer.
8. The group as transitional object promotes the emergence of the real self and facilitates the mastery of the self as the patient experiments with objects in a new way. Giving and receiving empathy, reassurance, understanding, and self-assertion in group leads to freeing of impulses, and the capacity for greater closeness emerges.

ROLE OF THE GROUP LEADER

The task of group leaders is to ensure that the group members maintain abstinence while providing them with the opportunity to experience enough anxiety and frustration to promote the emergence of their typical destructive and maladaptive characterological patterns and coping styles. At the same time, enough support and gratification is required to ensure that they will not act out either in group (minimizing destructive transference distortions and pathological projective identification) or outside of group (dropping out of group or returning to alcohol or drug use to help manage painful affect) until they learn how to cope with adversity and stress in a more productive manner. Alcoholics and substance abusers usually do not respond well to passive or emotionally withholding group leaders or to strategies that do not provide emotional gratification, support, and responsiveness.

Generally, addicted patients do not handle well the regressive pull that can be experienced in group if the group leader utilizes techniques that are applicable to Tavistock or classic psychodynamic theory as outlined by Bion (1961), Ezriel (1973), or Rice (1965). This is not to imply that the group leader ensures that the group and its members are gratified in an infantile manner. Not only is this unrealistic, antitherapeutic, and ultimately impossible, it feeds the group members' narcissism and omnipotent expectations for immediate gratification. Rather, establishing a climate of *optimal frustration* provides the delicate balance necessary to ensure that enough of the alcoholics' and substance abusers' dependency needs are met until they are able to gradually internalize control over their own destructive impulses and emotions.

To attain this end, group leaders must be more active and gratifying than they would be if they were treating nonaddicted patients. Yalom's (1985) emphasis on cohesion as an important curative factor takes on added significance when working with this population. Following Pines's (1998) suggestions, good-enough selfobject bonds or attachments need to be created with the group so the group itself becomes a selfobject. Group cohesion and attachment are essentially intertwined and necessary if the group is to provide the support and gratification required during early recovery. Arensberg (1998) agrees: "Obviously, for a group to work, a good-enough and safe-enough environment and group composition must exist" (p. 21). The creation of a climate that fosters understanding of self and self in relation to others helps group members understand the ways that their narcissistic vulnerabilities and difficulties with attachment can lead to alcohol and drug use.

GROUP COHESION

The concept of cohesion plays a dominant role in attachment-oriented group psychotherapy, not only during the early stages of group development but throughout the entire course of addiction treatment. Relationships—or more correctly, the alcoholic's and addict's inability to establish healthy affect regulating attachments—are key factors in both the etiology and resolution of addictive disorders. Group psychotherapy, with its myriad of relationship possibilities—member-to-member, member-to-group, and member-to-leader—provides a vehicle that not only reveals deficits in the individual member's attachment styles, but also more importantly furnishes a therapeutic culture that can be reparative. The optimal culture and emotional atmosphere that the group leader looks to establish is one that is cohesive.

The concept of cohesion is central to understanding the significance that this construct plays in successful group treatment with all diagnostic categories, not just substance abusers. Cohesion refers to those factors that define the essence of all attachment relationships that get established in group and that provide the necessary context within which therapy or treatment occurs. Cohesion is to group psychotherapy what the therapeutic alliance is to individual therapy. Just as treatment effectiveness in individual therapy will be limited if a therapeutic alliance is not established, little will be accomplished without cohesion first being developed in group.

Studies comparing rankings of Yalom's twelve therapeutic factors reveal that cohesion is the single most important factor in successful treatment; especially when conducting groups for substance abusers (Flores 1997). These findings support

Yalom's clinical opinion that the establishment of a cohesive environment is first necessary before any other therapeutic forces in group can be activated. Yalom (1985) states: "Group cohesion is the *sine qua non* of effective long-term therapy, and the effective group therapist must direct his or her efforts towards maximal development of these therapeutic resources," (p. 111). When comparing and describing the therapeutic factors in group, Yalom makes an important distinction between those therapeutic factors which are mechanisms for change, and those therapeutic factors which are conditions for change. Cohesion and the importance this factor plays in the creation of the condition for change cannot be overstated.

In a review article examining the relationship between the therapeutic alliance and successful treatment outcome in group psychotherapy, Burlingame and colleagues (2001) suggest that the literature shows cohesion in group is the primary organizing context within which all successful treatment in group occurs. Burlingame writes:

> Because member-to-member and member-to-group relationships are theorized and found to be primary therapeutic mechanisms in group therapy, development of the optimal therapeutic environment in groups requires that attention be directed not only to the therapeutic growth of the individual client members but also to that of the group as a whole. The astute group therapist knows that he or she is often able to contribute most to the group members by fostering relationships among the members and helping them to learn to help each other. The therapeutic task for many group members is to learn how to successfully negotiate these relationships. In this way, the group therapy format becomes a curative influence in its own right and not merely a "watered-down" version of individual therapy, in which group members compete for and have to share the therapist's time and attention. [p. 373]

Some authors (e.g. Marziali et al. 1997) have suggested that group cohesion and group alliance are two separate concepts. They differentiate between the two, limiting alliance as applicable only to the strength of the relationship between the group members and the group leader. Cohesion, in contrast, applies exclusively to the level of connection that members have with each other in the group. Burlingame and colleagues' (2001) definition not only integrates this unnecessary differentiation, it also represents a view that is more compatible with the way Irwin Yalom, Louis Ormont, and attachment theory applies the principle of cohesion. For instance, Ormont (1992) considers the establishment of a "sense of community" in the group as a parallel development to the attainment of cohesion in group. He suggests that if a group leader orchestrates the right mixture of emotional involvement and communication among all members in group, then an important source of therapeutic power will be harnessed. The individuals in the group have the potential to fashion something far more valuable together, as a unit, if they are an integral part of a therapeutic community. If the right atmosphere is created, Ormont writes, "These people will understand themselves better together as a consensual mass than they ever would with interpretation or singular insight" (1992).

Burlingame and colleagues present empirical evidence that cohesion predicts outcome and that a number of studies (e.g. Bednar and Kaul, 1994, Dresden et al. 1985) have concluded a strong positive relationship exists between cohesion in group and patient improvement. Burlingame and colleagues go on to review the literature, examining the member-to-member and member-to-group categories, before concluding that the following relationships between cohesion and successful treatment are empirically validated:

Patients who reported high levels of relatedness or attachment (e.g., feeling understood, protected, and comfortable with the group) also reported the most symptomatic improvement.

Improvements were found to be related to patients' self-reports that they liked the group; experienced intimacy; felt accepted; and experienced warmth, empathy, friendliness, consideration, genuineness, and working together to solve a problem.

Attraction to the group, even at a minimal level, is related to retention of group members in group, especially during the early phase of group treatment.

Higher rates of group attrition were related to poor outcome.

Group-level cohesion (e.g., self-absorption vs. involvement, trust vs. mistrust), as rated by an individual observer, was related to self-reported improvement and cohesion exhibited in the first thirty minutes of a session produced the best outcome results.

Members who felt personally valued and understood by the group leader had greater improvement. Conversely, poorer outcomes were associated with members who reported more negative feelings or experiences.

High positive emotional attachment to the group and its members increased disclosure and more intense feedback from group members, leading to more interaction and more positive outcome.

The development of early cohesion appears related to the group's ability to handle and tolerate conflict.

Establishing and Maintaining the Emotional Climate in Group

Burlingame and colleagues (2001, p. 375) identified six empirically supported principles that enhance treatment retention, cohesion, and successful treatment outcome:

1. A primary objective of the group leader should be facilitating group members' emotional expression, the responsiveness of others to that expression, and the shared meaning derived from such expression.
2. The group leader's presence affects the relationship not only with individual members, but also with all group members as they vicariously experience the leader's manner of relating, and thus the importance of managing one's own emotional presence in the service of others.
3. The timing and delivery of feedback should be pivotal considerations for leaders as they facilitate this relationship-building process.

4. Leader modeling real-time observations, guiding effective interpersonal feedback, and maintaining a moderate level of control and affiliation may positively impact cohesion.
5. The group leader should establish clarity regarding group processes in early sessions since higher levels of structure probably lead to higher levels of disclosure and cohesion.
6. Pregroup preparation sets treatment expectations, defines group rules, and instructs members in appropriate roles and skills needed for effective group participation and group cohesion.

Attachment theorists recognize that both member-to-member and member-to-group attachments are necessary because originally they serve a biological function to ensure survival. During early development, attachment helped secure assistance for the infant during times of threat or danger. However, as the individual grows older, affiliative relationships with peers and groups became more important because they involve greater reciprocity and a semantic order (Lichtenberg et al. 1992). Affiliative relationships are not based purely on physical proximity, but are mediated by a complex set of meanings and representatives. If long-term recovery is to be achieved, the capacity to establish affiliative relationships is crucial. One reason AA works as well as it does is because it provides the alcoholic the opportunity to substitute affiliative relationships for their addiction.

Providing gratification and being more responsive help facilitate an emotional attachment to the group. In more traditional psychodynamic group psychotherapy utilizing object relations theory, the group leader's task is to help group members work through the defenses each uses as an attempt to manage the anxieties associated with unacceptable or threatening forms of object relations in group. These anxieties are often related to unconscious instinctual drives, and the leader's task is usually to interpret these defenses and anxieties: However, drawing on Kohut (1977) and the theoretical perspective of self psychology, it is best not to interpret these anxieties or behaviors as distorted or maladaptive, but to help the alcoholic and substance abuser understand that these reactions are related to and a consequence of unmet developmental needs for selfobject responsiveness that are repeated in the here-and-now interactions of the group. This approach, heavily influenced by self psychology, is much more supportive and gratifying and less threatening or shameful than traditional approaches to treating vulnerabilities typically manifested by most alcoholics and addicts.

GROUP, TRANSFERENCE, SHAME, AND OBJECT HUNGER

Once group leaders have used the power and the leverage of the group to help substance abusers internalize their responsibility for abstinence from alcohol and drugs, they must then help them come to terms with the internal deficits that contribute to their substance abuse. This is not usually possible until substance abusers have had enough time and distance from their use of substances to allow their cognitive processes to stabilize and their emotional lability to be contained. It is during this stage of treatment that they can develop the capacity to explore and understand the relationship between their use of substances to regulate their affect and their difficulty with attachment.

The exploration of the destructive forces that prevent the development of mature mutuality can only take place in what Wolf (1988) refers to as the *empathic selfobject ambience*. Because the activation of shame related to object hunger, dependency, and hostility associated with the transference relationship often is too intense for the alcoholic and addict to tolerate in individual therapy, group therapy is required.

Transference intensity is reduced and spread out in group therapy. The group provides a holding environment, allowing the addict or alcoholic to achieve an appropriate mutually dependent relationship with other group members without the crippling interference of their own anger, dependency, or fear of intimacy. The group helps create a safe space between the addict and the group leader. Through identification, a more stable set of internal self and object representations (internal working model) will be incorporated.

The group format is better able to accomplish this task

because it provides many key elements that individual therapy cannot provide. Group therapy can more readily do this because it gives substance abusers a far wider array of individuals upon whom they can either depend or direct their anger. By virtue of the number of group members, the group format dilutes the intensity of the feelings that are sure to be activated in any close interpersonal relationship and that have to be worked through if characterological change is to occur. While this process is likely to be too threatening in a one-to-one relationship, the group provides a safer holding environment that gives substance abusers more "space," while permitting them to deal with the intense hostility and ambivalence they are sure to experience as their needs for approval, dependence, and caring surface. Usually, most addicts and alcoholics cannot tolerate the stimulation of "object hunger" or their own dependent yearnings that are activated in individual therapy as well as any in intimate relationships.

As Kosseff (1975) discusses, the group becomes

> A transitional object that protects the patient from the intensity of the fear of dependency on the therapist because this dependency is transferred to the group. The group carries within it a degree of freedom or support which the dyadic relationship cannot provide while at the same time serving as a bulwark against too great feelings of frustration and fear of punishment if he should function autonomously. [p. 237]

A clinical vignette will help illustrate this point:

> Mary, a recovering addict with nearly two years of abstinence, had been progressing nicely in her therapy group, which she had entered shortly after her discharge from an inpatient alcohol and drug treatment program. Along with the immediate comfort she was able to establish with the group, she also quickly developed an idealizing transference with her female group leader. Hanging on intently to her every comment, she would revel in any show of attention and support given her by the group leader. Her admiration came to an abrupt end after nearly a year in group when the group leader supported another group

> member's observation that Mary was intolerant of anyone disagreeing with her. Mary exploded into a rage, screaming she was "sick and tired of people betraying and blaming me," directing most of her anger at the group leader. Attempts at containment and interpretation by the group leader proved futile. However, Mary was able to gain some solace from other group members who expressed their understanding of her feelings because they too had felt similar feelings with others in their lives. Following this emotional explosion, weeks went by in which Mary refused to even look at the group leader, much less speak to her. Her only comments during the next two months were mumblings about leaving the group because she "no longer felt safe here." However, Mary had enough of an emotional connection with many of the other group members that she was able to respond to their urging that she stay because they cared for her and would miss her if she left. Consequently, Mary continued to attend the sessions regularly, eventually interacting more and more freely with the rest of the group members, while remaining somewhat cautious and distant from the group leader. Gradually, she was able to engage the group leader and even respond favorably to some of her interventions. Finally, one evening she was telling the group about an argument she had with her female supervisor at work. She looked directly at the group leader and openly confessed, "You know, I think I was distorting her comments and overreacting just like I did with you a couple of months ago."

No interpretation was required. The group had provided her with a safe holding environment and its group members had given her enough "good objects" to connect with until she was able to work through the intensity of the transference feelings with the group leader who represented the internalized bad-object parental figure. If the group members had not been able to provide enough safety for Mary by their "holding" of her, she would have likely dropped out of therapy or sought previous sources of gratification (alcohol or drugs).

Because the group expands transference possibilities, it

provides important advantages for long-term recovery. As the group continues to meet and relationships develop, affiliation-seeking behavior is activated. This permits more opportunity for the elicitation and exploration of internal working models, providing group members with a more favorable atmosphere for modifying and altering the repetitive nature of their destructive ways of relating. Once the group becomes an attachment object, it offers a larger number of potential selfobject candidates, cre-

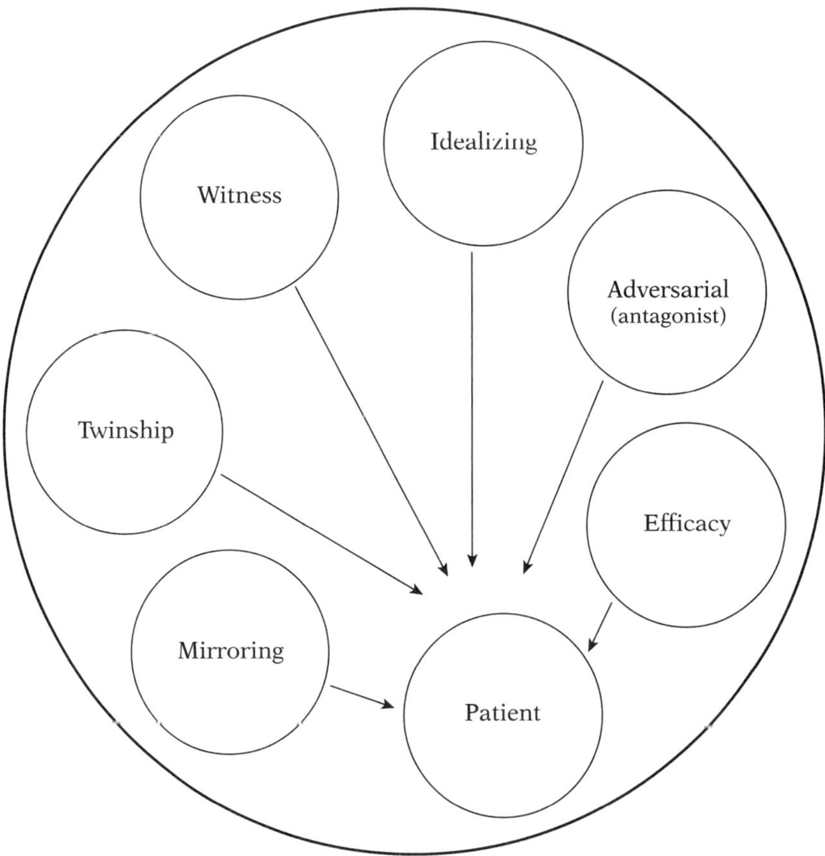

Figure 10–1
Group as an object (holding environment).
The selfobject is defined as someone who is experienced intrapsychically as providing functions that evoke, maintain, or positively affect the sense of self (emotional regulators).

ating more diverse transferences and greater possibilities for members to establish the particular *extended selfobject functions* (Harwood 1986) they require (Bacal 1985). The opportunity for *adversarial* and *efficacy experiences* (Wolf 1980) are increased, adding to the possibilities for the group members to experience a *self-delineating selfobject function*, which is basic for the emergence of a separate sense of self (Stolorow et al. 1987).

Figure 10–1 illustrates the expansion of selfobject transference possibilities in a group. A clinical vignette demonstrates how these selfobject functions can be activated in a group to increase therapeutic benefit.

> Betty was an attractive, energetic woman in her early thirties with one year of abstinence who entered a long-term, outpatient therapy group. The group quickly found her to be an exciting, involved group member who was very responsive to others in the group. However, they gradually discovered her propensity to treat them as disparagingly as she treated others outside of the group. She would make hasty intense attachments, then quickly become disillusioned or bored with her new relationships. Betty repeated this pattern within the group. She was very seductive with the men and dismissive of the women. The only daughter in a family of four sons and a dominant father, she had a love–hate relationship with men while seeing women as unimportant and inconsequential. Her attachment to the group and to one of the group leaders was strong enough to permit her to tolerate the different selfobject responses she evoked in others. Two men engaged her around her typical seductive patterns, while another man remained consistently confrontational of her manipulations. A fourth male member stayed consistently protective and supportive of her, even during her most provocative moments in the group. Two women engaged her competitively, while a third remained empathic and understanding of her difficulties with men. Another woman, Alice, became a new identified object for her. Alice's demeanor was totally opposite to that of Betty's, and so Alice was consistently able to get the male members in the group to respond to her in a supportive, respectful, and nurturing way because she was gentle

and unobtrusive. Betty learned that all quiet women didn't have to be masochistic like her mother. Through the course of her involvement with members of the group, Betty was able to evoke the selfobject responses she required to transform and alter the destructive relational patterns established in her family.

In summary, the group's value as a transitional object is in its facilitation of the identification process. It helps alcoholics and addicts do the following:

> (1) shift from a set of internalized split-images of self to a more unitary representation of self by identification with other group members; (2) shift from the part object seen as if it were the whole object (the therapist seen solely as bad object); (3) shift the fears of being engulfed by the group leader to a gradual recognition through other group members that this cannot happen because the group leader is not so powerful and because they, by sharing the leader with the patient, interfere with the patient's longing for fusion. [Kosseff 1975, p. 237]

Kosseff (1975) sums up this process:

> The group helps the patient let go of primitive idealizations of the therapist and his omnipotence by pointing out both the reality and the shortcomings of the therapist. As the patient is able to face these less positive attitudes toward the therapist, he is able "to change places" with him and see himself in a more worthwhile light. Where the patient in individual treatment would tend to overlook differences between his view of the therapist and the reality of the therapist, the other group members jar the patient's efforts at continuing pathological identification with the therapist or themselves and force him to acknowledge, and ultimately accept, his differences from others. Where the therapist's relative silence in individual treatment may tend to foster such pathological identification, visible group behavior and interaction force objective recognition of differences. What had been a sealed-off, dead-end identification with the therapist, a giving up of the real object and a substitution of an internalized, possibly idealized object, along with a

> giving up of the real potentialities of the self in favor of a false compliant self, now gives way to a recognition of the self as good and different from others. As the danger of fusion and immolation with the therapist subsides, the patient develops the hope and possibility of separation and true individuation. [p. 237]

Often after alcoholics have completed treatment, they want to return for visits, especially when anxious. This is where the lifelong availability of the AA program provides an even clearer illustration of this transitional function. Many individuals have difficulty weaning themselves from the AA program and are likely to seek continued contact with it. They gain continual confidence from the AA activities that win approval from the AA community. In this way, the unfolding of a sense of self-approval, defined as object constancy, can be discerned. What was not completed in childhood may take place later on as the program itself gradually acquires a maternal function, first as a transitional object and later, after individuals have internalized some of values of the program, as the source of object constancy.

LATE-STAGE GROUP THERAPY

The group leader must remember that an intervention made for a newly recovering alcoholic may be totally inappropriate for an alcoholic with one, two, or even ten years of sobriety. Late-stage treatment requires that chemically dependent individuals take a hard look at their character pathology and the defenses that prevent them from accurately perceiving their difficulties relating to others on a truly intimate level. Eventually they must learn how to form healthy attachments, and since it is impossible to be close to anyone and not fight, they must learn how to resolve interpersonal conflicts without relying on chemicals to self-soothe or regulate affect.

11

Attachment and the Therapeutic Alliance

> The improvement of psychotherapy may best be accomplished by learning to improve one's ability to relate to clients.
> *Lambert and Barley (2001)*

> The finest moments of life come through mutuality and comradeship.
> *Will Durant (1926)*

There are few things in the field of psychology and psychotherapy for which the evidence is as strong as that supporting the importance of the therapeutic alliance (Beutler 2000, Horvath 2001, Norcross 2001, Strupp 1998). There is an abundance of research evidence that the therapist's ability to establish a therapeutic alliance is the single most important contributing factor to successful treatment outcome (see following). Thousands of studies and the historical accumulation of expert clinical opinion dating as far back as Freud's early papers (1913) acknowledge the significant importance of the many ways that the working alliance determines treatment outcome. More recent empirical investigations of different attachment styles—of both the therapist and patient—have shed new light on the ways that alliances either fail or succeed in therapy.

These findings have important implications because they dictate to a large degree how therapy needs to be conducted when working with the addicted patient. Attachment-oriented Therapy (AOT) focuses on the relationship and the implicit rules (see Chapter 5) that guide the transformational power inherent in any authentic intimate relationship. Because substance abuse and all addictive driven behavior are to some degree a compensatorily determined substitute for a person's inability to derive satisfaction from relationships and close personal contact, the therapeutic challenge of engaging the alcoholic and addict in a therapeutic alliance is both enormously difficult and enormously important.

PRINCIPLES OF ATTACHMENT-ORIENTED THERAPY

Because the therapeutic alliance has emerged as a consistent predictor of positive treatment outcome across an entire range of different psychotherapy approaches, it has sparked an interest in the generic elements common to all forms of therapy. AOT can therefore be viewed as a "pan-theoretical" approach that transfers across all models of psychotherapy and ideological perspectives. From this perspective, AOT is not so much an approach to therapy as it is an attitude about therapy. It is less concerned with the techniques or the theoretical model that guides the therapist's interventions as it is concerned with *who* is applying the treatment and in what *way* the therapist is managing the therapeutic relationship. Any approach to therapy, no matter how sophisticated or substantially grounded in solid scientific theory, will only be as effective as the person conducting it. It is not so much *what* the therapist does as it is *how* the therapist creates the proper emotional climate of the relationship, because it is this environment that promotes the patient's engagement in the therapy venture. Kohut (1977) suggested that the origins of the specific pathogenesis in an individual's early development is not so much related to the particular rearing practices of the parents as it is to the emotional climate of the home. In a similar fashion, it is not so much the specific practices of the therapist applying treatment that influences successful treatment outcome as it is the creation of the proper therapeutic climate.

Therapy that follows the guidelines of AOT does not adhere to the bias of the classic psychodynamic developmental model in which maturity or mental health is equated with independence. As Bowlby and Kohut suggest, normal development is not the movement from dependence to independence, but rather the movement from immature dependence to mature interdependence or mutuality. This shift in perspective is especially important in the treatment of substance abusers. Helping the addict or alcoholic obtain mature dependency on people has obvious implications for treatment. The regulatory power of mature dependency or a secure attachment relationship is absolutely necessary if substance abusers are to relinquish their reliance on substances—a destructive dependency that erodes whatever existing capacity for affect regulation they originally possessed. Independence, or more correctly the addict's and alcoholic's counterdependence, is a force that fuels the substance abuser's narcissistic position and isolation, both of which are the cornerstones of every addictive process.

Attachment theory holds the view that mental health or maturity is defined by a person's capacity to move toward interdependence rather than independence from relationships. Staying connected is the primary aim of this model. Remaining in relation, even when the patient is detached, angry, or avoidant, is accomplished not by clinging to the patient, but rather by remaining empathically understanding of the patient's attachment fears and difficulties with relationships. Negotiating the vicissitudes typically involved in the give and take of any relationship eventually helps the alcoholic and addict move toward experiencing even more subtle and satisfying ways of being in relation. Eventually, the substance abuser learns how to transfer these subtleties outside the therapeutic milieu in the form of mutuality with others.

Mutuality can be defined as any growth-enhancing relationship that benefits both parties. It is not about being enmeshed or codependent; it is more about the efforts to know and understand another's experience. While this is true for both the addicted and nonaddicted, it is an especially important capacity for the alcoholic and addict because, as Jeffery Roth (2002) says, "Addiction is a disease of isolation." Being joined by another empathically in an atmosphere of mutual respect and trust helps reduced the addicted individual's sense of alienation and aloneness. Mutuality from this perspective provides each person in the relationship with the simultaneous affect regulation that is the hallmark of emotional stability and mental health. Lewis and colleagues (2000) state, "Total self-sufficiency turns out to be a daydream . . . Stability means finding people who regulate you well and staying near them" (p. 86).

All interventions need to occur in the service of moving the relationship along. As will be discussed, a key to successful treatment is the therapist's capacity and skill at working through the inevitable conflicts that arise in any relationship. This model looks at the relational resilience of substance abusers. What is their capacity to stay connected to others when there are disagreements and conflicts? How soon will they be able to move back into relation when there is a rupture in the alliance? AOT is focused on the ebb and flow inherent in all long-term attachment relationships.

This approach, while concerned with the dangers of enmeshment and infantile gratification, also differs from the more classic psychodynamic model, which has countertransference concerns about the therapist getting too involved. AOT is more concerned with the therapist not being involved enough or being too distant. Consequently, AOT is not so much a change in technique, or even a change in theory, as it is a change in principle. More emphasis is placed on the importance of the relationship and the development of mutual respect, trust, and responsibility. When patients can bring themselves more fully and authentically into a relationship, they not only embrace and get to know the other, but also embrace and get to know themselves, which can never be accomplished in isolation, only in relation.

Talking intimately with another about themselves is a developmental function that not all adults achieve. Communication about one's feelings in relation to another person is also a skill that many alcoholics and addicts do not possess. Knowing oneself and sharing that knowledge with another requires the capacity of putting one's feelings into words, a developmental task that requires the acquisition of inner speech or what Meares (1993) refers to as self-narrative. Attachment theory, especially because of the work of Margaret Main (1995) and her development of the Adult Attachment Interview (AAI), has shown a connection between attachment status in childhood and narrative styles in adulthood. Fonagy and colleagues (1994) discuss the reflexive self function (RSF), which is the ability to think about oneself in relation to another—a necessity for intimacy. Using narratives to accurately recount one's past (insight) is a key determinant in knowing oneself and knowing others. As Holmes (1996) says, "Acquiring inner speech means becoming intimate with oneself; knowledge of oneself goes hand in hand with knowledge of others" (p. 14).

A clinical example helps illustrate this principle:

> Andrew was more than five years sober and very actively involved in AA when he sought out a psychotherapy group. After a number of weeks in the group, Andrew's style of relating became painfully obvious to the group leader and the other group members. He had great difficulty relating to others interpersonally about the emotional material stirred up in the here and now of the present relationships in the group. Andrew could be supportive and compassionate of others' painful experiences or stories, but he could not stay engaged with others once the interpersonal exchange required that people relate beyond the historic content of their experience. Some of Andrew's narrative style may have been shaped in part by his repeated exposure to AA meetings, where the telling of one's stories is often stereotypically scripted and "crosstalk" is strongly discouraged. When Andrew spoke of himself, he could not keep others engaged. Group members would become distracted or drift off because his exchanges became bogged down in the minute details of his painful past history. They could feel sorry for Andrew, but they could not feel drawn in by him. The problem wasn't that it was unusual for new group members to feel compelled to tell their story when they first joined the group. New members usually spend some time letting other group members know their history. Andrew's problem was that he remained stuck in his narratives. His stories became rote and stereotyped. It took a concerted effort by the group leader to steer the others away from their eventual

indifference or boredom and their stereotyped responses to Andrew (e.g., "Oh, that's horrible, you had a terrible childhood; I can't believe they did that to you," etc.), and guide them to deal directly with the feeling that Andrew evoked in them. Using his knowledge of Margaret Main's work on narrative styles and attachment, the therapist was able to cut across the dichotomy between historical truth and narrative truth. By focusing on the form of Andrew's narratives, rather than their content, the group leader was able to help the group and Andrew see that Andrew's preoccupation with his history was a way for him to stay attached to his past pain and hurt in the hope of evoking protective attachment behavior in potential caregivers. The group leader's actions here are an important reminder that therapists are more helpful when they attend as much to the *way* their patients talk as to *what* they talk about.

ADDICTION AND THE WORKING ALLIANCE

Attachment theory applied to psychotherapy in general and addiction treatment in particular has important far-reaching implications for how the patient needs to be approached in therapy. Attachment theory is not so much a new theory as it is a new way of thinking about relationships, about the crucial developmental functions attachment provides for developing children, and about the important regulatory functions it provides for mature adults.

However, as important a skill as the ability to establish a working alliance is, it alone will not solve most of the dilemmas that the majority of patients, especially those suffering from addictive disorders, bring to the therapeutic encounter. A good theory and solid training in the proper application of the techniques that are guided by that theory are also essential. But as Lambert and Barley (2001) suggest, it is the therapist's ability to relate that creates the capacity for attachment and leads to the establishment of a working alliance, without which little influence can be exerted on the patient's behalf. If an attachment is not created, the therapist has little opportunity to apply the technical skills that the theory dictates. Strupp (1999) explains why the integration of theory, technical skills, and the ability to establish a therapeutic alliance is so important:

> Technical skills, I believe more strongly than ever, are the hallmark of the competent psychotherapist. They are encompassed by what I have termed the skillful management of a human relationship toward therapeutic ends. To my way of thinking, these skills are undergirded by a theory of therapy (in keeping with Kurt Lewin's dictum that nothing is as practical as a good theory) which acts as a road map guiding the therapist's interventions. One of the telling observations we made in the Vanderbilt I study (Strupp and Hadley 1979) comparing the performance of experienced therapists with that of untrained but kind college professors was the frequently encountered comment by college professors that after a few hours of "therapy" (I use the quotation marks advisedly), they "ran out of material to talk about." In other words, they were adrift in a sea of material they were at a loss to organize and process. In the final analysis such a theory may be relatively straightforward but it must embody a rationale of what constitutes the "problem" and what should be done to alleviate it. By the same token, the therapist must be cognizant of the intricacies of psychopathology, the nature of defensive operations, developmental history, and the vagaries of human communication. [p. 35]

Following Strupp's recommendations, attachment theory defines the problem of addiction as both a consequence of and solution to an individual's incapacity to establish healthy emotional regulatory relationships. The resolution or "what should be done to alleviate the problem" requires that the therapist first persuade the addict or alcoholic to detach from the object of their addiction, because until they do they will not be able to attach to treatment or recovery. Creating and maintaining the attachment or therapeutic alliance with alcoholics and addicts require a special set of skills and knowledge about what constitutes addiction so that like the kindly professors in Strupp's

Vanderbilt Study, the therapist will not be "adrift in a sea of material that they [are] at a loss to organize and process."

A clinical example shows how attachment theory can help a therapist organize a seemingly unrelated sea of material presented by a new patient with an addiction history:

> Susan's former therapist in New York City referred her for therapy after a recent job promotion required she transfer to a new executive position at corporate headquarters in Chicago. When making the referral, her previous therapist spoke fondly of Susan, saying she had worked hard in therapy for the last five years and made tremendous progress overcoming a cocaine addiction and a very troubled childhood marked by both emotional and physical abuse.
>
> "However," her therapist cautioned, "she has one persistent affliction she just can't seem to overcome. She's a compulsive shopper and she's constantly in debt."
>
> Susan came for her first appointment immaculately dressed, decked out in a sleek black Armani suite, Ferragamo high heels, a gold Rolex, and a stylish leather Coach purse hanging from her narrow shoulders. A tall, thin, attractive woman, Susan looked like she had just stepped out of an advertisement in *Vogue* magazine.
>
> She was also an emotional mess.
>
> Distressed to the point of distraction, she spoke discouragingly of the overwhelming stress of the recent move, her new job, the death of her father, a breakup with her boyfriend, and the loss of her therapist. Her face was drawn and taut, her eye-contact poor, and her fingers revealed the bruised and bloody results of her nervous picking at her fingernails and cuticles. She was not sleeping, eating, or going to AA meetings.
>
> "I've even stopped exercising," she lamented. "That's at least the one thing I've always managed to do even when I was in the worst throes of my cocaine use."
>
> "Why have you stopped exercising?" the therapist asked.
>
> Susan stared blankly at the floor for a few seconds

before answering, "I think it's because I don't want to leave my apartment. I don't want anyone to see me in this pitiful condition."

"You're isolating," the therapist said. "That's deadly for an addict."

"I know." Susan looked up, smiled weakly at the therapist, and nodded. "I just seem to be unable to help myself. The only thing I'm doing is working," Susan paused and shook her head, ". . . and shopping."

The therapist opened his mouth to speak, but Susan didn't wait for a response.

"My credit cards are charged to the max. Neiman Marcus is sending me threatening letters. Saks Fifth Avenue has threatened to close my account." Susan frowned. "I wish they would close my account. I owe them fifty thousand dollars." Susan buried her head in her hands. "I can't believe I've done this." She looked up at the therapist, an angry scowl on her face. "They're worse than the drug dealers I used to deal with. Did you know that if you're a preferred customer, they'll assign you your own special salesperson who calls you when they get something new in to give you the chance to be the first person to see the latest from Armani."

"They do sound like drug dealers calling to let their best customers know when the latest high-quality stash has arrived from Colombia."

"Exactly!" Susan balled her hands into a fist. "Here I am fifty thousand dollars into debt with them and they're still extending my credit, and they're so damn nice and understanding about it."

"Do you know why you keep taking their calls?" the therapist asked, even though he knew what the answer might be.

A deep sadness washed over Susan's face. "Yeah, I know. Barbara, my private sales consultant, is so sweet to me. She's the only person who calls me anymore. She's at least someone to talk to who's friendly. I know it's her job, but I really do think she likes me. And I can talk with her." Tears welled up in Susan eyes. "It's so damn sad. I've become this pitiful that I hunger so much for someone to be nice to me."

"No, I don't think that's pitiful at all. We all have this need, this hunger for someone to be kind to us." The therapist leaned toward her and made an assuring gesture with his hand. "The problem is not that you hunger for it. The problem is where you're trying to get it. It's like that old country-and-western song, a number of years back, you're 'Looking for Love in All the Wrong Places.'"

Susan cracked a weak smile. "I think you're right. But how did I get into this mess and how do I get out of it?"

"You treat this like any other addiction," the therapist replied. The good news is that you have a model, a template for dealing with this. You know what worked with your cocaine addiction. You just need to apply those same principles to your shopping."

Susan wrinkled up her face. "I'm confused. I don't see the similarities."

"Look," the therapist said, as he held up his hand and began counting on his fingers. "First, you're overwhelmed by your emotions and the stress in your life. Second, you're using your shopping the same way you used your drugs—to medicate your feelings. Third, you're isolating. The only people you're really talking to or have any contact with are the 'dealers.' Fourth, you're feeling ashamed of your behavior, which is only further eroding your self-esteem and self-respect."

Susan hesitated and looked at the four fingers the therapist now held up in front of her. She slowly nodded. "Maybe you're right."

"Listen, Susan," the therapist said. "Addiction is all about isolation and trying to manage painful feelings either by yourself or using something other than people to help with those feelings. Because of all the losses you've had in the last few months, the people who used to help keep you stabilized are no longer available—your therapist, your boyfriend, even your home AA group. You're either turning to the wrong people, like Barbara, your Saks sales rep, or you're using things like your shopping to keep you distracted from the loneliness and isolation you feel."

RESEARCH AND THE THERAPEUTIC ALLIANCE

Empirical evidence supports what experienced clinicians have always intuitively known. The accomplished and skilled therapist knows that the development and maintenance of the therapeutic relationship is a primary curative component of successful therapy because it is the quality of the relationship that provides the context in which specific techniques exert their influence. Add to this recognition the emerging evidence that addiction is inversely related to a person's capacity for intimate attachments, and the significance of the relationship among attachment, a working alliance, and successful treatment takes on profound implications. A brief review of the research that shows how different attachment styles affect an individual's capacity to establish a therapeutic alliance and the impact a strong therapeutic relationship has on treatment outcome helps explain why AOT is so crucial in the treatment of addiction.

During the last ten years the American Psychological Association (APA) has supported a succession of task force investigations (Chambless and Hollond 1998, Chambless et al. 1996, Nathan 1998, Task Force on Promotion and Dissemination of Psychological Procedures 1995) that have produced elaborate lists of empirically supported psychological treatment recommendations. All these task force investigations have been aimed at the identification of a variety of specific disorders that respond favorably to a series of well-controlled randomized studies, all of which adhered to an approved and accepted degree of methodological vigor. Those treatments that qualified as empirically validated procedures or empirically supported techniques have usually followed a restricted manualized individual therapy approach for a fixed number of sessions and have been limited to adult patients.

One strength of the task forces' approach to treatment lies in their concise and clear recommendations that help keep the therapist "on model," which requires that the more experienced therapists restrain themselves from using techniques learned from other types of individual or group treatments. These standardized approaches to treatment have been undoubtedly influenced by the task forces' research emphasis and the researchers' experience with numerous clinical trials, which require that one define what one is doing and make sure that it is being done according to a standardized manual. Consequently, all treatment approaches that fit the criteria of empirically validated or empirically supported therapy procedures end up reading like a treatment manual.

While the rigorous application of procedure is a primary strength of the task forces' work, it is also the source of its primary weakness. Because manuals are used to train providers and monitor therapist activities via some measure of adherence, treatment is standardized to ensure that everyone is doing the same thing. Such an approach has its advantages and disadvantages. One unavoidable pitfall is that manuals, in their zeal to standardize treatment, go to considerable lengths to eliminate the therapist as a person and central agent of change. In the process, the therapist variable can be compromised, even though this variable accounts for the greatest outcome variance in successful treatment (Norcross 2001). Unfortunately, many empirically validated manualized therapies suffer from a propensity to depict therapists as disembodied individuals who perform procedures only on axis I disorders. As Norcross suggests, this stands in marked contrast to the seasoned clinician's experience of psychotherapy as an intensely interpersonal and affective pursuit with another person whose diagnostic category is often shifting as treatment evolves. The inescapable fact is that the therapist and the relationship can be as empirically validated as standardized applications of psychotherapy treatments.

Responding to this bias and discrepancy in the direction that previous task forces have taken, Division 29 (Psychotherapy Division) of the APA decided to identify, operationalize, and disseminate information on empirically supported *relationships*, as opposed to treatment techniques that fail to account for the therapist and the relationship variable. After a series of studies and reviews of hundreds of empirical research studies, the task force made the following conclusions:

The therapy relationship makes substantial and consistent contributions to psychotherapy outcome independent of the specific type of treatment.

Practice and treatment guidelines should explicitly address therapist behaviors and qualities that promote a facilitative therapy relationship.

Efforts to promulgate practice guidelines or evidence-based lists of effective psychotherapy without including the therapy relationship are seriously incomplete and potentially misleading on both clinical and empirical grounds.

The therapy relationship acts in concert with discrete interventions, patient characteristics, and clinical qualities in determining treatment effectiveness.

Adapting or tailoring the therapy relationship to specific patient needs and characteristics (in addition to diagnosis) enhances the effectiveness of treatment. [Steering Committee, and Recommendations of the Division 29 Task Force 2001, p. 495]

In conclusion, the president of the Division 29 Task Force argued that the curative power of the person of the therapist and his or her relationship with the patient can be as empirically validated as manualized treatments of psychotherapy methods, and more importantly, the effects of the therapeutic relationship have been shown to be more robust in its effect on treatment outcome (Norcross 2001). The following statement sums up Division 29's position on this matter:

> As a general trend across studies, the largest chunk of outcome variance not attributable to preexisting patient characteristics involves individual therapist differences and the emergent *therapeutic relationship* between patient and therapist, regardless of technique or school of therapy. This is the main thrust of three decades of empirical research. [Henry 1998, p. 128]

THE ALLIANCE: WHAT IS IT AND WHY IS IT IMPORTANT?

Some may trivialize the importance of the therapeutic alliance and characterize AOT as simply a good relationship with a caring, nice person—something that anyone could do without any special training. To the contrary, it takes more than a warm, nice person to do good psychotherapy. To prevent the importance of the therapeutic alliance being misinterpreted to be nothing more than a version of warmed-over Carl Rogers, it is important to clarify a few points. Norcross (2001), discussing the skills required to effectively establish a good therapeutic alliance, addresses the complexity involved in this process: "The research shows an effective psychotherapist is one who employs specific methods, who offers strong relationships, and who customizes both discrete methods and relationship stances to the individual person and condition. This requires considerable training and experience; the antithesis of 'anyone can do psychotherapy'" (p. 353).

As Strupp (1998) demonstrated in his classic series of Vanderbilt studies, the greatest contributor to premature dropouts and treatment failures is the management of the therapy relationship, especially when the patient's problems are complicated by extreme interpersonal criticalness, negativity, and dissatisfaction. Competent, talented, and experienced therapists are often unable to effectively deal with the problems of "negative complementary." Strupp explained: "By this I mean, in a nutshell, the ubiquitous human tendency to enact with significant others the interpersonal problems that constitute the 'illness' which psychotherapy is intended to mitigate" (Strupp, 1999, p. 35). Decades of research indicate the provision of therapy is an interpersonal process in which a main curative component is the nature of the therapeutic relationship. In a review article on this subject, Lambert and Barley (2001) found the empirical support for this position so robust as to lead them to suggest, "The improvement of psychotherapy may best be accomplished by learning to improve one's ability to relate to clients."

Fortunately, there is an abundance of research that shows that there are a multitude of variables that facilitate the accomplishment of being able to relate to clients, and in so doing facilitate the establishment of a strong therapeutic alliance, which will then positively influence successful treatment outcome. No doubt, the difficulties of working with individual patients vary. The literature indicates that the capacity to develop an alliance is not a simple function of the therapist's training or experience. Patients with more severe problems and low motivation, like many alcoholics and addicts, are more difficult to engage in the therapy process. Though the patient variables may vary, as do the demands of different treatments, the therapist needs to remain sensitive to the fact that the qualities of a good therapeutic alliance and the significant contributions it makes to positive outcome are remarkably stable and robust across a broad range of variables.

Horvath (2001), in a review article on the subject, summarized the importance of the alliance:

> Two decades of empirical research have consistently linked the quality of the alliance between therapist and client with therapy outcome. The magnitude of this relation appears to be independent of the type of therapy and whether the outcome is assessed from the perspective of the therapist, client, or observer. Although the strength of the connection appears to be relatively uniform throughout therapy, the client's report of the early alliance may be the most clinically useful indicator. In successful treatments, the therapist's and client's assessments of the alliance tend to converge over time. Recent research suggests that the therapist's skills and personal factors both influence the likelihood of developing a good therapeutic alliance with the client. Though the relation between the therapist's level of training and the quality of the alliance is inconsistent, it is likely that the more trained therapists are able to form better alliances with severely impaired clients. [p. 365]

Considering the implications that a good working alliance has on treatment outcome, it is crucial to understand all the ways that both the patient and the therapist contribute to the alliance. To fully appreciate all the intricacies that make up this endeavor, it is important to move past the early simplified concept of the alliance that limited it to the positive transference from the patient to the therapist (Freud 1913). Currently, the therapeutic alliance is defined in terms of agreement on the therapeutic tasks and goals, and the development of bonds of mutual trust, acceptance, and confidence between patient and therapist. However, to fully appreciate the contributions that each person makes to the therapeutic alliance, we must examine the therapist's and the patient's attachment styles.

ATTACHMENT STYLES AND THE THERAPEUTIC ALLIANCE

In a review article on attachment styles and treatment outcome, Meyer and Pilkonis (2001) presented an abundance of research evidence that different attachment styles influence not only the strength of the therapeutic alliance, but also how quickly it is formed. Both the therapist's and the patient's attachment styles contribute to the establishment of the alliance. Each brings something to the relationship, and it is the strength of their combined ability to relate that determines if the relationship is able to tolerate and repair the ruptures and empathic failures that inevitably occur over the course of treatment. Of course, the greater responsibility to work through the inevitable difficulties that arise in the relationship rests with the therapist. Put another way, therapy can be described as a relationship between two people where one person has fewer problems than the other, and that person, one hopes, is the therapist.

Attachment theory informs clinical work in a way that places increasing emphasis on the contributions of both the therapist and patient to the establishment of the therapeutic relationship. This has required a shift in the way that transference has historically and typically been understood and defined. No longer is transference seen as arising primarily from the patient. Views on this perspective have been modified to examine with greater specificity the impact of the therapist in the therapeutic encounter.

Self psychology and intersubjective theory (Stolorow et al. 1987) provide a theoretical perspective for understanding the interplay that goes on in any relationship, therapeutic or otherwise, that occurs between two or more people. All psychological phenomena take place within an interaction of the subjective world of one person with the subjective world of another. Systems are created by the interactions of one intersubjective experience with another's intersubjective world. Relationships are therefore co-created. As Gans and Alonso (1998) state, "Simply put, the way I am with you *partly* determines the way you are with me, an interactional effect that may be modest or substantial" (p. 312). Put another way, how I am with you and how you are with me is different from how you are with her or how I am with him.

In therapy, the intersubjective world of the therapist is influenced by, interacts with, and influences the intersubjective world of the patient. To a large degree, therapy is affected by how much the patient influences the therapist's own emotional and mental processes. The success of therapy is, in large part, determined by how much the therapist allows his or her actions to be influenced by the patient's emotional demands. As Brandchaft and Stolorow (1988) state, "In the therapeutic situation, the manifest pathology (and its subsequent course) is always *codetermined* by *both* the patient's disorder and therapist's ability to understand it" (p. 251). The manifest pathology never arises entirely from pathological endopsychic sources within the patient. Therapy is the interplay between the patient's attachment style or transferences and the therapist's attachment style or transferences. Transference can therefore be understood as the patient's attempt to transform the therapist to fit his or her internal working model, which dictates "how I have to behave in order to be in relation to you." To the degree that therapists become transformed, they are caught in their countertransference or the patient's projective identification.

In discussing the therapist–patient factor, it is important to differentiate between the commonly identified therapist variables (e.g., interpersonal style, empathy, warmth, congruence, authenticity) and the patient characteristics (e.g., motivation, attachment style, diagnosis, object relations, psychopathology) that contribute to both the therapeutic alliance and successful treatment outcome. These concepts are not mutually exclusive or distinct, but are interdependent and overlapping. Strupp

(1999), quoting Beutler and colleagues (1994), stated, "As correctly noted, the therapeutic relationship is not a therapist quality but is a set of processes that are dependent on both therapist and client" (p. 34). Beutler and Strupp are drawing the important distinction between the qualities of the therapist and the qualities of the patient. While each person contributes to the therapeutic relationship, it is not an entity that each innately carries; rather, it is something that is created through their mutual exchange. It is the skilled and talented therapist—and as research shows, the more effective therapist—who is able to establish and maintain a therapeutic relationship with patients, who by the nature of their difficulties and past experiences, are unable to do that. In fact, those patients who possess a more extreme form of this difficulty are the ones most likely to experience the most benefit.

THERAPISTS' CONTRIBUTIONS

Many years ago, Erv and Miriam Polster (1974) expressed the opinion that the personhood of the therapist was the key element of successful psychotherapy. They felt that most excellent therapists are exciting people who have access to a wide range of human emotions. They can be tender or tough, serious or funny, courageous or cautious. If their patients spend enough time with them, the Polsters say, it will rub off. Patients will have the opportunity to experience someone who knows how to accept, arouse, tolerate, and deal with frustration. Eventually, patients will learn a respect for what it is like to be a human being who can meet surprise and adventure without hiding these characteristics when they appear. This can be accomplished only if therapists have experienced life to the fullest. They must know fear, anxiety, courage, and dependence. They must not be afraid to love and be no stranger to anger. They must possess the capacity for what Karl Jaspers (1975) calls "unlimited communication" or be what Erv Polster calls "a connoisseur of contact." The therapist must also have the capacity for what Franz Alexander (1950) calls "dynamic reasoning"—the ability to see one's patients not only as they are now, but also how they became as they are. The therapist must be able to listen with what Theodore Reik (1954) calls "the third ear." However, while therapists always strive to understand, they must be able to tolerate the tension of not understanding rather than forcing their explanations or interpretations. As Reik says, "It is better not to understand than to misunderstand." Most importantly, the therapist must be able to visit and be comfortable with his own emotional demons as well as those of the patient. Martin Buber (1963) said that the emotional demand upon the therapist at times is such that few will attempt to venture into the world of "sick souls" with their whole being. Buber, as usual, eloquently described this venture:

> In certain cases, a therapist is terrified by what he is doing because he begins to suspect that something entirely other is demanded of him. Something incompatible with the economics of his profession, dangerously threatening, indeed, to his regulated practice of it. What is demanded of him is that he draw the particular case out of the correct methodological objectification and himself step forth out of the role of profession superiority, achieved and guaranteed by long training and practice, into the elementary situation between one who calls and one who is called. The abyss does not call to his confidently functioning security of action, but to the abyss, that is to the self of the doctor, that selfhood that is hidden under the structures erected through training and practice, that is itself encompassed by chaos, itself familiar with demons, but is graced with the humble power of wrestling and overcoming, and is ready to wrestle and overcome thus ever anew. Through his hearing of this call erupts in the most exposed of the intellectual professions, the crisis of its paradox. In a decisive hour together with the patient entrusted to and trusting in him, he has left the closed room of psychological treatment in which the analyst rules by means of his systematic and methodological superiority and has stepped forward with him into the air of the world where self is exposed to self. [p. 98]

Hans Strupp (1978) has succinctly outlined the process of the establishment of a good working relationship in therapy. The matching of therapist and patient characteristics are determined in large part by the successful management of the early sessions of therapy. Furthermore, a good human relationship is judged by Strupp (1978) to be a precondition for the therapist's technical interventions:

> There is ample evidence that any good human relationship—i.e., an interaction characterized by understanding, acceptance, respect, trust, empathy, and warmth—is helpful and constructive. If such a relationship is provided by one person (therapist) for another (patient) who is unhappy, demoralized, defeated, and suffering from the kinds of problems which our society has diagnosed as requiring the services of a specialist in mental health, the outcome will generally be "therapeutic," provided the recipient is able to respond to, or take advantage of, what the therapist has to offer. Some therapists believe that psychotherapy begins precisely at the point where a patient cannot profit from a good human relationship, and the professional is needed specifically by those persons who are chronically unable to seek out and profit from a good human relationship. [p. 9]

Strupp emphasizes repeatedly that it is not the utilization and techniques or the elucidation of historical antecedents that produce change in a patient. It is the reliving and modification of historically meaningful patterns that come alive in the here and now of the therapist–patient relationship. Therapeutic change is not carried by reason but by the emotional relationship between the patient and the therapist, and the therapist as a person plays a crucial part in determining how important and effective this relationship will be. A therapist who is just a nice person will fail to provide the entire range of stimulus that the patient will need in treatment. Therapists must be able to challenge, soothe, care, love, and, if necessary, fight with the patient if they are to provide the full range of emotional experience that can potentially come alive in any authentic relationship. Therapists should have free access to all their passions and should discipline them to achieve a therapeutic purpose. Whenever therapists are kind, altruistic, or generous, it should *not* be determined by their desire to be nice or thought of as kindly. Rather, their ability to soothe another and be generous should emerge out of the depths of their own self-worth and competence.

RESEARCH EVIDENCE

Positive regard (Farber and Lane 2001), congruence, genuineness (Klein et al. 2001), feedback and emotional engagement (Claiborn et al. 2001), attachment styles (Meyer and Pilkonis, 2001), self-disclosure (Hill and Knox 2001), countertransference management (Gelso and Hayes 2001), relational interpretations (Crits-Christoph and Gibbons 2001), and empathy (Greenberg et al. 2001) have all been shown to enhance the therapeutic relationship and consequently positively affect treatment outcome. These and other important related variables coalesce into three primary clusters of therapeutic skills—empathy, flexibility, and management of negative process—that determine to a large degree how successful therapy will be and whether the alliance will be established, maintained, and ultimately used to enhance treatment outcome.

EMPATHY

Research methodology does not always allow the intricacies of empathy to fit neatly into a research paradigm. Because of a number of factors, the question of causality—whether empathy increases positive therapy outcome or is just a corollary of it—cannot be concisely answered by a pure analysis of findings. Construct validity, insensitive or inadequate measures, and a restricted range of predictor variables all hamper good empirical data. Despite the limitations that empathy poses on scientific inquiry, four factors have been consistently identified as potential mediators among empathy, the enhancement of the therapeutic alliance, and successful treatment outcome.

Empathy as a Relationship Condition

Empathy strengthens the relationship, expands satisfaction with the therapist, increases safety, provides a secure base, and enhances treatment retention. A relationship cannot be firmly established without trust, and there is little chance for trust to develop without empathy. Empathy is closely related to successful treatment outcome. Research results demonstrate that measures of alliance strength increased following reports that therapists' actions or comments were indicative of their patients' inner experience. These findings remained consistent whether patients or independent observers did the ratings. Feeling understood is positively related to patient satisfaction, safety, and self-disclosure. Evidence also indicates that empathy is correlated with therapy retention, and at least one important study indicated that this is significantly true for alcoholics. Chafetz and colleagues (1962) found that after a single empathic counseling session, alcoholics were ten times more likely to seek treatment and forty to fifty times as likely to stay in treatment.

Empathy as a Corrective Emotional Experience

Empathy helps reduce the feeling of isolation and alienation. It alters neurophysiology and increases self-respect and self-worth. Previous levels of developmental arrestment are resolved, resulting in a greater capacity for trust, autonomy, assertiveness, relaxation, gratification, and self-care. Hans Strupp (1999) in particular has focused on the importance of empathy throughout his years of outcome research. However, he speaks to the imprecision of the use of the word, cautioning the reader that the term *empathy* is often used in a glib fashion. He goes on to suggest that this is unfortunate because he sees "empathy as being closely related to the ability to LISTEN." The ability to listen empathically not just to what is being said but also to what is not being said is "one of the finest qualities a therapist can—and should—possess." He quotes from Fromm-Reichmann (1950) on the subject (p. 34):

> The psychotherapist must be able to listen. This does not appear to be a startling statement, but it is intended to be just that. To be able to listen and to gather information from another person in this other person's own right, without reacting along the lines of one's own problems or experiences of

> which one may be reminded, perhaps in a disturbing way, is an art of interpersonal exchange which few people are able to practice without special training. [p. 7]

Strupp goes on to draw on his forty years of psychotherapy training and outcome research to add, "What makes being listened to with interest, respect, and compassion so immeasurably poignant is precisely the lack of such experiences in the background of so many patients" (p. 35). Self psychology adds some important perspectives on the important implications of this very basic human need. "If you listen carefully," Paul Ornstein once said, "your patients will tell you how they want to be analyzed." Unlike many highly directive, time-limited approaches, where the therapist knows best and the patient is a passive recipient of the therapist's expertise, self psychology takes the stance that the patient is always right. Ornstein goes on to explain how the proper use of empathic attunement usually provides clues to what the patient needs (Ornstein, 1982 Verbal Communication).

A clinical vignette illustrates this point:

> Pete is a 40-year-old attorney who originally sought therapy because of his wife's concerns about his marijuana use and escalating outbursts of anger. At the first meeting, Pete readily admitted that he was also concerned about his marijuana use, adding that he had already decided to stop using pot once he called to set up the appointment. "It's just a relic left over from my college days. I really don't need it anymore."
>
> "It's good to hear that you are willing to take an honest hard look at yourself and take some action to do something about behavior you see as destructive," the therapist said.
>
> "Quitting pot will be easy compared to trying to control my temper." Pete leaned back in his chair, furrowed his brow, and gave the therapist a worried look. "To be honest with you, I've wanted to stop smoking for years now, but every time I tried, my temper outbursts got worse. I'm worried that my anger is just going to get completely out of control. At least the pot calmed me down some."
>
> Pete proceeded to describe how his temper created

problems at work, home, and with friends. Pete grimaced, "It's embarrassing. I can have the worst case of road rage at times that gets sparked by the silliest things. My wife doesn't even like me watching the evening news. I start screaming at the announcers."

"How long has this been going on?" the therapist asked.

"My whole adult life." Pete leaned forward. "You've got to help me. My boss called me in the other day and said another outburst could cost me my job. No one wants to work for me anymore, it's gotten so bad."

"I see the concern in your face and hear the fear in your voice. Your afraid your anger is getting out of control."

Pete leaned back and sighed, "Well, you got that right. I am out of control and it frightens me."

"You said your anger has been out of control your entire adult life. How was it before, when you were a child?"

"You kidding?" Pete scowled and shook his head. "No one was allowed to be angry in my family except my father."

"Really! Why don't you tell me about it."

Pete hesitated. "You think this is related? Will talking about my father help?"

The therapist shrugged and smiled. "Maybe. Why don't we give it a try."

Pete gripped the arms of the chair and spent the rest of the session describing a very narcissistic father, who demanded to be the recognized head of the household. At times, the father would hold Pete's mother and siblings as virtual hostages while he would spend literally hours recounting his latest sales triumph of the week. A rigidly pious and sanctimonious religious man, Pete's father would parade his family before the church's congregation every Sunday when they were children. Now that all the siblings were fully grown, Pete's father would weekly send them all religious clippings and copies of letters written to him by prison inmates, proclaiming what a great man he was to be furnishing them with religious guidance. The father demanded that his correspondence be read and responded to.

The outpouring from Pete about his father proceeded uninterrupted for the next forty minutes.

When Pete paused for a breath, the therapist gently interjected a comment: "Pete, we're about out of time. It sounds like the subject of your father is an important one. It's something I think we'll need to explore more next time."

Pete looked up at the clock, his eyes wide with surprise. "Wow! Where'd the time go? I guess I had a lot to say, huh?"

The therapist nodded and chuckled, "I think so. Undoubtedly, you have a lot of things to say about him that he never gave you the chance to say when you were growing up."

The next few sessions were repeats of the first one. Pete would get on a roll about his father and talk animatedly, nonstop for the entire session. Any attempts by the therapist to respond or make a comment on anything Pete said were quickly brushed off. At times when the therapist would make an observation, Pete would halt his monologue for a moment, nod some weak acknowledgment or give the therapist a quick irritated look, and proceed as if the statement hadn't been uttered.

At the end of the last session, after the therapist had to repeatedly remind Pete that they had to end the session, Pete smiled and proclaimed, "Sorry for running over again, but there's so much to tell you." As Pete rose to leave, he announced, "I don't know how this is happening, but I haven't exploded at my wife or gotten angry at anyone at work for two weeks."

Despite Pete's reported success, the therapist made a decision to engage Pete more the next session because he was concerned that Pete's self-absorbing monologues were repetitious of his father's narcissistic ramblings. Fifteen minutes into the session, the therapist was prepared to interrupt Pete in the middle of one of his monologues, but stopped himself when he heard Pete convey in parallel process what it was he needed in their relationship if therapy was to repair the developmental deficit in his experience.

"Damn it!" Pete looked up at the therapist and banged his fist against the chair. "You know at the end of the session last week when I said that I didn't know how this therapy was helping?"

The therapist nodded.

"Well, I exploded at my wife the other day. I realize now what it is that pisses me off so much." Pete glared at the therapist. "It's when she interrupts me. Shit! That really angers me. It's my father all over again. He would never listen to me. If I had something to say, he would either stop me with that look or that dismissing wave of his hand. Once when I tried to yell over him and demand that he listen to what I had to say, he threw me to the ground and pinned my arms with his legs and screamed at me that he would kill me if I ever tried to talk over him again."

"That's horrible to be on the receiving end of that kind of rage," the therapist said.

"You're right." Pete looked into the therapist's eyes. "It was frightening. I thought he was going to kill me."

Pete proceeded to describe a series of repeated events in his life that revealed a consistent pattern of repressed and unexpressed rage that he had to repeatedly swallow. As he grew older, his anger would get ignited each time he felt ignored or interrupted. The mobilization of his rage was the only way Pete could fight back against the overwhelming feelings of insignificance and personal unimportance that threatened to overtake him any time he felt interrupted or dismissed.

His therapist, through empathic attunement, was able to hear clearly what Pete needed if his developmental arrestment was to be repaired. Pete required a soothing selfobject that would understand and contain his years of painful dismissal and interruption. Over the course of the next two years, Pete's anger subsided because of the containment that his therapist provided. Pete proceeded to see similarities between his monologues and his father's narcissism. Interpretations were never required for this realization. An uninterrupted and nondismissing holding environment that allowed him to discover for himself was all that was needed.

Empathy as a Pathway for Better Object Relations

The capacity for intimate relationships is made possible through empathic connections with others. The ability to accurately read others' feelings and emotional signals not only leads to a deeper richness in relationships, it also improves one's proficiency in picking better lovers, friends, and spouses. Self psychology, more than any other clinical perspective before it, has placed the importance of empathy at the center of its theoretical edifice. Empathy, as Kohut defined and applied it, captures the essence upon which all initiative for engagement and interventions rest. The judicial use of empathy is also self psychology's primary tool of data collection as well as its principal instrument for building the therapeutic alliance. However, empathy should never be confused with sympathy or being nice. Kohut (1984) defined empathy as "one person's attempt to experience the inner life of another while simultaneously retaining the stance of objective observer" (p. 175). Distinguishing between the two functions of empathy, Kohut (1982) defined the first as an information-gathering activity and second as a powerful emotional bond between people.

Expanding on the function of bonding or attachment, Kohut (1982) stated, "The mere presence of empathy has also a beneficial, in a broad sense, a therapeutic effect—both in the clinical setting and in human life in general" (p. 397). Kohut is suggesting attachment, emotional bonding, and attunement are not only powerful therapeutic forces in therapy but also essential ingredients in defining happiness and mental health. Because attachment and emotional attunement are reciprocal physiological influences, they provide a profound and more necessary function than many recognize. Lewis and colleagues (2000), discussing the importance that marriage and attachment provide in keeping couples stabilized, point to the important regulatory function that secure attachment supplies:

> Because loving is reciprocal physiologic influence, it entails a deeper and more literal connection than most realize. Limbic regulation affords lovers the ability to modulate each other's emotions, neurophysiology, hormonal status, immune function, sleep rhythms, and stability. If one leaves on a trip, the other may suffer insomnia, a delayed menstrual cycle, a cold that would have been fought off in the fortified state of togetherness. [pp. 207–208]

However, they add that the skill of becoming and remaining attuned to another's emotional rhythms requires a solid investment of years. The physiological realities that dictate our central nervous system's requirement for the familiarity that comes with prolonged attachment doesn't often fit with society's (or managed care's) demand for quick solutions and rapid answers. "Some couples cannot love because the two simply don't spend enough time in each other's presence to allow it" (p. 205). Their astute observation that the physiological and biological realities of our emotional life do not lend themselves to influences that are time-limited or short term has important implications for treatment requirements.

Empathy as a Emotional Container

Empathy provides a holding environment that allows otherwise overwhelming emotions to be processed and decontaminated. With the containment that empathy provides, the individual develops a sense of mastery over previously frightening or forbidden feelings, leading to a greater capacity for affect regulation, self-soothing, and transmuting internalization. The skillful use of empathy not only helps therapists understand their patient's experiences better, it also helps them assess the limitations of their patient's capacity for certain experiences. Through vicarious introspection and empathic identification, the therapist is able to determine what range of affect is missing from the patient's emotional life. The absence of an expected feeling provides insight into the level of the patient's developmental arrest. However, as important as empathy is, it alone is not enough. Empathy reaches its full therapeutic potential when the therapist is able to convey to the patient an empathic response that expands the patient's experience. Empathy, understanding, or what has been popularly called Rogerian reflection must be done in a way that amplifies the patient's sense of self. Properly used, empathy helps patients gain a more comprehensive view of themselves and a deeper appreciation of their denied or disowned archaic needs. Archaic needs, from a self psychology perspective, pertain to the unmodified, infantile demands for immediate gratification, perfect attunement, and merger fantasies with the omnipotent parental object. Because of environmental failures, these archaic needs have been split off and repressed, depriving the individual of the opportunity to transform infantile disappointments to a mature acceptance of life's limitations.

The more skillful and accurate a therapist's empathic responses are, the more regression will be promoted. With increased regression, the more a patient's archaic needs will be activated. Conversely, if the therapist isn't a caring, sensitive person, archaic needs won't be activated and all treatment will stay on the surface and be directed to symptom reduction or symptom relief. It is here that self psychology demonstrates why it is an in-depth psychology and parts company from the Rogerian approach. Self psychology makes an important distinction between activating archaic needs and trying to gratify them. Gratification won't work because archaic needs are bottomless pits—this is what every addiction is about. Addictions are misguided attempts to fill a hole that cannot be filled. The regressive pull of an empathic relationship or therapeutic alliance will activate the repressed, forbidden wish—the desire for gratification of previously unmet developmental needs.

Just as an arm broken in childhood cannot be set twenty years later in adulthood, any attempt to provide the adult in therapy with something that should have been provided for them as a child is doomed to fail despite the best efforts of the most compassionate therapist. Instead, patients require help, understanding, and explanations for what they are experiencing before they can work through the grief of what never was and accept what will never be. An empathic holding environment helps them work through not only the grief but also the anger and shame that are associated with the primitive, age-inappropriate, and childlike desires for immediate gratification that often accompany the activation of archaic needs.

FLEXIBILITY

A review of the literature on treatment outcome indicates that it is often difficult to disentangle the effects of the treatment approach from the impact of the person delivering the treatment. Some therapists are better able to respond flexibly to a patient's pathology, changing response sets and improvising to deal with negative complementarity, anger, resistance, or indifference. Norcross (2001) suggests that therapists who possess "relational flexibility" are better able to weather the difficulties in the initial sessions, which strengthens the alliance and improves treatment outcome. Research suggests that therapists who place more emphasis on developing the alliance than on technical interventions, especially during the beginning of treatment, are more effective. Actively soliciting the patients' perspective on various aspects of the alliance and inviting them to collaborate in the negotiation of the goals of treatment is also associated with better treatment outcome.

It appears that the talented therapist shows more flexibility in response to a patient's attachment style and communication patterns, often adopting the patient's ideas or expressions. The value of an open, flexible stance in therapy as opposed to excessive control or rigid expectations is a consistent theme in the literature. For instance, such personal attributes as uncertainty, rigidity, criticalness, aloofness, tension, and distractibility in a therapist are all related to alliance ruptures. Therapists' techniques such as inappropriate self-disclosure, long withholding silences, too much structure, and unyielding use of transference interpretations also contribute negatively to treatment outcome, alliance ruptures, and failures at establishing a working alliance.

Ruptures in the therapeutic alliance can also occur when

therapists fail to appreciate the vast number of ways that patients may need to use their therapeutic relationship. Scott Rutan (1985) has a unique view to offer on this subject. He says the astute therapist must stay closely attuned to the different ways that the patient may need to engage the therapist. Rutan warns that problems are likely to arise when the patient approaches the therapist out of one relational mode and the therapist respondes out of another. Rutan says that a relationship in therapy is always threefold:

1. *Transferential*: The therapist serves the function of a transferential object, eliciting in the patient old distorted relational patterns and attachment styles.
2. *Professional*: The therapist is viewed as a technical expert, whose years of training and experience qualify him or her to be approached as a person who possesses special skills and knowledge on human development and behavior.
3. *Authentic individual*: The therapist is approached as a human being in relation to another human being who is separate and authentic in his or her own right.

A clinical example illustrates this point:

Steve, a 36-year-old, single Caucasian man, had originally been referred for outpatient therapy following a relapse and a subsequent hospitalization related to his relapse. Prior to his hospitalization, Steve had been active in Alcoholics Anonymous for nearly four years and had returned to drinking even though he had diligently worked the steps of the AA program, had a sponsor, and attended daily AA meetings. Therapy progressed nicely for nearly two years before Steve felt secure enough in the relationship to talk openly about his history of sexual abuse. The next year of treatment was grueling and painful as Steve spent session after session working through agonizing memories and excruciating details of the humiliating minutiae of the sexual abuse and derogation. Over the course of therapy, it became apparent to both Steve and his therapist that the unresolved trauma had led to his previous relapse. They both knew that if Steve was to achieve what AA calls serenity and acceptance, he needed to explore in painful recall all the horrors that were inflicted upon him when he was a child.

During this time of recall and the working through of repressed memories, Steve relied on the guidance of the therapist as he maneuvered through the murky waters of recall that were cloudy by distorted memories, fantasies, and fear. One day Steve showed up for the session and engaged the therapist with a demeanor that was markedly different from his usual one. Usually Steve vacillated between transferential idealization of the therapist and cautious suspiciousness, clouded by mistrust and doubts about this authority figure's motives and intent. At other times Steve relied on the therapist's recommendations, trusting that the therapist's years of experience with addiction and trauma would guide him in the direction that he needed to go.

This day was different. Steve did not present with his usual apprehension about uncovering new memories or his defensive stance, questioning his therapist's intentions.

"How are you doing today?" Steve asked, smiling broadly as he sat down. "It's a great day out, isn't it?"

"It appears to be. But to be honest, I've been cooped up in this office the better part of the day. What's it like out there today?"

"Gorgeous spring day." Steve stretched his long legs out in front of him and leaned back against the chair. "I got tickets for the Mets' game tomorrow," he announced. "First-base side, next to the dugout."

"Baseball tickets? I didn't know you were a fan."

"Yep," Steve nodded. "Have been my whole life. But not always a Mets fan. I used to love the Cincinnati Reds." Steve sat up and leaned forward, his face full of enthusiasm. "Now, that was my team."

"The Big Red Machine." the therapist beamed back at him.

"Yes!" Steve's eyes shined bright with excitement. "How did you know about them?" Steve quickly glanced at the diploma on the wall. "That's right, you went to the University of Cincinnati."

"I did," the therapist nodded. "And I grew up in Ohio, so I've been a Reds fan since I was a child."

"Me, too." Steve slapped his hands on his legs and laughed out loud. "Ha! I didn't know you were from Ohio. I grew up in Indiana, right by the Ohio River."

"I know," the therapist nodded.

"Oh, of course you know that." Steve's face flushed. "For a moment there, I forgot how much you know about my past." Steve paused and searched the therapist's face for a moment. "I bet I haven't told you about the time my father took me to a Reds baseball game when I was a young kid."

"No, you haven't. Was that at the new stadium or old Crosley Field?"

"Crosley Field!" Steve clapped his hands together in excitement. "You know about Crosley Field?" Steve didn't wait for an answer. "Yes, he took me there to see a game just a couple months before they started to build the new ballpark."

"That was a great old ballpark, wasn't it? I saw quite a few games there as a kid myself."

Steve leaned back in his chair, a serene, satisfied smile on his face. He stared at the wall over the therapist's head, looking like he was watching imaginary images flash past on the wall above him. Tears welled in his eyes and his voiced cracked as he spoke. "Those were good times. That was the one thing my father and I could always share. Our love for baseball."

Steve spent the remainder of the session talking about the richness of his relationship with his father. He spoke of forgotten times of security and love, before his parents divorced and his mother moved him to Chicago, where the abuse began. His therapist's decision to meet Steve in the authenticity of the moment, instead of interpreting Steve's talk of baseball as transference or resistance allowed a deepening of their relationship. Therapy from that day forward took on even a deeper, more collaborative direction.

As this vignette illustrates, therapists must stay aware of the way their patients may need to be in relation with them. Holmes (1996) agrees with Rutan about the importance of flexibility when treating patients. It is the more flexible therapist who is more likely to be responsive to the particular idiosyncratic needs of the individual patient. Some patients may require a therapist they can hate and some may require a therapist they can love. Holmes (1996) states:

> For one group the task of analysis is to root out the hatred and envy that the analytic situation inevitably arouses. From this can emerge the respect for the other that is the basis of true intimacy. The omnipotence of projective identification attempts to deny the reality of hatred and detachment, and eventually has to be faced in the depressive position. On the other side the therapist sees a patient who has been deprived of the experience of secure attachment. The analyst's job is to repair that deficit, to restore the sufferer's faith in the power of the bonds of love, and to accept, for the time being, the patient's need to idealize, demand admiration, to imagine lifelong companionship with her helper, and only gradually, under conditions of optimal disillusionment, to proffer the reality of detachment, and so become more autonomous. [p. 68]

Experience, Training, and Talent

Holmes and Rutan are addressing a special set of skills that often differentiates the talented and experienced therapist from novice therapists. Experienced therapists are less likely to let themselves be restrained by their theory. However, talented therapists are more likely to be well grounded in a theory that experience helps modify so that its delivery is less stiff or mechanical. Like a talented abstract artist, they know when and how to break the rules. One need only examine Picasso's early work to see how skilled he was early in his career at maintaining and mastering the proper form and composition in his drawings and paintings. Only after years of painstakingly mastering the basics did Picasso know what rules could be broken and how they could be applied creatively. So it is with the experienced and talented therapist who can be flexible in his application of technique. Theory does not completely dictate the experienced therapist's actions; it only guides it.

Examination of videotapes of experienced and novice therapists supports these observations. Novice therapists from different theoretical perspectives are distinctly different in applying their techniques in treatment, while experienced therapists coming from different theoretical perspectives resemble each other more in direct application even though they may have different rationales or explanations about why they do what they do. It appears that experience dilutes theoretical or ideological differences, and skilled, experienced therapists are drawn by their experience to do similar things that prove effective in treatment. Experienced and talented therapists are often disciplined improvisationalists who have stronger self-regulatory skills and a more flexible repertoire than novices and their less talented counterparts. Research evidence strongly suggests that the therapist's contributions to the establishment of the therapeutic alliance requires more than just the therapist's being nice. It requires experience, training, and talent. However, what defines talent? How do you measure it? Can it be taught? Hans Strupp has grappled with these questions in his repeated attempts over the years to assess how psychotherapy training programs can enhance the delivery of what has been identified as the most important contributing factor to successful treatment—the therapist–patient relationship variable. Strupp (1999) describes the factors that contribute to the therapeutic alliance, which he calls "the contemporary construct of the therapy relationship which has consistently been found to be a central contributor to therapeutic progress":

> At this juncture I am not entirely clear about the extent to which these qualities are innate although I tend to think that they are part of what might be called the "native talent" of a good psychotherapist. Like any talent, therapeutic talent is undoubtedly trainable and perfectible; otherwise, what would be the justification of our training programs? On the other hand, I have encountered in my research a distressingly large number of therapists whom I can only characterize, by analogy to musical talent, as "tone deaf." I also believe that the basic therapeutic qualities I mentioned above, as well as technical skills, are more

> or less normally distributed. If so, we would expect about 68% of all therapists to be more or less "average," with only about 16% as truly outstanding and a similar percentage as substandard. [p. 34]

In a similar vein, Liese (1998), discussing addiction treatment and the Project MATCH Study, questioned the research findings because the researchers failed to control for the therapist–patient relationship variable:

> Of particular interest to me in Project Match is whether significant therapist differences were nested within treatment groups in the study. Were there some extraordinarily *talented* clinicians in the three treatment conditions? Were there some extraordinarily *untalented* clinicians? If so what can we learn from these clinicians? How was their talent (or lack thereof) manifested? How did talent relate to treatment adherence (as measured by standardized adherence scales used in the study)? How were *talented* and *untalented* clinicians similar to or different from each other? Did their talents (or lack thereof) effect outcome? Or even more relevant to the original goals of the study, did certain therapist *talents* interact with certain patient characteristics to predict outcome? [p. 17]

Binder (1999) feels that talented and experienced therapists have know-how and an artistry that influences the conduct of therapy. They demonstrate skills, a knowledge of what to do in actual clinical situations that cannot be acquired solely through didactic course work, supervision, or following prescribed technical strategies and tasks that treatment manuals dictate. "We all know whether we are playing golf, playing music, or doing psychotherapy, a complex set of skills cannot be developed by merely reading and talking about them" (p. 711). As numerous studies have shown, the mere adherence to prescribed technical prescriptions and strategies is by itself rarely predictive of good treatment outcome. All experienced therapists know that a typical therapy relationship is characterized by patients with either ill-defined problems or shifting diagnostic entities in a unique environment of uncertainty, instability, and potential conflicts. It is, as Binder suggests, the talented therapist who deviates when necessary from the prescribed approach when situations and difficult patients require flexibility in the therapeutic encounter.

> Nancy, a 41-year-old recovering alcoholic, had reached a standstill in her therapy after two years of abstinence. Prior to seeing her present therapist, Nancy had struggled with her drinking for nearly twenty years. She had been in and out of different treatment programs and had gone through a series of therapists with little relief or success. All other attempts to curb her drinking using Moderation Management, cognitive-behavioral, and even aversion therapy, failed to help. Because of her father's religious fanaticism and fundamental beliefs, Nancy could not tolerate AA and its spiritual emphasis on recovery. It was only when she was able to develop a working alliance with a therapist who encouraged abstinence without forcing her to go to AA that a significant level of progress was achieved. Her marriage, health, and depression all improved dramatically. However, Nancy remained plagued by a repetitive maladaptive interpersonal pattern that proved difficult for her to alter. Despite all efforts so far by her and her therapist, Nancy could not shake her negative, defeatist attitude and her malignant self-loathing. She entered her session as she had done for the last few weeks, lamenting her life and the hopelessness of her situation.
>
> "Let's face it, Doctor, I haven't been getting anywhere the last few months," Nancy sighed heavily. "I think I'm just going to have to accept that I won't ever be able to change the way I feel about myself."
>
> "It's hard not to get discouraged. You've been battling this feeling your whole life," the therapist said.
>
> Nancy looked up at the therapist and forced a weak smile. "You're such a dear. You keep hanging in there with me and despite my pitiful wallowing in my misery, you never seem to get discouraged."
>
> "I don't consider your pain to be pitiful, just difficult," the therapist smiled back at her.
>
> "Thank you for saying that. I always feel understood

and never judged by you." Nancy folded her well-manicured hands in her lap, fidgeted with the large diamond ring on her finger, and gracefully crossed one long muscular leg over the other.

Her therapist examined this attractive woman, dressed fashionably in her Armani skirt and silk blouse. Married to a successful husband, with two handsome children, Nancy appeared to have no reason to be miserable or dissatisfied with her life. However, her therapist was becoming concerned by the recalcitrant quality of her distorted self-image. Insight and positive regard seemed to be producing diminishing returns.

"You keep reminding me how these feelings I have about myself are related to the poverty and emotional impoverishment of the home I grew up in," Nancy said, pulling at the golden chain around her neck. "But I'm discovering that there's a big difference between knowing one thing and feeling another. No matter how much I understand how and where this started, it doesn't change how I feel."

"Of course it doesn't," the therapist said. "That's what makes this so frustrating for you."

"Frustrating? I wish it did make me frustrated. You keep reminding me that if I could get in touch with my anger and direct it outward that it would help break me free of this incessant self-hatred that keeps me trapped." Nancy looked up at the therapist. "Maybe you're the one getting frustrated with me?"

The therapist smiled. "Nice try, Nancy. We've talked about this before. You're so used to everyone eventually getting frustrated with you that you expect it'll only be a matter of time until I do. When will I ever pass this test?"

"Oh, you passed it months ago." Nancy patted a wrinkle out of her Armani skirt. "I guess I just have to check you out from time to time to make sure you're not getting tired of me yet."

"Because you get so frustrated with yourself so easily, it's hard to believe that I wouldn't?"

"Something like that," Nancy nodded and sighed

again. "I wish I could see me the way you do. Maybe I would be more objective, less critical in my judgments of me."

"Well, imagine yourself sitting there," the therapist pointed at the chair. "Describe her to me. What do you see?"

"What?" Nancy looked up at the therapist, a startled look on her face. "What do you mean?"

He waved his hand again at the chair. "Describe her to me," the therapist repeated. "What is she like? Give me an objective opinion of her."

A crooked smile crossed Nancy's face. She looked at the empty chair. "I would describe her as a good woman. A kind, friendly person who would go out of her way to help someone," Nancy chuckled, and looked nervously at the therapist.

"Go on," he encouraged her. "Tell me more."

"She's a neat woman, really. If I met her somewhere or lived next door to her, I would want to get to know her better. She looks like someone I would find very interesting."

The remainder of the session was spent with Nancy talking about herself in third person. Over the next couple of months, the therapist would invite her to repeatedly speak of herself as if she were another person. Because of this change in perspective, Nancy was able to get unstuck. The therapist's decision to go against the common wisdom of keeping patients talking in the first person to help them "own" and get closer to their experience went against all the conventional rules of good therapy. He improvised. The therapist tried something different that he didn't usually do because of what he judged to be a set of unique circumstances about her situation.

Improvisation—whether it is the jazz musician creating an innovative riff or the quarterback scrambling out of the pocket on a broken play—is the cardinal characteristic of the talented musician, athlete, or therapist. The talented and flexible therapist has at his or her disposal an enormous repertoire of response contingencies and is more likely to be able to effectively manage the difficulties that arise in the therapeutic alliance. Binder (1999) states:

> I propose that the highest form of therapist competence, the essence of therapist expertise, is the capacity for improvising in situations where established working models do not suffice. The most proficient form of improvisation is reflection-in-action, in which working models are fine-tuned or radically modified through a special sort of problem-framing and problem-solving dialogue with the patient. Improvisation appears to be an important, sometimes requisite, capacity for dealing with perhaps the most difficult challenge facing the psychotherapist, namely the management of negative therapeutic process. Often referred to as hostile transference/counter-transference patterns of cyclical maladaptive interpersonal enactments, negative therapeutic process is pervasive and underestimated as a source of therapeutic failure. [p. 714]

MANAGEMENT OF NEGATIVE PROCESS

The single most consistent therapist contribution to treatment failure is the therapist's inability to deal effectively with negative process. Negative process and alliance ruptures are unavoidable occurrences during the course of any type of therapy, regardless of the theoretical approach or model. It is the therapist's capacity for recognizing negative process and effectively repairing ruptures in the therapeutic alliance that contribute most to positive treatment outcome. Unidentified or unrepaired ruptures either impede therapeutic progress or lead to premature terminations.

Therapists tend to overestimate and misjudge the value of their status in the relationship, particularly in the opening phases of therapeutic work. Some evidence exists that the ways the therapist judges the alliance are different from the patient's perceptions of what is important. Therapists are more likely to evaluate the alliance by the agreement of goals and tasks of therapy, especially the sense of responsibility assumed by the patient for therapeutic progress. Patients, in contrast, place much more emphasis on whether the therapist is friendly, helpful, and understanding. Most importantly, it is the talented therapist who is more likely to notice negative process and skillfully deal with it.

The skillful therapist is also aware that dealing with negative process is not a spectator sport and requires more than telling the patient how to alter his or her maladaptive relational patterns. Lewis and colleagues (2000) state:

> Describing good relatedness to someone, no matter how precisely or how often, does not inscribe it into the neural network that inspires love. Self-help books are like car repair manuals; you can read them all day, but doing so doesn't fix a thing. Working on a car means rolling up your sleeves and getting under the hood, and you have to be willing to get dirt on your hands and grease beneath your fingernails. Overhauling emotional knowledge is no spectator sport; it demands the messy experience of yanking and tinkering that comes from a limbic bond. If someone's relationship today bears a troubled imprint, it does so because an influential relationship left its mark on a child's mind. When a limbic connection has established a neural pattern, it takes a limbic connection to revise it. [p. 177]

Ackerman and Hilsenroth (2001, p. 173), discussing the therapist's personal attributes that contribute negatively to the alliance, say that more needs to be known about how the therapist contributes to the rupture of the working alliance. Quoting Strupp (1980b), they add:

> Major decrements to the foundation of a good working alliance are not only the patient's characterological distortions and maladaptive defenses, but—at least equally important—the therapist's personal reactions. We believe the notion that therapists are well adjusted individuals with little negative contribution to the therapeutic process has been over estimated. Therapists (even those who are very well trained and experienced), like others, often find it difficult to deal constructively with interpersonal conflicts in which they are actively involved. [p. 173]

REPAIRING ALLIANCE RUPTURES

One of the most difficult yet most important factors influencing treatment outcome is the therapist's ability to identify and address weakness or ruptures in the therapeutic alliance. The ability to identify ruptures and negative process is a skill that proves difficult for even experienced therapists. Some initial research on the subject (Rennie 1994, Safran et al. 2001) suggests that it is vital that the therapist be skilled at picking up clues that the alliance is in trouble and help patients participate in an open discussion about their dissatisfaction. This is often not an easy task because as Rennie's (1994) findings suggest, patients often believe that protecting their therapist is the best way to maintain the relationship, and in many cases or circumstances it is understandable that they would be reluctant to talk openly about their concerns.

A conference presentation by Steven Skulsky (2002) illustrates how it sometimes takes alarming circumstances to propel therapists to be aware of the subtle messages they can give their patients about their need to be protected from criticism and negative commentary.

At the conference workshop, which focused on the ways that therapists contribute to their patient's reluctance to talk openly about all their feelings in relation to their treatment, the moderator urged therapists to continually commit themselves to constantly challenge the ways they refuse to look at the parts of self that are grandiose and defensive.

Steven Skulsky, the presenter, spoke of a triad of destructive forces that contribute to this problem:

1. Arrogance
2. Stupidity
3. Lack of curiosity

"In other words," Skulsky said (verbal communication), "narcissism. If we think we already know, there's not going to be any desire to find out."

Rather than risk the uncomfortableness of not knowing, we avoid the uncertainty of new experiences. Skulsky cautioned therapists that they often stay with what they are comfortable with unless something forces them to learn from new emotional experiences.

Relying on the work of Wilford Bion, Skulsky points out that all real learning is emotional learning and that in order to grow emotionally, you have to learn from new emotional experiences. "But," he adds, "and this is what Bion has taught us about emotional learning: we all *hate*, not just dislike, we *hate* intense emotional pain or discomfort." All deep emotional learning is about learning to identify and understand what defenses we use that prevent us from facing emotions that frighten us. Consequently, we will avoid opening ourselves up to new experiences unless circumstances drag us, often kicking and screaming, into new experiences.

Skulsky then described how a recent heart attack, produced by his lack of exercise and excessive weight, propelled him to face and relinquish the idealization of self, and start honestly looking at things as they really are.

"It took my almost dying of a heart attack," Skulsky explained, "before I could open up and admit my frailties and imperfections. Before I could relinquish this phallic image of myself that was more than the real one, I had to face deep emotional feelings that I was unwilling to experience."

Skulsky's patients were the first to notice his transformation. "My patients in group would tell me, 'Your almost dying has been a godsend. We used to be afraid to tell you when you screwed up. Your need to think or to hold on to the image that you were a good therapist inhibited us. We can be more honest now. This crisis has given us the freedom now to tell you when you screw up.'"

Skulsky goes on to clarify how any unresolved experiences will leave us vulnerable for defensive operations to surface. "Healthy psychics, like healthy bodies," Skulsky explains, "require that we pay attention to what kind of nourishment or food we take in. Our hunger for emotional truth is just as intense and necessary as our body's hunger for food and water. We need the right balance between security operations, defensiveness, and managing anxiety on the one side, balanced by the discovery of ways to open up and experience new aspects of our existence, despite the anxiety that this discovery might produce."

"People," Skulsky says, "are not given a great deal of emotional awareness. We are instead given a *capacity* for emotional experience. A *capacity* that develops only to the degree that we are willing to work on learning, risking, and integrating new emotional experiences." Referring to a Jungian metaphor used by James Hillerman, Skulsky says, "People are not given a soul—a deep emotional life. Instead, they are given the possibility of soul. How much soul you have depends upon how much you deal with your own soul-like experiences; how much the pain is faced, how much the anxieties are confronted."

Drawing on parallels between Freud's early development of psychodynamic theory and the Judeo-Christian heritage, Skulsky explains that emotional learning is founded on two important shared foundations:

1. *The covenant*: We must find higher values for the sake of which we will abandon lower order instincts and needs. What are the higher order sublimations and values that we will postpone some gratification for?
2. *No false idols*: How do we constantly challenge ourselves to take a look at the pieces of self that are grandiose and defensive because to do so will stir up anxieties and unpleasant emotions that we are too frightened to face?

Therapists' willingness to discover how their narcissistic vulnerabilities are contributing to the avoidance of negative commentary has important implications for the identification and resolution of ruptures in the alliance. As research shows, there is a direct correlation between successful treatment outcome and repairs in alliance ruptures. Self psychology has long recognized that optimal frustration and rupture repair lead to a greater capacity for transmuting internalization and the building of psychic structure. In other words, the patient is able to internalize more emotional control, gains a greater capacity for the immediate delay of gratification, and becomes less reliant on external sources of affect regulation. Through the resolution of disappointment that accompanies all empathic failures, a number of important developmental achievements are mastered:

1. The ability to resolve narcissistic injuries and repair ruptures in the therapeutic alliance generalizes to all relationships, leaving patients with increased hope. They come to believe and have faith that they can have disagreements with important people in their lives and that these disagreements will not destroy the relationship.
2. Confidence in their ability and skill at conflict resolution leave patients less vulnerable to slipping into despair.
3. There is an increased tolerance for ambiguity and differences in their relationships. They become less rigid, more flexible, and more forgiving of self and other.
4. Intimacy and satisfaction in relationships are increased. Patients develop a sense of, "I can be who I am and you can be who you are, and we will disagree or not understand each other at times. But if we continue talking, we will come to a point of compromise, or at the very least agree to disagree."
5. Most importantly, patients develop a sense of mastery over their emotions. No longer will they, as Spinoza said, be of human bondage to the whims and fluctuations of their affective states. "We all want," Skulsky (2002) explains, "that satisfactory experience" that was repeatedly captured in the movie *Home Alone*." Each time the young boy foiled the bad-guy burglar trying to break into the house—those persecutory objects trying to do damage to our inner-psychic homes—he would make a fist and say, "Yes." This sense of, "*Yes*, I can handle this!" will leave patients with a newfound confidence in their coping ability.

Even if therapists accept Skulsky's challenge and work hard to become more aware of their patients' reservations about being openly honest about the therapist's failings, it is often difficult to address the conflict in a way that is beneficial. A number of studies cited by Safran and colleagues (2001) showed that therapists are often prone to responding defensively, hiding their own uncomfortable feelings behind their techniques. Psychodynamic therapists rely on an excessive use of transference interpretations, and cognitive therapists focus on the patients' cognitive distortions. Responses that demonstrate flexibility and empathy on the therapist's part lead to less damage of the alliance. A clinical vignette illustrates the misuse of transference interpretation:

> During the tenth session of a group psychotherapy training experience, a young woman angrily confronted the group leader, stating he was arbitrary, indifferent, and aloof. The group stopped in its tracks and the group members all sat poised on the edge of their seats, for this was the first confrontation of the leader, and the group was eager to see how he would respond. Finally, after a very agonizing few seconds, the group leader replied, "Do I remind you of your father?" The woman, relieved at the opportunity to move the exchange from the heat of the authentic encounter of the present relationship to the safety of a past relationship, quickly agreed that there were similarities between him and her father. She and the group therapist then proceeded to explore the more familiar terrain of her relationship with her father. The initial crisis of the confrontation had been watered down and the rest of the group sat back, relieved on some level that this issue could be dealt with on less threatening ground. Although the group members were relieved to be allowed to move away from the overt expression of anger in the group, they had been cheated out of a valuable therapeutic experience. They were, in fact, given a demonstration of how to avoid direct confrontations and negative process. The issue between this woman and the group leader was unresolved. In fact, it remained unresolved for the rest of the group members during the remainder of the group experience, for her accusation was very true. The group leader was, indeed, arbitrary, indifferent, and aloof. His urgency to move into the woman's past

> relationship with her father was reflective of his own need to avoid facing the painful accuracy of this woman's accusations. Transference is only transference if it is inappropriate to the present.

In contrast to the above example, several studies suggest that when therapists are able to respond nondefensively, attend directly to the alliance, adjust their responses and behavior, and address the rifts as they occur, the alliance actually improves and gets stronger. The patient's willingness to assert negative feelings about being misunderstood and the therapist's willingness to engage in a mutual effort to repair the rupture lead to a resolution of the impasse. Unilateral termination by the patient tends to take place when this process does not occur. Not only does the repair allow treatment to continue and prevent premature dropouts, but also evidence suggests that the repair of the rupture leads to an increased strength in the alliance. This is even true when alliances that had been ruptured and repaired were compared to therapeutic relationships that remained steady or increased uninterrupted during the course of treatment.

Attachment theory lends some support for the type of stance that the therapist needs to take in cases of negative transference or ruptures in the alliance. Bowlby's (1979b) seminal article, "On Knowing What You Are Not Supposed to Know and Feeling What You Are Not Supposed to Feel," addresses the type of therapeutic environment the therapist needs to create if the patient is going to feel secure enough to protest. Holmes (1996) noted, "The capacity of the caregiver to recognize and accept protest is as much a foundation of psychological health as the absence of major separation. The denial of trauma and suppression of protest were seen by Bowlby as crucial determinants of neurosis" (p. 6). Bowlby felt that parental attunement and the ability to accept protest without retaliation or excessive anxiety form the basis for secure attachment. In a similar fashion, the therapist who can manage the patient's hostility or anger without retaliation or fear is likely to have greater treatment success.

PATIENT CONTRIBUTIONS

While psychotherapy research has succeeded in demonstrating that treatment works, there is also a great deal of evidence that most of the treatment gain is determined by patients' coming to perceive the therapist as a competent, trustworthy, accepting, and caring individual who is responsive to their presenting difficulties. These perceptions are not dependent on the therapist's theoretical orientation, training, or technique. Nor are these perceptions consistently evident from one patient to another. While it is apparent that the characteristics of patients determine, in large part, whether they will be able to perceive the favorable qualities of the therapist, it is not clear why some patients click with some therapists and not others. Certainly, the convergence of patient and therapist values and personalities plays a large part in the establishment of the therapeutic relationship. Since there is strong evidence that success in both psychotherapy and alcoholism treatment is very much dependent on the establishment of a good working alliance, the nature of a patient's contribution to the therapeutic relationship and the working alliance is important to understand.

What interpersonal skills patients bring to psychotherapy determine to a large degree the potential success of the therapeutic encounter. The more patients have to offer the therapy situation and the less severe their pathology, the more likely treatment will be successful. Conversely, the more severe the patients' disorders, the less the chance they will benefit from treatment, no matter how skillful or talented the therapist may be. Research shows that patients' personal characteristics are the single most important contributing factor to the strength of the alliance. However, the effectiveness of this relationship in producing desirable therapeutic change is also determined in large part by the therapist's personality and his skill at managing interpersonal relationships, especially with patients who have a history of difficulties in this area. Some patients, such as severely psychotic individuals, cannot tolerate the closeness of an authentic interpersonal relationship. Patients who are severely intoxicated, chronic substance abusers, or who suffer from severe character disorders have great difficulty forming a true working alliance with a therapist.

INITIAL PHASE OF TREATMENT

The patient's willingness to enter treatment is determined by a number of important factors. The most significant is the level of the patient's experienced distress. The effectiveness of the initial stages of treatment is enhanced by the therapist's ability to mobilize the patient's expectancy for help, and this is influenced in large part by the patient's ability to possess a favorable expectation of treatment. This requires that the patient be able to accept some dependence on the therapist. Good responders to psychotherapy expect treatment to help them, and they are better integrated socially and less mistrustful than poor responders. The ability of a person to respond favorably is not so much a sign of excessive gullibility as it is of easy acceptance of others in their socially defined roles. However, the more suggestible patients are and the greater their experienced distress, the more likely they are to stay in treatment (Frank 1978).

There are a number of important factors that will enhance the patient's willingness to perceive the therapist as a source of help. Certainly, the therapist's ability to inspire the patient's confidence in him as a credible psychotherapist is essential. There is not a close correspondence between these inferred attributes, as rated by the therapist, the patient, or outside observers. The most consistent relationship found between therapeutic outcome and inferred therapist qualities are those derived from the patient's perception of the therapist rather than from either the therapist's perception of himself or the ratings of outside observers.

The patient's willingness to continue treatment is in turn dependent in large part on the patient's personal liking of the therapist. It has also been found that if the patient perceives the therapist to be a credible person, there is more of a chance that he will find the therapist more attractive. The concepts of credibility and attractiveness are not mutually exclusive. Research has demonstrated that those who are perceived as experts and who engender trust produce greater influence over attitude and behavior change. Patients are consequently more accepting of explanations or interpretations that vary with their own perceptions of the world and belief systems, especially when a therapist who is perceived as attractive and credible presents the interpretations or explanations. The acceptance of the advice given is thus dependent on the patient's perceived estimation of the therapists' competence, skill, anticipated thoroughness, and mutual attractiveness. Like credibility, attractiveness interacts completely with issues of interpersonal similarity and compatibility.

As would be expected, it was found that patients with secure attachment styles were able to form working alliances more quickly, were functioning best at the end of treatment, and had more positive treatment outcome (Meyer and Pilkonis 2001). They were also more likely to rate their initial contact with their therapists more positively, describing them as warm, accessible, and responsive. In contrast, a number of studies have shown that the weakness of the alliance at intake or after the first session is a good predictor of premature termination (Barber et al. 1999, Mohl et al. 1991, Plotnicov 1990, Tyron and Kane 1993). While patients with dismissive or anxious attachment styles were more difficult to treat and usually had greater problems initially establishing a working alliance, once they finally did emotionally connect with the therapist, however, improvement was sometimes more dramatic. Patients with dismissing attachment styles reported a poor alliance in the middle but a very strong alliance in the later stages of treatment. It was hypothesized that patients with dismissive and preoccupied attachment styles often yearn for intimacy and fear abandonment, thus often striving harder to establish a close alliance, given their concern over potential rejection. Under certain conditions, the more severely impaired patients with insecure attachment styles may show the best relative trajectory. This suggests that once the therapist is able to engage the more troublesome patient in the therapeutic process, the chances for successful and often dramatic improvement are greatly enhanced.

Recent developments in attachment theory have offered a conceptual framework that illuminates how different attachment styles reflect patterns of relatedness that are indicators of a person's internal working model. Research has shown that attachment styles or internalized patterns of relatedness are found to be enduring characteristics that continue to affect the quality of interpersonal interactions throughout adulthood.

Bowlby's internal working model is one proposed mechanism for explaining how one's internalized view of self and other determines the way one has to behave in order to stay in relation to the other. These implicit rules of relatedness, unless enacted in the therapy relationship, often go undetected, resulting in either compliance or premature termination.

THE TESTING HYPOTHESIS

Attachment theory and self psychology posit that during the therapeutic encounter, patients often unconsciously attempt to alter these pathogenic beliefs and rules. Patients "test" the relationship in order to determine if the rules that were adopted in childhood will be sustained or refuted in the contemporary relationship with the therapist. If the therapist passes the test, the patient no longer finds it necessary to retain these archaic rules, and, without the need for an interpretation, modifies previously self-imposed preservative behaviors.

Self psychology holds a very similar view on the importance of enactment in the therapy relationship. Stone (1996) states:

> Self psychology proposes that patients search for a therapeutic experience that will provide a remedy for a previously deficient selfobject experience, thereby enabling the individual to stabilize an up to that point unstable defective Self and restart growth. An archaic selfobject is not experienced by the disordered patient as a separate person but as part of the Self, which serves to fulfill an incompletely developed structure . . . Patients work to overcome their fears that they will be retraumatized in the treatment situation as they have in the past. The process of disconfirming earlier pathogenic beliefs enables patients to restart growth. Empathically available selfobjects fill developmental deficits and stabilize the Self, which experiences greater cohesion and may resume pursuit of its goal and ideals. [p. 170]

Stone adds that while it is possible to discern some of these pathogenic beliefs by careful diagnosis, others unfold during the treatment process. Sometimes therapists fail to even notice that they are being tested until they have either failed or passed the test.

A clinical vignette illustrates this often unnoticed dilemma:

> Paul had a blemished and very troubled history of multiple relapses with crack cocaine. Following his latest relapse, Paul's frustrated sponsor referred him to therapy, explaining to the therapist, "Because nothing else seems to be working." Even though Paul had been actively involved in AA for years, he had been unable to put together more than three months of sobriety at a time. His motivation and willingness to work the steps of the program were beyond reproach. His sponsor was as confused and frustrated as everyone else who knew the young man. He was doing everything that he was told to do, and still he kept relapsing.
>
> His therapist soon learned that Paul had been in and out of therapy with at least five different therapists within the last two years. When asked early in the initial interview why had he had so many different therapists, Paul laughed good-naturedly and said, "I seem to have a knack for getting them to fire me."
>
> "Fire you?" the therapist asked. "Why do they keep firing you?"
>
> "I think it's because I keep relapsing," Paul shrugged. "They get frustrated with me, I guess. It usually comes down to them giving me an ultimatum. They tell me they can't keep working with me on an outpatient basis, that I need to agree to go into inpatient treatment," Paul shrugged. "They say my addiction's too dangerous. I guess I scare them, because I can do some pretty self-destructive things when I'm high on crack."
>
> "So the ultimatum is that they want you to go into inpatient treatment or else?"
>
> Paul nodded. "Yeah. But hell, I've been in inpatient treatment twice before. It works fine as long as I'm in there, but each time I get out, I relapse. I don't think that's the answer."
>
> "Well, why don't you tell me what you think the answer is."

A surprised looked crossed Paul's face. "Wow, I don't think anyone ever asked me that before. Everyone else is always telling me what to do. Do you really want to know what I'd like and what I think is the answer?"

The therapist leaned back in his chair and nodded. "Yes, I would."

"I'd like to try this on an outpatient basis." Paul made a motion with his hands. "An inpatient program isn't going to give or tell me anything I don't already know. Hell, I know more about the program and addiction than a lot of those counselors working there." Paul hesitated. "Now, I'm not telling you that I got it all figured out. I know what AA says about 'self-will run riot.' I've got a good job. I can't afford to risk losing it if I go to some hospital. I'll do whatever you suggest, but I need someone to hang in there with me and help me, not control me."

"You don't like being controlled?" the therapist asked.

Paul smiled. "I know what you're thinking. What addict does like being controlled, and that addiction treatment is all about turning over control to a sponsor and a higher power. I know all that. If I have a problem, it's that I let people control me too much."

"What do you understand about that?"

Paul and his therapist spent the rest of the session talking about Paul's compliance. It quickly became clear that Paul's fear of abandonment prompted him to behave in an overly compliant manner in all his relationships—professional and personal. His drug use appeared to be in part related to a rebellious acting out. He and his therapist talked about other less self-destructive ways that he could display his need for autonomy and independence in a relationship. Before the session ended, Paul added one more piece of information.

"Oh, I almost forgot. I was adopted," Paul scowled. "I don't think it's that important, but my last therapist thought it was a big deal. So I guess I should tell you."

The therapist nodded. "I'm glad you did. I happen to agree with your last therapist. I think it is a big deal."

"Really?" Paul gave the therapist a quizzical look. "I

don't remember anything about it. I was only three or four days old when my foster parents took me in. So, I never even knew my mom or dad." Paul examined the therapist closely. "You still think it's a big deal?"

"Yes," the therapist said. "I still think it's a big deal. Let's talk about it more next time. But before we stop for today, let's go over what you're willing to do as far as AA meetings go."

Paul proved to be an eager, enthusiastic therapy client. He turned out to be engaging, insightful, clever, warm, and sensitive. A working alliance was quickly established. Determined to avoid another relapse and armed with what felt like a new committed collaboration with a responsive therapist, Paul readily agreed to any recommendations the therapist made. When it was suggested that Paul attend AA meetings, Paul sometimes attended two a day. When it was recommended that he get his phone number changed so he wouldn't receive surprise phone calls from his old crack dealers, Paul readily changed his phone numbers at work and at home. At his own initiative, Paul recruited not one but two new sponsors. Therapy progressed so quickly that his therapist suggested he might profit from a weekly ongoing therapy group. Paul promptly agreed. He quickly became a popular member of a hard-working therapy group. The same contagious enthusiasm he demonstrated in individual therapy was quickly manifested in group. His quick wit, pleasant demeanor, and supportive responses soon won over all of the other group members. Paul's sensitivity was contagious. The group quickly bonded with him.

Therapy moved along excellently for the next six months. Paul was able to put together the longest period of abstinence that he'd been able to achieve in nearly three years. Soon after he picked up his six-month chip, Paul began seriously dating a woman who he met in AA, who had more than five years of sobriety. The relationship developed quickly and before anyone in the group knew it, Paul announced that he was moving in with her. While some of the group members cautioned him about the speed of the relationship, most people were genuinely happy for him. Three weeks later, Paul relapsed.

Paul missed his next group meeting and two individual appointments. When he finally did return to therapy, he was remorseful and grief stricken. It was evident that the intensity of the new relationship with the woman he had just met had triggered some powerful feelings that he was not ready to master or understand. Conflicts had cropped up quickly in the relationship and Paul was not equipped to deal with them. His vacillation between compliance and passive-aggressive acting out proved too much for his girlfriend to tolerate and she quickly ended the relationship. Paul was devastated. His relapse was inevitable.

Toward the end of the session, Paul looked at the therapist and pleaded, "What should I do?"

"You need to do what you're already doing. You did the right thing by setting up this appointment and getting back into the AA program." The therapist smiled reassuringly at Paul. "We'll talk about this relapse and see what you can learn from it, so it won't happen again."

Paul looked relieved. "Thanks, I thought you might be angry and want to fire me."

"No, that won't happen. But we do have to talk about this relapse and see what you can do differently next time. The only thing worse than a relapse is an unexamined relapse."

Paul returned to the group and spoke at length about his relapse. The group was supportive and encouraging of Paul to get back into recovery. However, Paul's demeanor changed. He brooded more and withdrew into an obsessive preoccupation about the recently terminated relationship. He remained angry with the woman "for abandoning me." The more that he explained all that had occurred in the relationship, the more apparent it became to the group members that it was actually Paul who had abandoned the girlfriend first. She gradually grew more and more irritated with his refusal to follow through with his commitments and promises to her. When she became angry, he complied and made more promises that his passive-aggressive impulses would not let him fulfill. The group began to gently confront Paul. His attendance became more erratic. Within two months, Paul relapsed again.

This relapse proved to be more severe in duration and intensity. He missed a number of days at work because of his cocaine use and his boss soon placed him on probation. A pattern began to emerge both with the group and with work. His employer, like the group members, soon learned that they could not depend on Paul to be there when he said he would. In his individual sessions, his therapist was relentless in reminding Paul that he was doing to others what he feared they would do with him.

Paul refused to listen, and within another three weeks he relapsed again.

After Paul failed to show for the group session and his individual appointment, the therapist received an apologetic phone call two days later. Paul meekly asked if the therapist still wanted to see him. Paul sounded surprised when the therapist told him, "Of course I want to see you. We have our regular appointment next week, don't we?"

At the next appointment following his latest relapse, the therapist tried to get Paul to enter an inpatient program or a halfway house. Paul reacted with hurt indignation. "Okay, here it comes. What's the ultimatum? If I don't do what you want, you're going to abandon me, too?"

"No, I'm going to keep seeing you, no matter what you do. But I think the increased frequency of the relapses and the crack cocaine are clouding your thinking. I strongly encourage you to do something to stop this cycle. You're out of control."

Paul stared at the therapist. A mixture of relief and fear washed across his face. "I'll do whatever you want; just don't make me go into inpatient treatment. It's what my parents did to me when I first started using drugs in high school." Paul's face twisted up in an angry sneer. "They didn't want to bother with me and just shipped me off to some damn hospital. They abandoned me like everyone else."

"Paul, listen to me." The therapist held up his hand to get Paul's attention. "You're so focused on others' abandoning you that you don't see how you're abandoning everyone else."

"What do you mean that I'm abandoning them?" Paul set his jaw and stared defiantly at the therapist. "They're the ones who aren't there for me."

"You are caught up in something that I don't think you can see clearly," the therapist said. "I don't know how much of it is the cocaine and how much of it is the compulsion that you have to test everyone to see if they're going to abandon you or not."

Paul sat silently for a few seconds. He sighed, rubbed his chin, and looked intently into the therapist's eyes. "Why haven't you abandoned me?"

The therapist leaned forward and locked eyes with Paul. "Because I know what you're doing is a test. I don't know which is stronger, your fear that I will pass the test or your fear that I will fail."

The subject of Paul's relapses, his abandonment fears, and enactments became a constant theme in therapy over the next two months. However, nothing helped. Paul's relapses continued in frequency. He refused to try more intensive inpatient or outpatient treatment. He kept insisting that the therapist was just trying to find an excuse to abandon him "like everyone else in my life."

Paul couldn't be reasoned with and refused to follow the therapist's recommendations. The therapist felt strongly that Paul's fear that he would be abandoned by the therapist was in part driven by his compulsion to see if his worst fears would come true. The more the therapist assured him, the more anxious Paul became. He had the therapist trapped in a no-win situation. If the therapist refused to treat him unless Paul agreed to inpatient treatment, this stance would confirm Paul's testing hypothesis that he would be abandoned unless he "behaved." If the therapist continued to treat Paul as an outpatient, the therapist feared that he might be enabling him. The therapist decided that he would find a way to continue to confront Paul's addiction and self-defeating behavior while somehow continuing to maintain the relationship and alliance.

Paul relapsed again. After missing work for an entire week, his employer fired him. He failed to show up for his group therapy sessions, not bothering to call or letting the group know that he had decided unilaterally to terminate treatment even though he had made an agreement, as all group members had, that he would give the group four weeks' notice before leaving. A few days later, he made a phone call to the therapist leaving a message that he was too embarrassed to come in for any more appointments. Two weeks later, the therapist received one last phone call on his answering machine. Paul announced, "I've been clean now for six days and want to come back into therapy, if you are still willing to see me after all that I've done."

The therapist left him a return message. "Of course I'd be willing to see you. Schedule an appointment whenever you're ready."

The phone call never came.

Paul's case illustrates two related dilemmas that often confront therapists when they are working with an addicted patient. An addict's or alcoholic's pathology is often exacerbated by their drug use, resulting in a further deterioration of an already ineffective attachment style. At times, a powerfully addictive drug like crack cocaine makes interpersonal attachment practically impossible. The potent emotional rush and powerful reinforcing properties of the substances on the motivational centers of the brain compromise whatever existing structure was there before substances started to be abused. The subtleties involved in regulatory powers of an attachment relationship pale mightily in comparison to the persuasive powers of many drugs. The attachment to a drug and the reinforcing properties that many substances produce are far stronger than any emotional impact that can be generated by an attachment with another person. Also, as it was with Paul's case, the capacity to reason—to see what one is doing and understand why—is impaired to the degree that insight and self-understanding are for all practical purposes impossible.

Self-understanding and motivation are obliterated by the substance abuse.

THE ALLIANCE AND ADDICTION: SPECIAL CONSIDERATIONS

As Paul's case illustrates, treatment of the addicted patient often presents a set of special obstacles to the establishment of a working alliance. The biggest hurdle is the establishment of a collaborative working alliance. Unlike may individuals who enter therapy either highly motivated or suffering from what Henry David Thoreau called "quiet desperation," few alcoholics or addicts enter treatment of their own free will. They usually enter treatment under extreme outside pressure from their family, employer, or the court system, or are experiencing acute health problems related to their chronic substance abuse. They are either in denial or in severe emotional turmoil, suffering from guilt, depression, shame, and cognitive impairment—either incapable of forming, or unwilling to form, a therapeutic alliance. They often refuse to see that the majority of their problems are related to or exacerbated by their substance abuse. Many alcoholics and addicts are openly obstinate and angry because circumstances and influential others in their lives have forced them to seek a treatment that they feel they don't need or want. Even when addicts and alcoholics agree that they need treatment, they usually harbor a secret desire to use chemicals in a nonaddictive fashion, even though their history of abuse illustrates that they cannot. Their compliance with treatment is motivated more by their guilt and their wish to avoid further consequences than it is by a sincere desire to face their addiction to substances and the problems their chemical abuse has inflicted on their lives. Consequently, if addicts or alcoholics are not openly resistant and rebellious to treatment, they are working hard to create the impression of compliance so that they can meet whatever requirements are expected of them and get back to their habitual patterns of dealing with life's demands and interpersonal relationships.

Successful treatment of any kind is enhanced when the patient becomes an active participant in the therapy process.

Strupp (1999), in fact, cites as one of the crucial variables in successful treatment "an appropriate patient, that is, a person who is capable of achieving a modicum of insight and is motivated to work conscientiously in a therapeutic context that follows essentially the psychoanalytic model and who can tolerate the requirements of 'therapeutic neutrality'" (p. 34). Since in most cases with alcoholics and addicts the therapist is deprived of this important ingredient of successful therapy, special strategies are required. The development of the capacity to apply treatment to patients who are in a crisis, actively resistant to engagement in the therapeutic alliance, or passively compliant is a special skill that the addiction specialist needs to develop.

A CRISIS OPENS A PATIENT'S ATTACHMENT SYSTEM

Urgent circumstances often compel individuals to make massive shifts in their life perspectives and face their symbolic deaths. Brown & Yalom (1977), writing from an existential perspective, emphasize a crucial principle for interpersonal change: "This principle—that change is preceded by a state of dissonance or incongruity—has considerable clinical and social psychology backing" (p. 448). This is especially true for substance abusers, who, because of their excessive use of substances, have created a rift between their sober values and their addicted behavior. Addicts and alcoholics have often experienced a "stay in their own personal underworld, an experience which AA members refer to as hitting bottom" (Brown Yolom 1977 p. 448). Hitting bottom has a dual meaning for therapy and the creation of the therapeutic alliance. It is at once an obstacle and a potentially invaluable reference point. "As patients face their limits, their symbolic deaths, they are often able to make massive shifts in their life perspective. They may rearrange their priority of needs and trivialize the trivia in their lives" (Brown and Yalom 1977, p. 448).

However, the therapist needs to realize that for many alcoholics and addicts in the midst of hitting bottom, their window of opportunity for establishing an alliance may be brief and transient. The therapist has a small window of opportunity to influence the substance abuser to accept his or her diagnosis and establish a therapeutic alliance. Many substance abusers quickly "seal over" after the crisis passes, returning quickly to their dysfunctional attachment styles. The moment of opportunity slips away and the nascent therapeutic alliance is not fully developed.

In other situations, undiagnosed alcoholics and addicts gradually reveal the extent of their affliction during the course of outpatient therapy. The therapist, in this case, must address the issue of their substance abuse without "enabling" their continued use or disturbing the rudimentary development of the therapeutic alliance. The astute therapist must find a way to negotiate the substance abuser's detachment from substances so that the full impact of the attachment alliance to the therapist and the culture of recovery can be fully realized.

> An intake counselor at a local university hospital had referred Arnold, a 32-year-old stockbroker, for outpatient treatment. Arnold had called a local hospital for an appointment after listening to a radio advertisement describing the symptoms of adult attention deficit disorder (ADD). While Arnold did possess many of the symptoms (e.g., distractibility, impulsiveness, hyperactivity, etc.) and was quickly prescribed medication, the intake counselor was concerned about his drinking history. At the first appointment with the outpatient therapist, it was obvious that Arnold was a very bright, energetic, good-looking, and successful young man. He was also a very unhappy young man.
>
> When asked what had brought him to therapy and how could the therapist help, Arnold responded, "I'm not sure. The intake counselor at the university hospital thought you might me able to help me with my ADD."
>
> "Maybe you could start by telling me how you feel," the therapist suggested.
>
> "Feel?" Arnold smirked at the therapist. "I feel fine, I'm just bored at work and bored with my life in general."
>
> "Boredom doesn't sound like a good feeling to me," the therapist offered. "It must be difficult feeling that way."

"No. You don't understand. I feel fine," Arnold said, shifting nervously in his seat. "I just don't like what I'm doing. Nothing holds my interest for very long. That's my problem. Other than that, I feel fine."

At this point, the therapist decided to back off focusing on Arnold's feelings and asked, "Oh? Well then, why don't you tell me how long this has been going on? Maybe we can find a way to quickly fix it."

A smile of relief swiftly flashed across Arnold's face and he leaned back in his chair. "Great, I'd like that. You probably don't know this, but I'm the type of person who likes to meet problems head on and solve them quickly."

The therapist smiled. "Yes, I'm *quickly* getting that impression."

"Good. My job requires that I stay focused on my accounts and the stock market. I can't afford to get distracted." Arnold began to tap nervously on the arm of the chair. "And this damn medication doesn't seem to be helping anymore. I keep asking my psychiatrist to up it and he says we're at the maximum dose and wouldn't recommend that." Arnold looked at the therapist and frowned. "He told me to be patient and wait for the medication to work."

"He obviously doesn't know you well. I get the impression that patience is not your strong point."

"Well, you're right about that," Arnold laughed and pointed at the therapist. "You're sharp. I like that."

"I also get the impression that you don't care a lot about focusing on feelings. You appear more into identifying the problem and doing something about it," the therapist said, as playfully as he could.

Arnold smiled. "I like people who call a spade a spade. You're right about feelings. I'm not into this touchy-feely stuff. In fact that's one reason why I've hesitated coming to see one of you shrinks. Everything is always about feelings with you guys, isn't it?"

The therapist shrugged. "Often it is. But there are other things that matter, also."

Arnold arched his eyebrow. "Really? That hasn't been my experience."

"Your experience?" the therapist asked. "I thought you hadn't been to a therapist before."

"I haven't. But my mother has for years and it hasn't helped her a bit. She just gushes more and more all the time."

The therapist and Arnold proceeded to spend the rest of the session talking about Arnold's experience with his emotionally labile mother. After a lifetime of repeated failures at talk therapy, she had finally been correctly diagnosed with bipolar disorder five years ago. Even though her symptoms were greatly reduced by medication, her noncompliance with her recommended therapeutic dosage proved problematic. The rest of the session stayed focused on Arnold's distrust of therapists and his conviction that talking about feelings, especially in his mother's case, had only made matters worse. His therapist chose not to introduce the information that the intake counselor had given him about Arnold's alcohol consumption, deciding that the establishment of a working alliance had to take precedence during this rudimentary stage of their relationship.

Arnold agreed to set up another appointment. He was pleased with the way that session went and continued to see the therapist on a regular basis for the next two months. Arnold avoided the topic of his drinking, and the therapist waited patiently for an opening to introduce it. Most of the time was spent on Arnold's fear of his emotions. The therapist learned that Arnold felt passionately about many things, but was terrified that if he gave into feeling his emotions completely, he would be overtaken in much the same way his mother had been. Arnold was convinced he would become psychotic like her if he didn't work hard to keep his emotions under wraps.

"That most be hard work, keeping your feelings under constant check," the therapist said one day during their session. "How do you manage to do that?"

"Lots of ways. I run. I workout. Anything to keep myself busy helps."

"Ever use alcohol?" the therapist asked innocently.

"Sometimes." Arnold eyed the therapist suspiciously. "Why do you ask?"

"Just curious." The therapist waved his hand nonchalantly. "It had crossed my mind before when you had mentioned that the weekends were the times you felt most out of control or most intensely."

"What are you getting at?" Arnold stopped his incessant tapping and sat up in his chair. "What's the connection with my drinking and the increased intensity of my feelings on the weekend?"

"I've gotten the impression that drinking is one way you manage your feelings." The therapist examined Arnold carefully. He felt that he had enough of a relationship with Arnold now that he could risk a gentle confrontation around a subject that had been avoided up to now. "It seems your drinking is a kind of self-medication."

"So?" Arnold frowned. "Everyone drinks to relax. What's so strange about that?"

"Nothing, except that it may be that your drinking is actually making your emotions more intense and more difficult to manage." The therapist spoke the words with a complete absence of judgment. "It may be that your drinking is making your problem worse, not better."

A confused look washed across Arnold's face. "What? Making it worse . . . how?"

"You said that the last two times you and your girlfriend got into one of your worst fights was when you were drinking. I think you told me that you said a lot of cruel things to her that you didn't mean. You said you didn't know what had gotten into you, that it was so unlike you."

Arnold unfolded his arms and stroked his chin with his hand. "Maybe you're right." He looked up at the therapist. "You think that time I got into an argument with one of my clients during that two-cocktail lunch is another example?"

"Could be. What do you think?" the therapist asked.

"Maybe you're on to something here." A thoughtful look crossed Arnold's face. "If you're right, how do we fix it? You know how I am about problem solving."

"It depends," the therapist answered.

"On what?"

"If you're an alcoholic or not."

"An alcoholic?" Arnold's mouth dropped open. "What makes you think I'm an alcoholic?"

The therapist held up his hand and began counting on his fingers. "One, there's a history of alcoholism in your family; two, you had a DUI arrest three years ago; three, your girlfriend has repeatedly expressed concerns about your drinking; and four, your drinking, by your own indications, has increased over the last couple of years." By the time the therapist had finished counting, he was holding up four fingers in front of Arnold's face.

Arnold sat stunned for a few seconds before composing himself. He stroked the creases on his slacks and gave the therapist a piercing look. "Okay, let's say I'm an alcoholic. Can I cut down on my drinking, control it, and start to drink normally?"

The therapist shook his head. "No, if you're an alcoholic, by definition, you cannot drink normally. Now if you don't think you're an alcoholic, there are other options for you. But before we explore those options, you have to decide if you're an alcoholic or not. If you are one, the only treatment that works is abstinence and the best way to achieve that is through AA."

"AA?" Arnold shook his head. "No way I'm going to any AA meetings. Anyway I'm not sure I'm an alcoholic. Maybe I'm someone who just has a little bit of a drinking problem."

"Having a little bit of a drinking problem is like being a little bit pregnant. You're either an alcoholic or you're not," the therapist said emphatically. "Listen, Arnold, you've said you're a no-nonsense guy who likes to face problems head on and fix what has to be fixed. I would recommend you do the same thing with your alcoholism as you would with a stock you hold that's going belly up. You'd sell it and cut your losses."

Arnold grinned at his therapist. "Okay, I like that approach. I would recommend to my clients that they get some expert advise on what to do with their portfolio. What would you recommend I do?"

"I think you're an alcoholic for all the reasons I've stated. I would recommend we continue doing what we have been doing in here and that you stop drinking and start going to AA. If you're totally against AA, I won't push you on that. My experience tells me that all this works best if someone is also going to AA while they're dealing with the other stuff in therapy."

Arnold sat silently for a minute before swallowing slowly. "I don't agree with you. I don't think I'm an alcoholic and I think I can control my drinking. It looks as if we're at a crossroads here. I'm not sure what to do next."

"What we do next is to keep doing what we've been doing." The therapist smiled approvingly at Arnold. "You don't have to agree with me on this. Let's try it your way and see if it works. If it doesn't, you always have the option of trying something else."

A look of relief washed across Arnold's face. "Great, let's talk about how we do this."

The next few weeks were marked by Arnold's increased openness in the session. Associations related to his parents' rigidity and lack of confidence in his ability to make decisions were explored and worked through. Since the therapist did not want to risk a rupture in the alliance just because Arnold did not agree with his diagnosis or the treatment recommendations, the therapy alliance was deepened and strengthened. However, the burst of progress that Arnold initially demonstrated could not be sustained. Therapy limped along for the next six months with Arnold experiencing periods of mixed success with his controlled drinking and sporadic episodes of abstinence. Eventually Arnold was able to give up his drinking when he felt ready to make that commitment.

As in Arnold's case, the therapeutic alliance takes on added significance with addicts and alcoholics since many of them enter treatment suffering from intrapsychic deficits related to unmet developmental needs. From this perspective, the therapist deliberately opposes the previous traumatizing relationship with past attachment objects and uses the force of the corrective emotional relationship to repair deficits in self that have been produced by early neglect and abuse. Ormont (2001) sees the emotional recovery of the developmentally arrested patient as a corrective experience that occurs through the therapeutic relationship that is achieved by "providing what was not provided during the individual's formative years" (p. 345).

12

Addiction and Attachment-Oriented Therapy: Long-Term Implications

> There will come a time in every child's life when the only reason your child will listen to what you have to say is because they love you and know that you love them.
>
> *Attachment-Oriented Parenting Institute*

If research supplies the evidence and the relational models of attachment theory and self psychology provides the theoretical foundation for attachment-oriented therapy (AOT), it is Martin Buber's (1955) philosophical anthropology that furnishes AOT with its soul, its center, and its spiritual core. AOT is highly compatible with the ideological leanings of dialogical psychotherapy (Friedman 1985), an approach that offers practical insights into applying an understanding of Buber's philosophy to therapeutic practice. Buber (1988) says, "If Psychology and Psychoanalysis are to be successful in their endeavor to understand and to heal men, they must be grounded in a realistic conception of what man is" [p. 8]. Buber, the Jewish existential philosopher, has spent a lifetime with his anthropological approach, trying to answer the question of what really defines man and how can we properly understand what makes him both unique and similar to all other bearers of consciousness.

Buber provides an answer to that question by asserting that we can never truly know each other in isolation, only in relation (1963). "We may come nearer the answer to the question what man is when we come to see him as the eternal meeting of the One with the Other," (p. 18). The school of dialogical psychotherapy in particular has long understood the therapeutic powers inherent in all authentic dialogue and genuine encounter. "Healing through meeting" and "personal making present" are crucial components of Buber's philosophical perspectives on the importance of I–Thou relationships. The "between" is the only true reality of existence or as Maurice Freidman says, "The action takes place between the boundaries" (p. 24). Buber (1988) concludes, "If all real living is meeting, all true healing takes place through meeting" (p. 21).

Buber was not a man of pat formulas, but someone who tried to meet each person and each situation uniquely. Despite the fact that much of Buber's fame and popularity rests on the development of the distinctions he made between the duality of the I–It and the I–Thou, psychotherapists often fail to completely appreciate all the implications of Buber's philosophical system. Buber's (1960) major contribution to psychotherapy is often interpreted simply as his emphasis on the importance of the I–Thou. As significant as the authentic meeting of another in genuine dialogue is to his dialogic approach, Buber's genius was not in the formulation of the I–Thou, for others did that before him. However, it was Buber alone who placed at the center of a monumental corpus the task of pointing the way to the essential difference between the direct, mutual meeting—into which one enters with one whole being, making oneself fully present—and the indirect, nonmutual relationship of subject and object, the I–It.

Only through the development of the "I" can the eternal "Thou" be confronted with its uniqueness. Buber (1988) writes, "The I confronts its detached self for a moment like a Thou, and then takes possession if itself and henceforth enters into relation in full consciousness" (p. 11). Because of its separateness I can now truly meet a Thou. People have the opportunity in such circumstances to recognize the paradox of their uniqueness and similarity. Consciousness here is higher because the element of choice is present.

> Entering into relation is an act of the whole being: it is the act by which we constitute ourselves as human, and it is an act which must be repeated ever again in ever new situations . . . This distance given, man is able to enter in relation with other beings distant from, and opposed to him, for the "overcoming"

> of distance does not mean simple unity, but the polar tension of distance and relation together. [Buber 1988, p. 12]

The importance of the discovery of an authentic, separate I cannot be overstated. Buber 1955 stated, "The principle of individuation, the fundamental fact of the infinite variety of human persons, of whom this one is only one person . . . gives it its kernel and skeleton" (p. 124). Therefore, before one can truly meet another, one must first know oneself. To the extent that we cannot know or be true to ourselves—to be what is innate or biologically ingrained in us to become—determines the degree of our emotional and psychological impairment. If the push or drive to actualize our uniquely determined self is obstructed, we will, Buber said, remain spiritually sick and vulnerable to physical illness and psychopathology. The paradox for Buber, as it is for self psychology and attachment theory, is that the discovery and development of "self" (the I of the I–Thou) requires the presence of the other. The other can be both the source of the impediment and the stimulus for the restoration and vitalization of the self.

Like Kohut and the self psychologists after him, Buber sees the therapeutic encounter as providing the reparative environment, which permits the arrested projectory of emotional growth to commence or continue. Acceptance and confirmation, in the limited Rogerian sense, is not the goal of therapy; it is only a means for helping others complete their arrested and unfinished potential. Acceptance differs from confirmation in the way that Buber defines the two terms. The former is related to seeing and meeting the other person as he is. Confirmation means validating not just what the other is, but also what the other can become—his or her potential.

> Confirmation can be misunderstood as *static*. I meet another—I accept and confirm him as he now is. But confirming a person *as he is* is only the first step. Confirmation does not mean that I take his appearance at this moment as being the person I want to confirm. I must take the other person in his dynamic existence, in his specific potentiality. In the present lies hidden what *can become*. This potentiality, this sense of unique direction as a person, can make itself felt to me without our relationship, and it is that I most want to confirm. In therapy this personal direction

> becomes perceptible to the therapist in a very special way. [Buber 1988, pp. 28–29]

THEORETICAL UNCERTAINTY

If there is one phrase that is a key to interpreting and understanding Buber's philosophical system, it's his concept of the "narrow ridge." This phrase signifies Buber's standpoint, the edifice upon which the I–Thou relationship stands. "I wanted, by this [narrow ridge], to express that I did not rest on the broad upland of a system that includes a series of sure statements about the absolute, but a narrow rocky ridge between the gulfs where there is no sureness of expressible knowledge but the certainty of meeting what remains undisclosed" (1963, p. 13). Buber stresses the importance of "holy insecurity," when truly meeting another. An I–Thou encounter requires the necessity of turning loose all abstract categories and the certainty that comes with facts. Instead of retreating into the certainty of doctrines, theories, and other closed systems, the therapist must meet the other in the authentic experience, and only after the meeting can their encounter be properly understood. To do less, to encounter another while holding oneself back is pretending and inauthentic. Buber stated (1955):

> Help without mutuality is presumptuousness, it is an attempt to practice magic. The doctor or the psychotherapist who tries to dominate his patient stifles the growth of his blessing. As soon as the helper is touched by the desire, in however subtle a form, to dominate or to enjoy his patient, or to treat the latter's wish to be dominated or enjoyed by him as other than a wrong condition needing to be cured, the danger of falsification arises, besides which all quackery appears peripheral. [p. 95]

Sometimes, though, the therapist will have to know when to hold oneself back and be silent. If the therapist's primary motive for speaking is to demonstrate how competent, brilliant, or helpful he or she is, problems are likely to occur. When the alcoholic's or addict's getting better is important to the therapist only as a reflection on the therapist's ability to cure, progress in therapy is compromised.

A clinical example illustrates this potential dilemma:

> Even though Pete was ten years into recovery from his alcoholism, he still carried many unresolved narcissistic vulnerabilities. One primary recurring difficulty was his intolerance of others and his need always to be in control. A large intimidating man, Pete started the session complaining angrily about his new wife's timidity and his annoyance at her difficulty making decisions.
>
> "I'm sick and tired of having to act like the parent in this damn relationship." Pete spit out the words. "She's always asking if it's okay to do this or do that." Pete screwed up his face and mockingly spoke in a high-pitched feminine voice. "Can I let the dog out now? Is it all right if I turn on the TV? It won't bother you will it, *dear*?"
>
> The therapist listened empathically, immersing himself as much as he could into the depths of Pete's experience. He worked to grasp an empathic understanding of the frustration that one might experience at not having a strong partner to lean on in a relationship. He let Pete know that having to make all the decisions in a marriage would be discouraging and annoying. What the therapist restrained himself from saying was more important. The therapist did not say how Pete had created the situation by first choosing to marry someone who was so passive and sweet, a trait that Pete found endearing at the beginning of the relationship. Also, Pete's physical size, loud voice, and provocative presence intimidated most people. The therapist wanted to point out to Pete how he was "training" his wife to become even more submissive and compliant because of his intimidating behavior.
>
> Instead, the therapist remained empathically attuned until Pete's anger spent itself and Pete gradually began to talk softly of his deep sense of loneliness and isolation in the marriage.
>
> "When I try to talk with her or my friends about my feelings, it only makes things worse. Everyone wants to tell me what I'm doing wrong."

"Feeling misunderstood by others only drives you deeper into your defensive anger, creating even greater feelings of isolation and misunderstanding," the therapist said.

"Yes. I hate it." Pete shook his head. "I start thinking, why in the hell do I want to talk to anyone about how I feel; it only makes matters worse."

The therapist continued to stay attuned to Pete's affect states and empathically responsive to his feelings. Slowly but surely, Pete came to his own realizations about the way he was contributing to his own difficulties in the relationship.

"I can see how I have created this timidity in her. I hate that, too," Pete frowned. "When I get critical and attack her, it only makes her more hesitant and cautious around me." Pete ran his hand through his hair. "I know it doesn't work and only makes matters worse, but sometimes I feel powerless to stop myself."

By the end of the session, Pete's feelings and thinking had become consolidated. Through the therapist's attunement and his lack of need to show Pete the errors of his ways, the therapist was able to provide a holding environment that allowed Pete to discover for himself what he was doing that was self-defeating. The therapist stifled his own need to be right or brilliant, permitting Pete to experience the satisfaction that comes from struggling and discovering one's own answers.

As this vignette illustrates, Buber's emphasis has rested particularly on the healing-through-meeting process that is such an intricate part of true dialogue. Buber's therapist must therefore enter, completely and in reality, in the act of self-reflection, in order to become aware of human wholeness. In other words, he must carry out this act of entry into that unique dimension as an act of his life, without any prepared philosophical security; that is, he must expose himself to all that can meet him when he is really living. The patient, Buber feels, is often floundering; he cannot be interested in the therapist as a person, for in a relationship that has an object to accomplish, the two cannot be equals.

Maintaining the healthy balance between separateness and mutuality is not always easy to accomplish. With certain vulnerable individuals, as consciousness of one's separateness grows, it becomes more difficult to overcome distance through relationships. There is a temptation to accentuate the distance and take refuge in the pseudo-security of the world of things, creating a vacuum that often gets filled by alcohol, drugs, and other obsessive distractions and compulsive addictions. However, as Buber (1963) emphasized, distance becomes the presupposition for relation. Distance once given allows one to enter in relation. In other words, an I always precedes an I–Thou relationship. Psychotherapy as it should be practiced demands much, perhaps in some cases much more than therapists can give in a situation, under those circumstances. The reason it demands so much is that it requires one to enter the realm of the suffering, uncertainty, and authentic dialogue.

A clinical example illustrates the potential power that an authentic relationship can have when dealing with an individual struggling in the midst of a devastating addiction.

> Shortly after his discharge from a thirty-day inpatient treatment program for his alcoholism and depression, Ted followed the recommendations of the treatment program and sought out an individual therapist. He proceeded to progress nicely in therapy for the next two years, making his weekly therapy sessions, taking his prescribed antidepressant medication, and consistently going to AA meetings. His marriage, which had been on the verge of divorce when he had first entered the hospital, was now a source of security and support. A job promotion helped ease some of the financial pressures, and Ted was once again feeling confident and successful.
>
> Even though he stayed committed to his weekly individual therapy sessions, he began to cut back on his AA meetings. Soon, he began telling his therapist that he wanted to come off his medication. "I want to do this alone," Ted announced one day. "I just don't like being dependent on anything."
>
> His therapist expressed concern about Ted's decision, gently reminding him that some elements of his grandiosity

may be returning. "You know that's what got you in trouble last time. Soon you'll begin thinking, 'I can't be one of those alcoholics. I'm different. I'm special.'"

Ted refused to listen. Soon he was off his medication. A few weeks later, he announced, "I had a couple beers at the ballgame the other night and nothing terrible happened." Ted looked at the therapist proudly. "No lightning came down and struck me or anything."

"What did your AA group say?" the therapist asked.

"Aww," Ted waved his hand dismissively. "I stopped going to AA a few weeks ago." Ted shrugged and forced a weak smile, examining the therapist's face for some sign of a reaction.

"I didn't know you had stopped going to AA."

"Yeah, I didn't tell you. I figured you might try to talk me out of it," Ted said.

"Well, you're right. I probably would have told you not to give up AA and the medication all in the same month." The therapist frowned. "But since you've done it, let's watch closely to see what happens. You haven't been thinking of stopping therapy too, have you?"

"The thought has crossed my mind." Ted scratched his forehead. "I thought you might be unhappy that I started drinking again."

"Unhappy is not the right word," the therapist said. "I'm *concerned* that you may be giving up all your support systems too quickly." The therapist leaned forward. "So, you must think you're not an alcoholic anymore."

"Huh?" Ted shrugged. "I guess I haven't thought much about it."

"Well, I strongly encourage you to think carefully about it. Because if you are an alcoholic, you won't be able to drink and your depression will likely return."

Ted scowled. "If you're right, I must not be an alcoholic. I drank the other weekend and nothing happened. I even had a glass of wine last night." Ted sat up and patted his chest. "I'm still here thinking clearly. I didn't go off on any binge."

"Come on, Ted," the therapist smiled. "You've been around AA enough to know that most alcoholics can have a few drinks and control it for a short time. That's not that unusual. It's what happens six or twelve months down the road that's important."

"Okay, you're right," Ted grimaced and nodded. "I'm willing to keep coming for a while. But I feel great right now and that's all that matters."

The session ended with Ted agreeing to continue therapy while he conducted his experiment with drinking. The next couple months were uneventful. Ted continued to report more successes with his controlled drinking and reveled in reemerging confidence. A couple of weeks later, however, a shift in his demeanor and attitude began to surface. He complained about his wife's lack of support and wondered whether the marriage was the right one for him. She started expressing more concern about the increased levels of alcohol he was consuming.

Within two months, Ted's depression had returned with a vengeance. Caught up in the throes of his drinking, depression, and his narcissistic defenses, Ted could not see clearly that he was spinning out of control. Concerns voiced by his wife and close friends fell on deaf ears. Ted refused to see what everyone else saw.

Fifteen minutes into the session, after Ted had spent the entire time complaining how "everyone just needs to get off my back; I got this thing under control. If I can just get a break and some understanding, everything will be all right," the therapist took a deep breath and held his hand up to stop Ted in midsentence. "Ted, look at me." With his voice full of emotion, the therapist said, "You are in relapse. You are right back where you were two years ago when you first went into rehab. I am not going to sit here and watch you destroy your marriage and drink yourself to death. I want you back on medication and I want you back in AA."

Ted stared at the therapist. He opened his mouth to protest, then stopped and leaned back in his chair, speechless.

The therapist's voice cracked with emotion. "I want your word that you'll leave here and pick up a white chip at a meeting tonight."

Ted leaned his elbows on his knees and cupped his hands around his head. “Okay, okay,” Ted said wearily. “If you think that’s what I need to do, I’ll do it.”

The therapist met Ted in the authenticity of the moment. This was no passive comment from an uninterested observer or a detached professional giving voice to an important theoretical concept. The message was delivered the only way that Ted, in his depressed stupor and alcohol-clouded thought process, could hear. In this example, Ted’s therapist took a position that was very similar to the one that attachment-oriented parenting recommends, that there will come a time in every child’s life when the only reason your child will listen to what you have to say is because they love you and know that you love them. In a similar fashion, there will come a time, as was the case with Ted, that the only reason patients will listen to the therapist is because the strength of the attachment bond or the therapeutic alliance will compel them to.

CONCLUSIONS

Buber’s message is an important one because alcohol and drug treatment is falling prey to the same difficulties that confront all forms of medical care. More and more emphasis is placed on greater technology, large group practices, multimillion-dollar corporate hospital chains with revolving treatment personnel, state and federal bureaucratic–dominated treatment policies and multiple specialties—all factors that tend to oppose a close therapist–patient relationship. Buber like others after him (e.g., Bowlby, Kohut) offers an important reminder of the need to restore or reestablish the necessary human connection between the patient and the person or persons providing the care and treatment if the individual is going to fully benefit from these advances in technology.

The long-term goals of AOT are mutuality and secure attachment, which help break the substance abuser’s cycle of alienation and isolation. However, as important as attachment is, the maintenance of a sense of separateness is equally so.

The polarity between attachment and autonomy has to be carefully managed. Secure attachment can be established only once insecure and ambivalent attachment styles are relinquished (Ainsworth 1989). If long-term treatment requirements are successfully achieved, the substance abuser will begin to understand and experience healthy mutuality. Every alcoholic and addict must learn the important task of resolving conflicts without resorting to alcohol or drugs.

The goal of substance abuse treatment is also very similar to the goal of analysis for individuals suffering from narcissistic disturbances. As Kohut (1984) wrote, cure in therapy is obtained when a person can establish healthy relationships outside of the therapeutic milieu. AOT accomplishes this in a number of ways. It provides a predictable and consistent holding environment that allows substance abusers to have their attachment and selfobject needs met in a way that is not exploitive, destructive, or shameful. Because of unmet developmental needs, substance abusers have strong and overpowering needs (object hunger) for human responsiveness that they feel are insatiable, and they feel shamed and frightened by their neediness. Through their identification with others in group therapy and twelve-step programs like AA, they have the opportunity to accept in themselves what they could not previously accept because they had felt so unique in their badness. Acceptance at this level of emotional vulnerability can be tolerated only by substance abusers if they feel understood at a very basic empathic level (immersion experience) by another who is as vulnerable as they are. This can be provided only by someone who is perceived of as a peer or equal, not by someone who is in a one-up position. True mutuality is the necessary catalyst for shame reduction and attachment. Therapy, both individual and group, if conducted along the lines of attachment theory, can provide this experience much more effectively than other forms of therapy.

I hope this book leaves the reader with the same understanding that I hope therapists and group leaders leave to their individual patients and group members when they terminate therapy—an understanding of addiction, AA, and therapy; some direction and specific guidelines for recovery; and most importantly some hope for the future. Despite all our efforts to give, guide, and support, each of us is ultimately alone when it comes to our life, recovery, and growth. This is the inevitable plight of the human condition. As Buber and the existentialists repeatedly remind us, we are ultimately alone and solely responsible for our fates. Nevertheless, while we are individually alone and responsible, this does not imply that we cannot be helped, supported, and encouraged by others in our life and in our community.

As therapists, whether individually or in group, we can give substance abusers something that they will be able to carry with them after therapy ends. Specifically, we can give them what everyone needs—an attachment experience and a sense of community in which they feel they are accepted and belong. Feeling alienated, empty, and not understood is a struggle that chemically dependent people experience. AA gives them a sense of belonging and of being understood at a very basic level. This is why the themes of attachment, trust, and safety have been so prominent throughout this book. While people want to be accepted, loved, and recognized, they want it unconditionally. The primary conflict for us all, the addicted as well as the nonaddicted, is to belong and be connected to something larger than ourselves without losing ourselves. Alcoholics and addicts perhaps feel this a little more intensely, and this may be why their demand for autonomy and independence takes on such rebellious, self-centered, and demanding properties. They fear that belonging to someone or something will cost them their individuality. This is a constant theme for all of us. Can I be close and truly intimate without losing myself, or will my need for independence come at a cost of alienation and isolation? Can I tolerate being alone without giving up my autonomy to get my need for human closeness met?

Therapy, directed along the lines prescribed in this book, can meet the needs of this human dilemma. It first allows the chemically dependent person to get close and be intimate with others who are accepting of him without a cost to his identity and autonomy. It then encourages his individuality while giving him the tools to get close to others without compromising his separateness. Ultimately, it allows alcoholics and addicts to deal with the emotions and conflicts triggered by all intimate encounters without relying on alcohol and drugs to sedate, buffer, or alter their feelings.

In many ways good therapy, much like Alcoholics Anonymous, can be viewed as a holding environment—a cohesive, safe community where people can get at the depth of understanding the relationship between their private and public selves. At the same time, addicts and alcoholics can be encouraged and allowed to evolve in separate ways at their own pace. As suggested by Wallace (1975) earlier in this book, recovery is a time-dependent process. During the early stages of recovery, the alcoholic and addict need to be welcomed to join and become attached to a safe, trusting, and healing culture. Later, as they gradually evolve through different stages of their recovery, they will learn how to be separate and close without losing their identity or isolating themselves from others. As AA so correctly points out, the AA member is a *recovering* alcoholic. He or she is never *recovered*. Our growth and evolution continue throughout the different stages of our lives. Attachment-oriented therapy, as a part of an alcoholic's or addict's recovery, helps propel this process. It is a process that doesn't end once the person leaves therapy or gets sober, for the issues of belonging and being alone remain constant themes in our lives. Therapy helps the recovering person learn ways to successfully adapt to this very central human process.

References

Ainsworth, M. D. S. (1969). Object relations, dependency and attachment: a theoretical review of the mother–infant relationship. *Child Development,* 40, 969–1025.

———. (1989) Attachment beyond infancy. *American Psychologist,* 44, 709–716.

Ackerman, S. J. and Hilsenroth, M. J. (2001). A review of therapist characteristics and techniques negatively impacting the therapeutic alliance. *Psychotherapy,* 38(2), 171–185.

Alcoholics Anonymous. (1939). *Alcoholics Anonymous.* New York: AA World Services.

Aledort, S. L. (2002). The Omnipotent Child Syndrome: The Role of Passionately Held Bad Fits in the Formation of Identity. *International Journal of Group Psychotherapy,* 52, 67–88.

Alexander, F. (1950). *Psychosomatic medicine.* New York: W. W. Norton.

Alonso, A. & Rutan, J. S. (1993). Character change in group therapy. *International Journal of Group Psychotherapy,* 43, 439–452.

Amini, F. (1996). *Attachment Theory & Group Psychotherapy.* American Group Psychotherapy Association 35th Annual Conference. Feb. 23. San Francisco, CA.

Arensberg, F. (1998) A consideration of Kohut's views on group psychotherapy. In N.H. Harwood & M. Pines (Eds), *Self experience in group.* (19–23). London: J. Kingsley Pub.

Bacal, H. A. (1985) Optimal responsiveness and the therapeutic process. In A. Goldberg (Ed) *Progress in Self Psychology.* New York: Guilford Press, pp. 202–226.

———. (1992). Contributions from self-psychology. In R. Klien, H. S. Bernard, & D. L. Singer (Eds), *Handbook of group psychotherapy* (55–86). Madison, CT: International University Press.

Barber, J.P., Luborsky, L., Critis-Christoph, P., Thase, M.E., Weiss, R., Frank, A., Onken, L., & Gallop, R. (1999). Therapeutic alliance as predictor of outcome in treatment of cocaine dependence. *Psychotherapy Research*, 9, 54–73.

Bartholomew, K. (1990). Avoidance of intimacy: an attachment perspective. *Journal of the Society for Personal Relations.* 7, 147–178.

Bateson, G. (1971). The cybernetics of self: A theory of alcoholism. *Psychiatry,* 34, 1–18.

Beebee, B. (1993) Contributions from Infant research. Film shown at the 16th Annual Conference on the Psychology of the Self. Toronto, Canada, October, 1993.

Beutler, L.F., Machado, P.P., & Neufeldt, S.A. (1994). Therapist variables. In A.E. Bergin & S.L. Garfield (eds.). *Handbook of psychotherapy and behavior change* (4th ed.) New York: Wiley and Sons, pp. 229–269.

Beutler, L.F. (2000). David and Goliath: When empirical and clinical standards of practice meet. *American Psychologist*, 55, 997–1007.

Binder, J.L. (1999) Issues in Teaching and Learning Time-Limited Psychotherapy, *Clinical Psychology Review*, 19, 705–719.

Bion, W.R. (1961) *Experiences in groups*. New York: Basic Books.

Blum, K., Cull, J.G., Braverman, E.R. & Comings, D.E. (1996). Reward Deficiency Syndrome. *American Scientist*, 84, 132–145.

Bollerud, K. (1995). A model for treating sexually abused substance abusers. Paper presented at The Addictions: Contemporary Treatment Issues, Harvard Medical School, March 3–4, 1995.

Bowlby, J. (1958). The nature of the child's tie to his mother. *International Journal of Psycho-Analysis* 39, 350–373.

———. (1973) *Attachment and loss: Vol. 2. Separation: Anxiety and anger*. New York: Basic Books.

———. (1979a) *The making and breaking of affectional bonds*. London & New York: Routledge.

———. (1979b) On knowing what you are not supposed to

know and feeling what you are not supposed to feel. *Canadian Journal of Psychiatry*, 24, 403–408.

———. (1980). *Loss: Sadness and Depression*. New York: Basic Books.

———. (1988) *A Secure Base. Clinical Applications of Attachment Theory.* London: Routledge.

Brandchaft, D. & Stolorow, R. (1988). The difficult patient: Intersubjective perspective. In N. Slavinsky-Holy (Ed.), *Borderline and narcissistic patients in therapy* (pp. 243–266). Madison, CT: International Universities Press.

Brown, D. G. (1985). Bion and Foukles: Basic assumptions and beyond. In M. Pines. (Ed.), *Bion and group psychotherapy* (192–219). London Tavistock Routledge.

Brown, S. (1985). *Treating the alcoholic: A developmental model of recovery.* New York: John Wiley & Sons.

Brown, S.A., Inaba, R.K., Gillin, J.C., Steward, M.A., Schuckit, M.A., & Irwin, M.R. (1994). Alcoholism and affective disorder: Clinical course of depressive symptoms, *American Journal of Psychiatry*, 152, 45–52.

Brown, S. & Yalom, I. (1977). Interactional group psychotherapy with alcoholic patients. *Journal of Studies on Alcohol*, 38, 426–456.

Buber, M. (1955) *Between man and man.* Translated by R. G. Smith. Boston: Beacon Press.* Second publication date 1961.

———. (1960). *I and Thou*. Translated by Walter Kaufmann, New York. Charles Scribner's Son.

———. (1963). *Pointing the way*, Translated by Maurice Friedman. New York: Harper Torchbooks.

———. (1988) *The knowledge of man* Translated by Maurice Friedman. Highlands, NJ: Humanities Press International, Inc.

Burlingame, G. M., Fuhriman, A., & Johnson, J. E. (2001). Cohesion in Group Psychotherapy, *Psychotherapy*, 38, 373–384.

Carnes, P. (1983). *Out of the shadows: Understanding sexual addiction.* Minneapolis, Minnesota: Comp Care Publishers.

Carnes, P. (1991). *Don't Call It Love: Recovery from Sexual Addiction*. New York: Bantam Books.

Center for Substance Abuse Treatment. (1994). *Assessment and*

Treatment of Patients with Coexisting Mental Illness and Alcohol and Other Drug Abuse. Treatment Improvement Protocal (TIP) #9. U.S. Department of Health & Human Services, Washington, D.C.

Chambless, D. L., et al. (1996) An update on empirically validated therapies. *The Clinical Psychologist*, 51, 3–16.

Chambless D. L., & Hollon, S. D. (1998) Defining empirically supported therapies. *Journal of Consulting and Clinical Psychology*, 64, 497–504.

Chafetz, M. E., Blane, H. T., Abram, H. S., Golner, J., Lacy, E., McCourt, W. F., Clark, E., & Myers, W. (1962) Establishing treatment relations with alcoholics. *Journal of Nervous and Mental Disease*. 134, 395–409.

Claiborn, C. D., Goodyear, R. K. & Horner, P. A. (2001) Feedback. *Psychotherapy*, 38, 401–405.

Covington, S. S. (1997). Women, addiction, and sexuality. In: Straussner, S. L. A., and Zelvin, E., (Eds.) *Gender and Addictions: Men and Women in Treatment*. Northvale, NJ: Jason Aronson, pp. 71–95.

Crits-Christoph, P. & Gibbons, M. C. (2001) Relational Interpretations. *Psychotherapy*, 38, 423–427.

DeCasper, A. J., & Fifer, W. P. (1980). "Of human bonding; newborns prefer their mother's voices." *Science*, 208(4448):1174–6.

Diamond, N. (1996) Can we speak of internal and external reality? *Group Analysis*, 29, 303–316.

Dies, R. R. (1992). Models of group psychotherapy: Shifting through confusion. *International Journal of Group Psychotherapy*, 42, 1–18.

Durant, W. (1926). *Story of Philosophy*. New York: Simon & Schuster.

Ekman, P. (1992). An argument for basic emotions. *Cognition and Emotions*, 6, 3/40:169–200.

Ezriel, H. (1973). Psychoanalytic group psychotherapy. In L. R. Wolberg E. K. Schwartz (Eds.), *Group Therapy* (183–210). New York: Stratton Intercontinental Medical Books.

Fairbairn, W. R. D. (1952) *Psychoanalytic studies of the personality.* London: Routledge & Kegan Paul.

Flores, P. (1982) Modification of Yalom's interactional group therapy model as a mode of treatment for alcoholism. *Group*, 6, 3–15.

———. (1988). *Group psychotherapy with addicted populations*. New York: The Haworth Press.

———. (1997). *Group psychotherapy with addicted populations: An integration of twelve-step and psychodynamic theory*. Binghampton, NY: Haworth press.

———. (2001) Addiction as an Attachment Disoder: Implications for Group Psychotherapy. *International Journal of Group Psychotherapy*, 51, 63–81.

Flores, P. & Mahon, L. (1993). The treatment of addiction in group psychotherapy. *International Journal of Group Psychotherapy,* 43, 143–156.

Foulkes, S.H. (1975) *Group Analytic Psychotherapy.* London: Interface (Gordon and Breach Science Publishing Ltd.).

Fonagy, P., Steele, M., Steele, H., et al. (1994). The theory and practice of resilience. *Journal of Child Psychology and Psychiatry* 35, 231–257.

Frank, J. (1978) *Psychotherapy and the human predicament*. New York: Schocken Books.

Friedman. M.S. (1985) *The Healing Dialogue in Psychotherapy*. New York: Jason Aronson Press.

Fromm, E. (1950). *Psychoanalysis and Religion*. New Haven, CN.: Yale University Press.

Fromm-Riechmann, F. (1950). *Principles of intensive psychotherapy*. Chicago: University of Chicago Press.

Gans, J.S. & Alonso, A. (1998). Difficult Patients: Their Construction in Group Therapy. *International Journal of Group Psychotherapy*, 48, 311–326.

Ganzarian, R. (1992). Introduction to object relations group psychotherapy. *International Journal of Group Psychotherapy*, 42, 205–224.

Gelso. C.J. & Hayes, J.A. (2001) Countertransference Management. *Psychotherapy*, 38, 418–422.

Greenberg, L.S. Elliott, R. Watson, J.E. Bohart, A. (2001) Empathy, *Psychotherapy,* 38, 380–384.

Grant, I., Reed, R., & Adams, K. (1980). Alcohol & drug related brain disorder: Implications for neuropsychological research. *Journal of Clinical Neuropsychology.,* 2(4), 321–331.

Group for the Advancement of Psychiatry. Dual Diagnosis. (1993). In: *Residents' Guide to Treatment of People with Chronic Mental Illness.* Report No. 136. Washington, DC: American Psychiatric Press. 145–161.

Guntrip, H. (1974). *Schizoid Phenomena, Object Relations and the Self.* London. Hogarth Press.

Harwood, I. (1983) The application of self-psychology concepts to group psychotherapy. *The International Journal of Group Psychotherapy.* 33. 469–488.

———. (1986) "The need for optimal, available selfobject caretakers: Moving toward extended selfobject experiences." *Group Analysis*, 19, 291–302.

———. (1998) "Advances in group psychotherapy and self psychology: an intersubjective approach. In I. Hardwood & M. Pines (Eds) *Self experience in group*. (30–45), London: J. Kingsley Pub.

Harlow, H. F. (1958). The nature of love. *American Psychologist*, 13:673–85.

Hamilton, V., (1985). John Bowlby: an ethological basis for psychoanalysis. *In Beyond Freud*, Ed. J. Reppen. New York: Analytic Press.

Henry, W. P. (1998). Science, politics, and the politics of science: The use and misuse of empirically validated treatment research. *Psychotherapy Research*, 8, 126–140.

Hazan, C., & Shaver, P. (1994). Attachment as an organizational framework for research on close relationships. *Psychological Inquiry* 51–22.

Heyman, S. E. (1995). *What can neuroscience teach us about addiction?* Presented at: The Addictions: Contemporary Treatment Issues. March 3–4. Harvard Medical School. Boston, MA.

Hill, C. E. & Knox, S. (2001) Self-Disclosure. *Psychotherapy*, 38, 413–417.

Horvath, A. O. (2001) The Alliance. *Psychotherapy*, 38, 365–372.

Hofer, M. A. (1996). On the nature and consequence of early loss, *Psychosomatic Medicine*, 58, 570–581.

Holmes, J. (1996) *Attachment, Intimacy, Autonomy. Using attachment theory in adult psychotherapy*. Northdale, NJ: Jason Aronson, Inc.

Horner, A. (1979). *Object relations and the developing ego in therapy*. New York: Jason Aronson Press.

Irons, R.R. & Schneideer, J.P. (1996). Addictive Sexual Disorders. In Addictive Psychiatry. Miller, N.S. (Ed.). p.2–21. New York: Haworth Press.

Izard, C.E. (1971). *The Face of Emotion*. New York: Appleton-Century-Crofts.

Jaspers, K. (1975). On my philosophy. In W. Kaufman (Ed.), *Existentialism from Dostoevsky to Sartre*. New York: New American Library (orig. 1941).

Jerrell, J.M. & Ridgely, M.S. (1999) Impact of robustness of program implementation on outcomes of clients in dual diagnosis programs. *Psychiatric Services*, 50(1), 109–112.

Jonnson, V.E. (1973). *I'll quit tomorrow*. New York: Harper & Row.

Jones, R.K. (1970). Sectarian characteristics of Alcoholics Anonymous. *Sociology*, 4, 181–195.

Jordan, J. (1986). *The meaning of mutuality*. Work in Progress, No. 23. Wellesley, MA: Stone Center.

Kanas, N. (1982). Alcoholism and group psychotherapy. In E.M. Pattison & S.E. Kaufman (Eds.), *Encyclopedic handbook of alcoholism*. (1011–1021). New York: Gardner Press.

Kaplan, H.I. & Sadock, B.J. (1993). *Comprehensive group psychotherapy*. (3rd Ed.) Baltimore, MD: Williams & Wilkens.

Karen, R. (1994). *Becoming attached: first relationships and how they shape our capacity to love*. New York: Oxford University Press.

Kaufman, E. & Reoux, J. (1988). Guidelines for the successful psychotherapy of substance abusers. *American Journal of Drug and Alcohol Abuse*, 14, 199–209.

Kelly, G. (1963). *A theory of personality. The psychology of personal constructs*. New York: W.W. Norton & Co.

Kemker, S.S., Kibel, H.D., & Mahler, J.C. (1993). On becoming oriented to inpatient treatment: Inducing new patients and professionals to recovery movement. *International Journal of Group Psychotherapy*, 43, 285–302.

Khantzian, E.J. (1982). Psychopathology, psychodynamics & alcoholism. In E.M. Pattison & S.E. Kaufman (Eds.), *Encyclopedic handbook of alcoholism* (581–597). New York: Gardner Press.

———. (1994). *Alcoholics Anonymous—Cult or corrective?* Paper presented at Fourth Annual Distinguished Lecture. Manhasset,. NY: Cornell University.

———. An Interview with Dr. Edward J. Khantzian. In *Psychotherapy Book News,* July 29, 1999, 8–13.

———. Reflections on Group Treatments as Corrective Experiences for Addictive Vulnerability. *International Journal of Group Psychotherapy*, 51, 11–20.

Khantzian, E. J., Halliday, K. S., & McAuliffe, W. E. (1990). *Addiction and the vulnerable self.* New York: Guilford Press.

Kishline, A. (1994). *Moderate drinking: The moderation management guide for people who want to reduce their drinking.* New York: Crown Trade Paperbacks.

Klein, M. (1948). *Contributions to Psycho-Analysis 1921–1945.* London: Hargrove.

Klein, Mh H., Kolden, G. G., Michels, J. L. & Chisholm-Stockard, S. (2001) Congruence or Genuineness. *Psychotherapy*, 38, 396–400.

Knapp, C. (1996). *Drinking: A love story*. New York. Dell.

Kohut, H. (1972). *Thoughts on narcissism and narcissitic rage.* Psychoanalytic Study of the Child. 27, 360–400.

———. (1977) Preface in J. D. Blaine & A. D. Julius (Eds.), *Psychodynamics of drug dependence.* NIDA Publication No. ADM 77–470. Washington, DC: Superintendent of Documents, U.S. Government Printing Office.

———. (1978) Creativeness, charisma, group psychotherapy. In P. Ornstien (ed) *The Search for the self* (Vol. 2). New York: International Universities Press.

———. (1982) Introspection, empathy, and the semi-circle of mental health. *International Journal of Psychoanalysis*, 63, 395–407.

———. (1984) *How does analysis cure?* Chicago: University of Chicago Press.

Kohut, H. & Wolfe, E. S. (1978). The disorders of the self and their treatment: An outline. *International Journal of Psychoanalysis*, 60, 413–424.

Kosseff, J. W. (1975). The leader using object-relations theory. In Z. A. Liff (Ed.), *The leader in group* (212–242). New York: Jason Aronson.

Kraemer, G.W. (1985). Effects of differences in early social experience on primate neurobiological–behavioral development. In M. Reite and T. Fields (Eds.) *The Psychobiology of Attachment and Separation*. New York: Academic Press.

———. (1992). A psychobiological theory of attachment. *Behavioral and Brain Sciences*, 15:493–541.

Krystal, H. (1982). Character disorders: Characterological specificity and the alcoholic. In: M.E. Pattison & E. Kaufman (Eds.), *Encyclopedic handbook of alcoholism* (607–618). New York: Gardner Press.

Kurtz, E. (1979). *Not-God: A history of Alcoholics Anonymous*. Center City, MN: Hazelden.

———. (1981). *Shame and guilt: Characteristics of the dependency cycle*. Center City, MN: Hazelden.

———. (1982). Why A.A. Works. The intellectual significance of Alcoholics Anonymous. *Journal of Studies on Alcohol*, 43, 38–80.

Kushner, M.G., Sher, K.J., Wood, M.D., & Wood, P.K. (1994). Anxiety and drinking behavior: Moderating effects of tension-reduction alcohol outcome expectancies. *Alcoholism: Clinical & Experimental*, 18, 852–860.

Laing, R. (1969). *The self and others*. London: Tavistock Publications.

Lambert, M.J. & Barley, D.E. (2001). Research summary on the therapeutic relationship and psychotherapy outcome. *Psychotherapy* 38: 357–364.

Leshner, A.I. (1996). Understanding Drug Addiction: Implications for Treatment. *Hospital Practice*. October 15. 1–11.

———. (1997a) Drug Abuse and Addiction Are Biomedical Problems. Hospital Practice: A Special Report, April, pp. 2–4.

———. (1997b) Introduction to the special issue: The National institute on Drug Abuse's (NIDA's) Drug Abuse treatment Outcome Study (DATOS). *Psychology of Addictive Behaviors*, Dec., 4, 211–215.

———. (2001). Addiction: A brain disease with biological underpinnings. In *Voice*, Vol. 6, Issue 1. 1–3.

Leszcz, M. (1992). The interpersonal approach to group psychotherapy. *International Journal of Group Psychotherapy*, 42, 37–62.

Lewis, T., Amini, F., & Lannon, R. (2000) *A general theory of love*. New York: Random House.

Lichtenberg J. D., Lachmann, F. M. and Fosshage, J. L. (1992) *Self and Motivational Systems*. Hillsdale, NJ: Analytic Press.

Lichtenstein, H. (1961). Identity & sexuality: A study of their interrelationship in man. *Journal of American Psychoanalytic Association*, 9, 179–260.

Liese, B. S. (1998). Project MATCH and the Issue of Psychotherapy Talent. The *Addictions Newsletter*, 5, 1–25.

Lorenz, K. (1953). *King Solomon's Ring*. London: Methuen.

Madsen, W. (1974). *The American alcoholic*. Springfield, IL: Charles C. Thomas.

Main, M. (1991). Metacognitive knowledge, metacognitive monitoring, and singular vs. multiple models of attachment. In Attachment Across the Life Cycle (Ed.) C. Parkes, et al. London: Routledge.

Main, M. (1995). Recent studies in attachment: overview with selected implications for clinical work. In *Attachment Theory: Social, Developmental, and Clinical Perspectives,* (Eds.) J. Cassidy & P.R. Shaver, pp. 845–887. New York: Guilford.

Main, M. (1996) Introduction to the special section on attachment and psychopathology: Part 2. Overview of the field of attachment. *Journal of Clinical and Counseling Psychology*, 64, 237–243.

Mahler, M. S. (1968). *On human symbiosis and the vicissitude of individuation*. New York: International University Press.

Mahler, M. S. (1979). *The selected papers of Margaret Mahler, Volumes I and II*. New York: Jason Aronson.

Marlatt, G. A. (1983). Controlled-drinking: A commentary, *American Psychologist*, 38: 1097–1110.

Marlatt, G. A. (Ed). (1998). *Harm reduction: Pragmatic strategies for managing high-risk behaviors.* New York: Aronson.

Marlatt, G. A., Larimer, M. E. Baer, J. S. & Quigley, L. A. (1993). Harm reduction for alcohol problems: Moving beyond the controlled drinking controversy. *Behavior Therapy,* 24, 461–503.

Marrone, M. (1998) *Attachment and interaction.* London: Jessica Kingsley Pub.

Marziali, E., Munroe-Blum, H. & McCleary, L. (1997). The Contribution of Group Cohesion and Group Alliance to the Outcome of Group Psychotherapy. *International Journal of Group Psychotherapy*, 47, 475–497.

Matano, R.A. & Yalom, I. (1991) Approaches to chemical dependency. Chemical dependency & interactive group therapy—a synthesis. *International Journal of Group Psychotherapy*, 41, 269–294.

McHugo, G.J. Drake, R.E., Teague, G.B. & Xie, H. (1999). Fidelity to assertive community treatment and client outcomes in New Hampshire Dual Disorders study. *Psychiatric Services*, 50 (8), 818–824.

Meares, R. (1993). *The Metaphor of Play*. Northvale, NJ: Jason Aronson.

Meissen, G., Powell, T.J., Wituk, S.A., Girrens, K. & Arteaga, S. (1999). Attitudes of AA contact persons toward group participation by persons with a mental illness. *Psychiatric Services*, 50 (8), 1079–1081.

Meyer, B. & Pilkonis, P.A. (2001) Attachment Style, *Psychotherapy*, 38, 466–472.

Miller, M.S. (1995). *Treatment of addictions: Applications of outcome research for clinical management*. Binghamton, NY: Haworth Press.

Miller, W.R. & Brown, S.A. (1997) Why Psychologists Should Treat Alcohol and Drug Problems. *American Psychologist*, 52. pps. 1269–1279.

Minkoff, K.,(1995). *Assessment and treatment of dual diagnosis: Serious mental illness and substance abuse disorder*. Paper present at The Addictions: Contemporary Treatment Issues, March 3–4, Harvard Medical School, Boston, MA.

Minkoff, K. & Drake, R.E. (1992). Homelessness and dual diagnosis. In Lamb, H.R., Bachrach, L.L. & Kass, F.I. *Treating the Homeless Mentally Ill: A Task Force Report of the American Psychiatric Association*. Washington, D.C. American Psychiatric Press.

Mohl, P.C., Martinez, D., Ticknor, C., Huang, M., & Cordell, L. (19910. Early dropouts from psychotherapy. *Journal of Nervous and Mental Disease*, 179(8), 478–481.

Morahan-Martin, J., & Schumacher, P. (2000). Incidence and correlates of pathological Internet use among college students. *Computers in Human Behavior*, 16 (1), 13–29.

Morrison, A.P. (1989). *Shame: The underside of narcissism.* Hillsdale, NJ: Analytic Press.

Nathan, P.E. (1992). A response to Alcoholism, politics, and bureaucracy: The consensus against controlled drinking in America, *Addictive Behaviors*, 17(1), 63–65.

Nathan, P.E. (1998) Practice guidelines: Not yet ideal. *American Psychologist*, 53, 290–299.

National Association of State Alcohol and Drug Abuse Directors and National Association of Mental Health Program directors. (1998). *National Dialogue on Co-occurring Mental Health and Substance Abuse Disorders.* June 16–17, Washington, DC.

National Association of State Mental Health Program Directors. (1999). *Transforming Knowledge and Research into Practice in the Public Health Sector: Focus on Dual Diagnosis, Criminal Justice/Mental Health Interface and Psychiatric Rehabilitation/Recovery.* Best Practice Symposium Proceedings, New Orleans, LA, October 27–28, 1999.

Newsweek Magazine, (1996). *The Story of the Unabomer*. April 22, 1996.

Norcross, J.C. (2001) Purposes, Processes, and Products on the Task Force on Empirically Supported Therapy Relationships. *Psychotherapy,* 38, 345–354.

Ogden, T.H. (1982) *Projective identification and psychotherapeutic technique.* New York: Jason Aronson.

Ogden, T.H. (1983). The concept of internal object relations. *International Journal of Psychoanalysis*, 64, 227–241.

Orford, J. (1985) *Excessive appetites: A psychological view of addiction*. New York: Wiley.

Ormont, L. (1992). *The group therapy experience*. New York: St. Martin's Press.

Ormont, L. (2001) Meeting Maturational Needs in the Group Setting. *International Journal of Group Psychotherapy,* 51, 343–360.

Ornstein, P. (1981). The bipolar self in the psychoanalytic treatment process. Clinical & theoretical considerations. *Journal of American Psychoanalytic Association*, 29, 353–375.

Ornstein, P. (1982). *Self Psychology*. Lecture Series: University of Cincinnati, January–March, 1982.

Paparo, F. & Nebiosi, G. (1998) How does group psychotherapy cure? A reconceptualization of the group process: from self psychology to the intersubjective perspective. In I. Hardwood & M. Pines (Eds), *Self experience in group*. (70–82) London: J. Kingsley Pub.

Parsons, O.A. & Farr, S.P. (1981). The neuropsychology of alcohol & drug use. In S.B. Felskov & T.J. Boll (Eds.), *Handbook of clinical neuropsychology* (320–365). New York: John Wiley & Sons.

Pattison, E.M. (1979). The selection of treatment modalities for the alcoholic patient. In J.H. Mandelson & N.K. Mello (Eds.), *The diagnosis and treatment of alcoholism*. (229–255). New York: McGraw-Hill.

Peele, S (1989). *Diseasing of America: addiction treatment out of control.* Boston: Houghton Mifflin.

Pendery, M.L,, Maltzman, I.M., & West, L.J. (1982). Controlled drinking by alcoholics? New findings and a reevaluation of major affirmative study, *Science*, 217, 169–174.

Piaget, J. (1954) *The Construction of reality in the child.* New York: Basic Books.

Pinker, S. (1997). *How the Mind Works*. New York: W.W. Norton & Co.

Pines, M. (1998) The self as a group: the group as a self. In I. Hardwood & M. Pines (Eds.), *Self experience in group*. (24–29), London: J. Kingsley Pub.

Plotnicov, K.H. (1990). *Early termination from counseling: The client's perspective*. Unpublished doctoral dissertation, University of Pittsburgh, PA.

Polster, E. & Polster, M. (1974) Notes on the training of Gestalt therapy. *Voices: The Art and Science of Psychotherapy,* 10, 38–44.

Prochaska, J.O. & DiClemente, C.C. (1992). Stages of change in the modification of problem behaviors. In M. Hersen, R.M. Eisler, & P.M. Miller (Eds.), *Progress in behavior modification*, Vol. 28 (184–214). Sycamore, IL: Sycamore Press.

Project MATCH Research Group. (1997). Matching alcoholism treatments to lient heterogeneity: Project MATCH posttreatment drinking outcomes. *Journal of Studies on Alcohol,* 58, 7–29.

Ray, O. (1983). *Drugs, society, and human behavior.* (3rd. Ed.), St. Louis, MI: C.V. Mosby Co.

Reiger, D.A., Farmer, M.E., Rae, D.S., Locke, B.Z., Keith, S.J., Judd, L.L. & Goodwin, F.K. (1990). Comorbidity of mental disorders with alcohol and other drug abuse. *Journal of the American Medical Association*, 264, 2511–2518.

Reik, T. (1954). *Listening with the Third Ear: The Inner Experience of a Psychoanalyst*. New York: Farrar, Straus.

Rennie, D.L. (1994). Client's deference in psychotherapy, *Journal of Counseling Psychology,* 41 (14), 427–437.

Rice, A.K. (1965). *Learning for leadership.* London: Tavistock Publications.

Ridgely, M.S., Lambert, D., Goodman, A., Chichester, C.S. & Ralph, R. (1998). Interagency collaboration in services for people with co-occurring mental illness and substance use disorder. *Psychiatric Services,* 49(2), 236–238.

Robertson, J. (1953). *A two-year-old goes to the hospital.* Film. University Park, PA: Penn State Audio Visual Services.

Roth, J. (2002). Personal communication. *American Group Psychotherapy Association*, Feb. 26, New Orleans, LA.

Rutan, J.S. (1985). Paper presented at Harvard Medical School seminar on group psychotherapy, *Psychodynamic group therapy*, Nov 12. Boston, MA.

Rutan, J.S. & Stone, W.N. (1993). *Psychodynamic group psychotherapy*. (2nd. Ed.). New York: The Guilford Press.

Ryan, C. & Butters, N. (1980). Further evidence for a continuum of impairment encompassing male alcoholic Korsakoff patients and chronic alcoholic men. *Alcoholism*, 4, 190–198.

Safran, J.O., & Segal, Z.V. (1990), *Interpersonal process in cognitive therapy*. New York: Basic Books.

Safran, J.D., Muran, J.C., Samstag, L.W. & Stevens, C. (2001) Repairing Alliance Ruptures, *Psychotherapy,* 38, 406–412.

Schacter, D.L. (1990). Memory. In M. Posner (Ed.), *Foundations of Cognitive Science*. Boston: MIT Press.

Schneider, J.P. & Schneider, B.H. (1991). *Sex, Lies, and Forgiveness: Couples Speak on Healing from Sex Addiction.* Center City, MN, Hazelden Ed. Materials.

Schuckit, M. A. (1973). Alcoholism & sociopathy. Diagnostic confusion. *Quarterly Journal of Studies on Alcohol*, 37, 157–164.

Skulsky, S. (2002). *Affective Learning*. Paper presented at the American Group Psychotherapy Conference, Feb. 25, New Orleans.

Shane, M., Shane, E., & Gales, M. (1997) *Intimate attachments: Toward a new self psychology.* New York. Guilford Press.

Shore, J. J., (1981). Use of paradox in the treatment of alcoholism. *Health and Social Work*, 38, 11–20.

Sobell, M. B. & Sobell, L. C. (1973). Individualized behavior therapy for alcoholics. *Behavior Therapy*, 4, 543–556.

Sobell, M. B. & Sobell, L. C. (1993). *Problem drinkers: Guided self-change treatment*. New York: Guilford.

Sobell, L. C. (1995). *Natural recovery from alcohol problems*. Paper presented at workshop. The Addictions: Contemporary treatment issues, March 3–4, Harvard Medical School. Boston, MA.

Spitz, R. (1945). Hospitalism: an inquiry into the genius of psychiatric conditions in early childhood. *Psychoanalytic Study of the Child*, I, 53–74.

Squire, L. R., Knowlton, B., & Munsen, G. (1993). "The structure and organization of memory." *Annual Review of Psychology*, 44, 453–495.

Steering Committee (2001) Empirically supported therapy relationships: Conclusions and recommendations of the Division 29 Task Force. *Psychotherapy,* 38 (4), pp. 495–497.

Stern, D. N. (1985) *The interpersonal world of the infant.* New York: Basic Books, Inc.

Stern, D. N. (1995) *The motherhood constellation.* New York: Basic Books, Inc.

Stolorow, R. Brandchaft, B. and Atwood, G. (1987) *Psychoanalytic treatment: An intersubjective approach.* Hillsdale, NJ: Analytic Press.

Stone, W. N. (1992). The place of self psychology in group psychotherapy: A status report. *International Journal of Group Psychotherapy*, 42, 335–350.

Stone, W. N. (1996). Self Psychology and the higher mental functioning hypothesis: complementary theories. *Group Analysis* 29, 169–181.

Strupp, H. H. (1978) A reformation of the dynamics of the therapist's contribution. In A. German & A. Rozier (Eds.) The therapists' contribution to effective psychotherapy: An empirical assessment (62–91). Elmsford, NY: Pergamon Press.

Strupp, H.H. (1980) Humanism and Psychotherapy: A Personal Statement of the Therapist's Essential Values. *Psychotherapy: Theory, Research and Practice*. Vol. 17, 396–400.

Strupp, H. H. (1980b). Success and failure in time-limited psychotherapy further evidence (Comparison 4). *Archives of General Psychiatry*, 37, 947–954.

Strupp, H.H. (1998). The Vanderbilt I study revisited. *Psychotherapy Research*, 8, 335–347.

Strupp, H.H. (1999). Essential Ingredients of a Helpful Therapist. *Psychotherapy Bulletin*, 34, 34–36.

Strupp, H.H. & Hadley, S.W. (1979) Specific versus nonspecific factors in psychotherapy: A controlled study of outcome. *Archives of General Psychiatry*, 36, 1125–1136.

Sullivan, H.S. (1953). *The interpersonal theory of psychiatry.* New York: W.W. Norton.

Surkis, A. (1989). *The group therapist's quandary: To lead or to treat?* Workshop presented at Tenth International Congress of Group Therapy, April, Amsterdam.

Task Force on Promotion and Dissemination of Psychological Procedures. (1995). Training in and dissemination of empirically validated psychological treatments: Report and recommendations. *The Clinical Psychologist*, 48, 3–23.

Tiebout, H.M. (1954). The ego factors in surrender in alcoholism. *Quarterly Journal of Studies on Alcohol*, 15, 610–621.

Thune, C.E. (1977). Alcoholism and the Archetypal Past: A Phenomenolgical perspective on Alcoholics Anonymous. *Journal of Studies on Alcohol*, 38, 75–89.

Tournier, R.E. (1979). Alcoholics Anonymous as treatment and as ideology. *Quarterly Journal of Studies on Alcohol*, 40, 230–239.

Treadway, D. (1990). Codependency: Disease, metaphor, or fad? *Family Therapy Networker*, 14(1), 38–42.

Tyron, G.S., & Kane, A.S. (1993). Relationship of working alliance to mutual and unilateral termination. *Journal of Counseling Psychology*, 40, 33–36.

Vaillant, G.E. (1978). Alcoholism and Drug Dependence. In *The Harvard guide to modern psychiatry,* Nicholi, A.M. (Ed.) pp. 567–577, Belknap Press, Cambridge, MA.

Vaillant, G.E. (1983). Natural History of Male Alcoholism V: Is Alcoholism the Cart or the Horse to Sociopathy? *British Journal of Addiction*, 78, 317–325.

Vaillant, G.E. & Milofsky, E.S. (1982). The Etiology of Alcoholism: A Prospective Viewpoint. *American Psychologist*, 37, 494–503.

Vannicelli, M. (1992). *Removing the road blocks: Group psychotherapy with substance abusers & family members.* New York: The Guilford Press.

Walant, K.B. (1995) *Creating the capacity for attachment: Treating addictions and the alienated self.* Northvale, NJ: Jason Aronson Inc.

Wallace, J. (1975). *Tactical and strategic use of the preferred defense structure of the recovering alcoholic*. New York: National Council on Alcoholism.

Wallace, J. (1977). Alcoholism from the inside out: A phenomenological analysis. In *Alcoholism, development, consequences and interventions.* Estes, N.J. & Heinemann, M.E. (Eds.) pp. 3–14. C.V. Mosby Co., St. Louis, MI.

Wallace, J. (1977). Between Scylla and Charybdis: Issues in Alcoholism Therapy. *Alcohol Health and Research World*, Summer, pp 15–34.

Wallace, J. (1978) Working with the preferred defense structure of the recovering alcoholic. In S. Zimberg, J. Wallace & S. Blume (Eds.) *Practical approaches to alcoholism psychotherapy*. (pp. 19–29). New York: Plenum Press.

Wallace, J. (1984). *Myths and misconceptions about Alcoholics Anonymous!* New York: AA World Services.

Washton, A.M. (1989). Cocaine may trigger sexual compulsivity. *U.S. Journal Drug & Alcohol Dependency*, 13 (6):8.

Washton, A.M. (1992) Structured outpatient group therapy with alcohol & substance abusers. In J. Lowinson, P. Ruiz & R. Millman (Eds), *Substance abuse: A comprehensive textbook*. Baltimore, MD: Williams & Wilkens.

Weinberg, J.R. (1975). A.A.: An Interpretation for the Nonbeliever. Center City, MN: Hazelden.

Wells, H. L. (1982). Chronic brain disease: An update on alcoholism, Parkinson's disease, and dementia. *Hospital and Community Psychiatry*, 33(2), 111–126.

West, M. L. & Sheldon-Keller, A. E. (1994). Patterns of Relating: *An Adult Attachment Perspective*. New York: Guilford.

Wilkenson, D. A. & Carlen, P. L. (1981). *Chronic organic brain syndromes associated with alcoholism: Neuropsychological & other aspects*. In Y. Israel, F. Grace, H. Kalent, R. E. Popham, W. Schmidt & R. G. Smart (eds), Research advances in alcohol and drug problems, Vol. 6. NY: Plenum Press.

Winnicott, D. W. (1965), *The Maturational Process and the Facilitating Environment*. New York: International Press.

Wolf, E. S. (1980) On the developmental line of selfobject relations. In A. Goldberg (ed) *Advances in self psychology*. New York: International Universities Press.

Wolf, E. S. (1985). The search for confirmation: technical aspects of mirroring, *Psychoanalytic Inquiry* 5, 271–282.

Wolf, E. S. (1988) *Treating the Self: Elements of Clinical Psychology*. New York and London: The Guilford Press.

Yalom, I. D. (1974.) Group therapy and alcoholism. *Annals of the New York Academy of Science*, 233, 85–103.

Yalom, I. D. (1995). *The theory and practice of group psychotherapy*. (4th Ed.). New York: Basic Books.

Yalom, I. D. (1985). *The theory and practice of group psychotherapy*. (3rd. Ed.). New York: Basic Books.

Yalom, V. J. & Vinogradov, S. (1993). Interpersonal group psychotherapy. In H K. Kaplan & B. J. Sadock (Eds.), *Comprehensive Group Psychotherapy*, (3rd. ed., pp. 185–194). Baltimore: Williams & Wilkins.

Index

About the Author

Philip J. Flores, Ph.D. is a clinical psychologist who has worked extensively for the past twenty years in the area of addictive disorders and group psychotherapy. He is a Fellow of the American Group Psychotherapy Association and holds a Certificate of Proficiency in the Treatment of Alcohol and Other Psychoactive Substance Use Disorders issued by the American Psychological Association. Dr. Flores is adjunct Faculty at Georgia State University and Argosy University and is supervisor of group psychotherapy at Emory University. In addition to his book, Group *Psychotherapy with Addiction Populations,* he has published numerous articles and chapters on addiction and group psychotherapy. He has also presented numerous workshops locally and nationally on these two subjects. Dr. Flores and his wife, Lisa Mahon, Ph.D., continue to run several outpatient psychotherapy groups a week in their private practice.